ADVANCE PRAISE FOR
INSURGENT ECOLOGIES

"This powerful collection begins from the premise that insurgency is always a provocation, a forceful intervention that doesn't constitute a singular new order from whole cloth, but rather moves to radically destabilize authorized forms of knowledge, power, and organizations based on a plurality of environmental struggles. In cases that take us from eucalyptus plantations in Spain to energy infrastructures in Palestine, from the organizing of La Via Campesina's transnational feminist politics to just transitions movements in South Africa, readers get more than disconnected storylines of resistance — they get a lucid study of how place-based, seemingly disconnected environmental struggles can cohere into a radical, unified, revolutionary politics. It's an indispensable handbook for scholars and movements seeking to go beyond a narrow anti-neoliberal critique toward one that embraces radical anticolonial thought, that avoids the exclusivity of excess jargon, and that locates liberation in the struggle that Samir Amin called "convergence in diversity."

— **MAYWA MONTENEGRO**, assistant professor, University of California and author of *Abolitionist Agroecology, Food Sovereignty and Pandemic Prevention*

"In times of renewed and massive enclosures, including that of political imagination, Insurgent Ecologies irrupts as a necessary read. A powerful collection on subaltern ecological politics across different geographies, this book will surely remain an important reference for intellectual and political work against and beyond capitalism."

— **DIANA OJEDA**, professor of Geography and director of the Commons Program at the Ostrom Workshop, Indiana University

"Linking planetary ecological devastation and the climate crisis to inequality and precariousness, this excellent collection could not be more timely. In the radical political ecology tradition, it argues for systemic change in order to advance environmental and climate justice — in, against and beyond capitalism."

— **JULIAN AGYEMAN**, professor of urban and environmental policy and planning, Tufts University

"It's not only climate that's warming up, so is ecopolitics! The interplay of movements for liberating land, livelihood, labour, and sexuality creates a new kind of materialist lens for our 21st century politics. This book is a joy to encounter - pluriversal in both content and process."

— ARIEL SALLEH, author of *EcoSufficiency and Global Justice* and *Ecofeminism as Politics*

"With a trenchant critique of the dominant systems that enslave, immiserate, and destroy people and nature, this volume's contributors map out a way forward with nothing short of radical change in every realm of social and political life. As a wide-ranging and globe-spanning yet highly synthetic set of chapters, this volume is a must-read for political ecologists everywhere."

— AMY TRAUGER, professor of Geography, University of Georgia

"The Undisciplined Environments Collective offers a timely addition to the classics of radical political ecology. Going beyond stale critique or mere documentation of resistance practices, the book dares to put 'the radical' back to the core of political ecology, by centering on questions of strategic, systemic and revolutionary change, and asking what forms of universality and camaraderie can come out of the now fragmented and localized struggles against capitalist accumulation. A must read!"

— MARIA KAIKA, director of the Centre for Urban studies at the University of Amsterdam, and editor of *Turning Up the Heat: Urban Political Ecology for a Climate Emergency*

"This book is an invaluable tool for looking beyond capitalism and its 'fixes', and forging the unity of struggles that is needed to move past it."

— STEFANIA BARCA, University of Santiago de Compostela, author of *Workers of the Earth: Labour, Ecology and Reproduction in the Age of Climate Change*

"There has never been a more critical moment for imagining and bringing into existence a broad spectrum of post-capitalist realities. Insurgent Ecologies offers rigorous analysis and inspiring guidance on counterhegemonic thought and direct action for the realization of that radical vision of system change."

— DAVID NAGUIB PELLOW, University of California Santa Barbara, author of *What is Critical Environmental Justice?*

"This book points to broader questions of strategy and transformation through which it engages critically with the field of political ecology from a novel lens, i.e., that of political strategy and the possibility of engendering revolutionary transformations."

— **BENGI AKBULUT,** professor, department of geography, co-director of the Social Justice Centre, Concordia University

"Insurgent Ecologies is a critical collection paying urgent homage the brave frontline of the many whilst reminding the struggle everywhere that confrontation, resistance and contestation is the work in times of continued elite capture, coloniality and dispossession."

— **ELISE KLEIN (OAM),** associate professor, Australian National University

To all our families and comrades. To the insurgents of the earth.

insurgent ECOLOGIES

BETWEEN ENVIRONMENTAL STRUGGLES AND POSTCAPITALIST TRANSFORMATIONS

edited by
Undisciplined Environments Collective

Diego Andreucci, Gustavo García-López, Rita Calvário,
Panagiota Kotsila, Salvatore Paolo De Rosa,
Giorgos Velegrakis, Amelie Huber, Ilenia Iengo,
Marien González-Hidalgo, Irene Leonardelli, and Irmak Ertör

Fernwood Publishing
Halifax & Winnipeg

Copyright 2024 © Undisciplined Environments Collective

All rights reserved. No part of this book may be reproduced or transmitted in any form by any means without permission in writing from the publisher, except by a reviewer, who may quote brief passages in a review.

Copyediting: Sarah Michaelson
Cover design: Jess Koroscil
Cover artwork: B.Y. (Earth Liberation Studio)
Interior artwork: Lillian Sol Cuevas, B.Y. (Earth Liberation Studio) and Beehive Design Collective
Text design: Brenda Conroy and Lauren Jeanneau
Printed and bound in the UK

Published by Fernwood Publishing
Halifax and Winnipeg
2970 Oxford Street, Halifax, Nova Scotia, B3L 2W4
www.fernwoodpublishing.ca

Fernwood Publishing Company Limited gratefully acknowledges the financial support of the Government of Canada through the Canada Book Fund and the Canada Council for the Arts. We acknowledge the Province of Manitoba for support through the Manitoba Publishers Marketing Assistance Program and the Book Publishing Tax Credit. We acknowledge the Nova Scotia Department of Communities, Culture and Heritage for support through the Publishers Assistance Fund.

Library and Archives Canada Cataloguing in Publication

Title: Insurgent ecologies : between environmental struggles and postcapitalist transformations /
edited by the Undisciplined Environments Collective: Diego Andreucci, Gustavo García-López, Rita Calvário, Panagiota Kotsila, Salvatore Paolo De Rosa, Giorgos Velegrakis, Amelie Huber, Ilenia Iengo, Marien González-Hidalgo, Irene Leonardelli, and Irmak Ertör.
Names: Undisciplined Environments Collective, editor.
Description: Includes bibliographical references and index.
Identifiers: Canadiana (print) 20240407571 | Canadiana (ebook) 20240410289 | ISBN 9781773636917
(softcover) | ISBN 9781773637075 (PDF) | ISBN 9781773637082 (EPUB)
Subjects: LCSH: Social movements—Case studies. | LCSH: Social justice—Case studies. | LCSH:
Environmental justice—Case studies. | LCSH: Radicalism—Social aspects—Case studies. | LCSH:
Political ecology—Case studies. | LCGFT: Case studies.
Classification: LCC HM881 .I47 2024 | DDC 303.48/4—dc23

CONTENTS

Notes on Contributors xi

Acknowledgements xix

Foreword
    Ulrich Brand 1

Introduction
    Diego Andreucci, Gustavo García-López and Rita Calvário 3

PART ONE: SOVEREIGNTY   19

Introduction to Part One
    Diego Andreucci, Rita Calvário and Gustavo García-López 20

1   "Because of the Land"
    Insurgent Infrastructures of Social Reproduction in Palestine
    Omar Jabary Salamanca 25

2   Ecological Thought and Practice in the Kurdish Freedom Movement
    The Case of Bakûr
    Ercan Ayboga and Anselm Schindler 38

3   Articulating Sovereignties
    Convergences and Tensions between National-Popular and
    Community-Territorial Struggles in Ecuador and Bolivia
    Diana Vela Almeida, Geovanna Lasso, Marxa Chávez León and Diego Andreucci 51

4   Decolonial Encounters and Autogestion
    Struggles for Life and Sovereignty in Puerto Rico and Beyond
    Gustavo García-López 66

PART TWO: LAND   83

Introduction to Part Two
    Rita Calvário, Marien González-Hidalgo and Irmak Ertör 84

5   Uprooting Monocultures, Re-Rooting the Commons
    Everyday Struggles against Eucalyptus Tree Plantations
    in Rural Galicia
    Marien González-Hidalgo, Diego Cidrás and Joám Evans Pim 88

6   Migrant Agricultural Workers, Radical Food Activism, and the
    Struggle for Emancipatory Rural Change in Southern Europe
    Antonella Angelini, Giulio Iocco and Martina Lo Cascio 100

7   Food Sovereignty as Translation
    Strengthening Fisherfolk's Struggles and Cultivating
    Peasant-Fisher Alliances in Brazil
    Rita Calvário, Irmak Ertör and Zoe W. Brent, in conversation with Josana Pinto 114

PART THREE: CLIMATE — 129

Introduction to Part Three
Salvatore Paolo De Rosa, Gustavo García-López and Amelie Huber 130

8 See You on the Frontlines
   Direct Action Tactics of Convergence for Climate Justice
   Salvatore Paolo De Rosa 134

9 Imagining Just Transitions
   Julie Sze, in conversation with Gopal Dayaneni 150

10 Counterhegemonic Flows
   Expanding Renewable Energy Struggles in Turkey
   Ethemcan Turhan and Cem İskender Aydın 166

PART FOUR: FEMINISMS — 181

Introduction to Part Four
Panagiota Kotsila, Ilenia Iengo and Irene Leonardelli 182

11 Queer Cruisers and Sex Workers Resisting and Redefining
   Urban Socionatures in Tbilisi, Georgia
   Tornike Kusiani and Panagiota Kotsila 186

12 Radicalizing Food Sovereignty
   The Power of La Vía Campesina's Feminist Politics
   Annette Aurélie Desmarais and Rita Calvário 198

13 Communitarian Territorial Feminisms of Abya Yala
   Women Organized against Violence and Dispossession and
   the Experience of Community Networks in Chiapas, Mexico
   Delmy Tania Cruz Hernández 212

PART FIVE: LABOUR — 229

Introduction to Part Five
Giorgos Velegrakis, Diego Andreucci and Gustavo García-López 230

14 A Transformative Just Transition as the Driver to
   an Ecosocialist Future in South Africa
   Jacklyn Cock 234

15 Workers' Struggles in Colombia
   From the Defence of National Sovereignty to the Defence of Territory
   Tatiana Roa Avendaño 247

16 Belonging by Confrontation
   Living, Working and Struggling next to a Mine in Halkidiki, Greece
   Giorgos Velegrakis and Danai Liodaki 259

Conclusions
Undisciplined Environments Collective 271

Index 280

NOTES ON CONTRIBUTORS

Editorial collective

DIEGO ANDREUCCI is a postdoctoral research fellow at the Department of Geography, University of Barcelona, working on political ecologies of extractivism, energy colonialism and socioecological transformations.

RITA CALVÁRIO is a researcher at the Center for Social Studies, University of Coimbra. She is leading research on peasant movements, alternative food networks, rural women and gender issues, agricultural labour and the challenges of building more just food systems in Europe, with a focus in Southern Europe. Her main research interests are on political ecology, agrarian change, rural social movements, food sovereignty, socio-environmental struggles and emancipatory politics.

SALVATORE PAOLO DE ROSA is a researcher at the Center for Applied Ecological Thinking at the University of Copenhagen. He received his PhD in Human Geography from Lund University in Sweden in 2017, and since then he has worked in research and education at the KTH of Stockholm and at the Lund University Center for Sustainability Studies. He has published extensively in scientific journals, popular press and collective books. With a background in anthropology and political ecology, his research focuses on collective action, environmental conflicts and socioecological transformations towards climate and social justice.

IRMAK ERTÖR is a political ecologist and works as an assistant professor at Bogazici University, Istanbul. Before her current position, she was working at the Institute of Environmental Science and Technology, Autonomous University of Barcelona (ICTA-UAB) as a postdoctoral researcher in the ERC-funded ENVJUSTICE project focusing on global fisheries conflicts and environmental justice. She researches socio-environmental conflicts and social movements of fisher communities, community-supported fisheries, food sovereignty, blue economy/degrowth and environmental justice.

GUSTAVO GARCÍA-LÓPEZ is an engaged scholar, educator and apprentice organizer from the islands of Puerto Rico, working on transformative initiatives and movements for commons and environmental justice. He is currently FCT-CEECIND Researcher at the Center for Social Studies, University of Coimbra, coordinating the Ecology and Society Workshop (ECOSOC). He is also part of the Post-Extractive Futures Collective, an emerging initiative weaving networks of solidarity and radical care amongst movements. He lives uprooted from his lands but finds home and guiding stars in his daughter Maia, and is held in life by broad care networks of people, spirits, memories and ecologies.

MARIEN GONZÁLEZ-HIDALGO is a researcher at the Swedish University of Agricultural Sciences in Uppsala. She is inspired by critical engagements with feminist political ecology, environmental justice and social movements research and action-research; and especially interested in the analysis of the role that affect, emotions and healing practices play in environmental disasters, conflicts and mobilizations.

AMELIE HUBER is a project manager at EuroNatur Foundation in Germany. She co-coordinates the Save the Blue Heart of Europe campaign in the Western Balkans, an activist network mobilizing science, legal activism and policy advocacy to protect Europe's last free-flowing rivers from the ongoing hydropower boom. She holds a PhD from the Institute of Environmental Sciences and Technology (ICTA-UAB) in Barcelona and has carried out extensive research on the political ecology of hydropower development in the Eastern Himalayas/Northeast India.

ILENIA IENGO is a WEGO-ITN Marie Sklodowska-Curie PhD fellow in Feminist Political Ecology at BCNUEJ, Institute for Environmental Science and Technology, Autonomous University of Barcelona, Spain. She is a chronically ill scholar-activist from Naples, southern Italy, also member of the Ecologie Politiche del Presente laboratory. Her work lies at the crossroads of environmental humanities, feminist political ecology, and disability justice engaging with toxicity, embodiment and prefigurative urban politics.

PANAGIOTA KOTSILA is a "Ramon y Cajal" research fellow at the Institute for Environmental Science and Technology (ICTA-UAB), Universitat Autònoma de Barcelona. Her work examines the bio/necro-politics of public health, the neoliberalization of urban natures, and the grassroots struggles for urban climate and health justice, particularly in relation to racialized groups.

IRENE LEONARDELLI currently works as a postdoctoral researcher at the University of Calabria, Italy, focusing on agriculture and rural and mountain development from a feminist political ecology perspective. She holds a PhD from IHE Delft Institute for Water Education in the Netherlands, where she worked as a junior researcher and as a Marie Curie fellow of the Well-being, Ecology, Gender and Community-Innovation Training Network (WEGO-ITN). Her PhD work focused on processes of agrarian transformation and water governance in rural Maharashtra, India, from a feminist perspective.

GIORGOS VELEGRAKIS is an affiliated lecturer at the Philosophy and History of Science Department, National and Kapodistrian University of Athens. Previously a Marie Curie doctoral fellow, he has considerable research experience on issues of relevance to extractivism, political ecology, radical geography, socio-environmental conflicts and movements and STS. He is co-editor of The Political Ecology of Austerity: Crisis, Social Movements, and the Environment.

Other contributors

ANTONELLA ANGELINI is a business and human rights scholar and practitioner with an interest in transnational and hybrid normativity, particularly as expressed by non-conventional individual and collective actors, ranging from local communities to worker collectives and transnational worker alliances. She specializes in worker-led governance initiatives for domestic and global value chains and access to remedy for business-related harm.

ERCAN AYBOGA is an environmental engineer and activist who, while still in Germany, co-founded Tatort Kurdistan. He spends his time between Northern Kurdistan and Germany, the country in which he was born to Kurdish parents who arrived from Turkey. Ayboga is involved in the Mesopotamian Ecology Movement and the fight for the right to water. He worked on defending both the Hasankeyf archaeological site and the Kurdish families displaced by the Turkish government's Ilisu Dam project, and for fair access to water in Rojava, in Syrian Kurdistan. He is co-author of the book Revolution in Rojava (Pluto Press 2016).

CEM İSKENDER AYDIN is an ecological economist, currently working as an assistant professor at the Institute of Environmental Sciences in Boğaziçi University, Turkey. His research covers the topics of energy justice, energy and climate policy/politics, environmental justice and mapping environmental conflicts, and environmental governance.

BEEHIVE DESIGN COLLECTIVE is a wildly motivated, all-volunteer, activist arts collective dedicated to "cross-pollinating the grassroots" by creating collaborative, anti-copyright images for use as educational and organizing tools. We work as word-to-image translators of complex global stories, shared with us through conversations with affected communities. We work anonymously by crediting every graphic we make to the collective as a whole. We build and disseminate these visual tools with the hope that they will self-replicate and take on life of their own.

ULRICH BRAND is professor and current chair of International Politics, and head of the Research Network Latin America, at the University of Vienna. His research interests include international politics, critical analyses of globalization and its political regulation, and the role of the state and the economy. He is also a member of the Working Group "Beyond Development" in Latin America of the Rosa Luxemburg Foundation, and the author of The Imperial Mode of Living: Everyday Life and the Ecological Crisis of Capitalism (with Markus Wissen).

ZOE W. BRENT is a postdoctoral researcher based at the International Institute of Social Studies, and a researcher with the Agrarian Justice team at Transnational Institute. Her research focuses on issues of food and farm systems, environmental justice and social reproduction. She is also a fellow at Food First, Institute for Food and Development Policy in Oakland, California; there, she coordinates educational delegations exploring food sovereignty in the Basque Country, as well as the Land and Sovereignty in the Americas Collective.

B.Y. is a working-class artist who makes most of his art while at his day job. B.Y. has been involved in the climate movement for many years as an art lead for the Sunrise Movement. He is the founder of Earth Liberation Studio, an emerging art studio explores the themes of climate change, late-stage capitalism, ecosocialism, communism, anarchism, and revolutionary optimism. The work argues that a better world is possible — one where the climate crisis is solved, and humanity is freed from the chains of capital, debt, credit, and soul-crushing, alienating work.

MARXA CHÁVEZ LEÓN is an independent social researcher and feminist activist from Bolivia. She holds a bachelor's degree in Sociology from Universidad Mayor de San Andrés in La Paz, and a master's degree in Political Ecology and Alternatives to Development from Universidad Andina Simón Bolívar, Quito, Ecuador.

DIEGO CIDRÁS is a geographer with a particular interest in understanding nature-culture interactions in the management of contentious landscapes. Some of his research interests also include exploring local perspectives on rewilding, conflict management in protected areas, and the overall dynamic interactions between natural and social systems. He is currently working as an assistant professor in Human Geography at Universidade de Santiago de Compostela.

JACKLYN COCK is a professor emeritus in the Department of Sociology at the University of the Witwatersrand and was an honorary research professor in the Society, Work and Politics (SWOP) Institute. She has written extensively on militarization, feminism, labour and environmental issues. She was also founder of Earthlife Africa's Johannesburg branch.

DELMY TANIA CRUZ HERNÁNDEZ is a Hñähñú Indigenous, feminist, southern ecologist, and popular educator dedicated to grassroots, leftist and reflective practices. Delmy is co-founder of Mujeres Transformando Mundos (Women Transforming Worlds), and member of the collective Feminist Critical Views of Territory. Delmy teaches at the Center for Advanced Studies of Mexico and Central America, University of Sciences and Arts of Chiapas.

LILLIAN SOL CUEVAS is a PhD candidate at the International Institute of Social Studies in The Hague, Netherlands, where she researches energy futures, municipal public markets and gender issues in Mexico City in order to challenge the dominant imaginary. She has followed a dynamic and versatile career, including work in public policy, human and women's rights, sustainable development, energy and climate change, and as project coordinator, volunteer and public official in national and international NGOs, as well as the Mexican government.

GOPAL DAYANENI has been involved in fighting for justice through organizing, campaigning, teaching, writing, speaking and direct action since the late 1980s. He currently serves on the Staff Collective of Movement Generation: Justice and Ecology Project, is an active trainer, and has been a campaigner for Silicon Valley Toxics Coalition and Project Underground. Most importantly, Gopal is the father of Ila Sophia and Kavi Samaka Orion. He lives in Oakland in an intentional, multi-generational community of nine adults, eight children, and a bunch of chickens.

ANNETTE AURÉLIE DESMARAIS is the past Canada Research Chair in Human Rights, Social Justice and Food Sovereignty (2013–2023) at the University of Manitoba, Canada. She is a scholar activist, professor in the Department of Sociology and Criminology and the Department of Environment and Geography, and president of the National Farmers Foundation (nationalfarmersfoundation.ca/). Her main areas of research are agrarian change, peasant and farmer movements, and food system transformation. Her work is available at landfoodsovereignty.ca.

JOÁM EVANS PIM is a commoner at the Froxán Community in Lousame, Galiza (Spain), where he lives with his family. He is also an activist in political, environmental, cultural and human rights issues, particularly focused on defending and restoring common lands and confronting destructive mining and other environmentally degrading projects. He serves as Director of the Montescola Foundation and is Adjunct Professor of Peace and Conflict Research at Åbo Akademi University (Finland), where he lectures on civil disobedience, extractivist violence and environmental justice at the Master's Program on Peace, Mediation and Conflict Research.

GIULIO IOCCO is an independent researcher and labour rights activist. He has collaborated in scholar-activist research on the working and living conditions of migrant agricultural workers in Mediterranean Europe, the rise of right-wing populism in the Italian countryside, and worker-driven initiatives to promote decent work in, and alternatives to, globalized agri-food chains. He has been an activist of the Italian radical labour union FuoriMercato since 2015 and was co-coordinator of its working group on agroecology between 2019 and 2022.

OMAR JABARY SALAMANCA is a research fellow and co-director of the Observatory of the Arab and Muslim Worlds (OMAM) at the Université Libre de Bruxelles. His research concentrates on development, urban studies, political ecology and settler colonial studies, with a focus in Palestine and the Middle East. He is also interested in global histories and archival practices of anticolonial solidarity movements. Omar is an editor of Arab Urbanism, a member of the International Critical Geography Group and part of the Kitchen collective.

TORNIKE KUSIANI is an environmental, LGBTQIA+ and human rights activist from Georgia. During his time as an activist, he created the first-ever queer gatherings named Horoom and played a pivotal role in founding the Green Party in Georgia. Additionally, he initiated legal action against the Georgian government, leading to a case before the European Court of Human Rights in Strasbourg. Tornike's dedication to activism and research earned him recognition, including selection for the prestigious Chevening scholarship.

GEOVANNA LASSO is a researcher and activist on issues related to food sovereignty, political agroecology, political ecology, and environmental and social justice. She is an external professor at the University Politécnica Salesiana and the Universidad Andina Simón Bolívar. Her research focus is the territorialization/deterritorialization and the power/resistance strategies around food sovereignty, and against neoliberal austerity in Ecuador. Geovanna has been part of the coordination team of the Agroecological Collective of Ecuador since 2014.

DANAI LIODAKI is a doctoral candidate at the Leibniz Institute for Regional Geography in Leipzig and an early-stage researcher at CORAL-ITN. Coming from the National Technical University of Athens, she had a strong interest on questions of public space, public art and social movements claiming the right to the city and nature. Her current research focuses on alternative economic and political spaces and "alternative to development" issues.

MARTINA LO CASCIO is research fellow at the Faculty of Political and Social Sciences, Scuola Normale Superiore Pisa, studying how civil society actors drive change towards transformative environmental governance. She was researcher fellow at the European University Institute, taking part in the study "Is Italian Agriculture a 'Pull Factor' for Irregular Migration — And, If So, Why?" coordinated by Alessandra Corrado. Her research focuses on migrant labour in intensive agricultural production in Southern Italy.

JOSANA PINTO is a fisher and activist, member of the national coordination of the Movimento de Pescadores e Pescadoras Artesanais (MPP, Artisanal FisherFolk Movement) in Brasil, through which she struggles for the recognition and valourization of sustainable small-scale fishing, women fishers' health, and healthy fishing environments. She is also a member of the World Forum of Fisher Peoples.

TATIANA ROA AVENDAÑO is an engineer, activist and environmentalist. She is part of the Censat Agua Viva Colombia and the Southern Ecosocial Pact. She has participated in Oilwatch, the Colombia Free of Fracking Alliance and the Social Mining, Energy and Environmental Roundtable for Peace. She also participates in the Alliance for Water Justice, the "Beyond Development" Working Group of the Rosa Luxemburg Foundation, and the Abya Yala Political Ecology Working Group of CLACSO. She is the editor of Energías para la Transición (2021).

ANSELM SCHINDLER is a freelance journalist and activist from Germany, involved in the climate justice movement and the Kurdish Solidarity Movement, including the "Make Rojava Green Again" campaign, which is working towards the reforestation of Syria. He has written for German publications including Junge Welt, Tax and Neues Deutschland, and is a regular contributor to the Academy of Democratic Modernity (democraticmodernity.com).

JULIE SZE is professor of American Studies at UC Davis. She has written three books, most recently Environmental Justice in a Moment of Danger, and is editor of Sustainability: Approaches to Environmental Justice and Social Power. She has written over fifty articles and book chapters. She collaborates with scientists, engineers, social scientists and community-based organizers in California and New York. She is deeply committed to public scholarship and is an active mentor for first-generation and low-income students.

ETHEMCAN TURHAN is an assistant professor at the Department of Spatial Planning and Environment, University of Groningen. He was previously a postdoctoral researcher at KTH Environmental Humanities Laboratory between 2016 and 2020. His main research interests are situated at the intersection of climate justice and energy democracy with empirical attention to environmental movements and migration mainly in Turkey, Middle East and the Mediterranean.

DIANA VELA ALMEIDA is an assistant professor at Utrecht University. She combines political ecology, ecological economics, and feminist critical geography to study extractivism, neoliberal environmentalism, and socio-environmental resistance. Lately, her work focuses on analyzing green capitalism in the energy transition agenda in Europe and the role of social reproduction and unrecognized work in this transition.

ACKNOWLEDGEMENTS

Undisciplined Environments Collective

This book is indebted and dedicated to all those who live and die to make other worlds possible. It is born out of participation in, and accompaniment of, those struggles, and many parallel experiences seeking to undiscipline academia by engaging in other forms of doing research joined with action. It carries with it the deep belief that we must walk the talk and that amid so much violence and devastation, insurgencies are more necessary than ever. If it was not clear from the failures of governments to address the climate crisis for decades — the inaction to stop the livestreamed genocide in Palestine has lifted all veils, undressed the empire as a system that, driven by an unquenchable thirst for endless accumulation of wealth and power, is prepared to kill everything and everyone.

Insurgency is usually associated with armed rebellion. Here we mobilize it in a broader sense, referring to a range of actions and practices, of ways of doing and being that seek to undo the dominant structures of colonial, racist, patriarchal capitalism, and creating alternative modes of life. Insurgency is "the place of becoming, of the encounter that marks possibility and action," and above all, the territorial practices of dissident peoples, as one of the book's contributors, Delmy Tania Cruz Hernádez, reminds us.

It is common for authors to acknowledge that their works are indebted to many others. We take this to heart, positing our book's editorial work as a shared effort of the Undisciplined Environments Collective, not just a group of individual editors. This move recognizes that, even when some of our members may have worked more than others in this labour, ultimately, the book would not have been possible without the effort of all of us. This collective effort also extends to all of the book's amazing contributors, who, while not part of Undisciplined Environments, have honoured us with their trust in this project, telling their stories with a powerful combination of passion and clarity. These stories offer hope in a context where capitalism feeds on deepening despair, charting concrete visions and strategies for building grassroots power and converging across movements. Hope not as a naïve belief that everything will be alright, but as the joining of the pessimism of the intellect and the optimism of the will, as Gramsci famously said.

Our editorial collective is also indebted to many others. Since 2014, we have run a political ecology blog, born from the European Network of Political Ecology (ENTITLE) project, where we had incredibly supportive mentors and colleagues, such as Giorgos Kallis, Giacomo D'Alisa, Stefania Barca, Marco Armiero, Erik Swyngedouw, Maria Kaika, Gavin Bridge, Begum Ozkaynak, Beatriz Bustos, Christos Zografos, Costis Chadjimichalis, Lucie Greyl, Jonah Wedekind, Irina Velicu, Santiago Gorostiza, Melissa Garcia Lamarca, and Felipe Milanez." Later, we received the support of the Well-Being, Ecology and Gender and Community (WEGO) project, led by Wendy Harcourt, changing our name from ENTITLE to Undisciplined Environments, which was the name of ENTITLE's final conference. Over the years, our platform has been sustained through a wide range of contributions by hundreds of scholars and activists, and the readership of many more.

We also want to express gratitude to the Fernwood team who believed in the project from the start, offering their professional and comradely support along the way — especially Fionna Jeffries with her wonderful leadership, Anumeha Gokhale with her strategizing for the book's marketing, and Lauren Jeanneau with her amazing work in the book design and production — and to the two peer-reviewers whose thoughtful and generous reading helped us to improve the book manuscript. And of course, our collective labour would not be possible without the many people who care for us every day: from our partners, friends, comrades, and family, to those who clean the offices where we work and the public spaces we traverse, all the way to those who grow and harvest our food and transport it to our neighbourhoods. And finally, back to those whose struggles we honour and participate in, against this genocidal and ecocidal system, for life and dignity for all.

FOREWORD

Ulrich Brand

In our times, crises of and discontent with capitalism are often politicized by the Far Right. Their proposals to deal with these crises question neither capitalist social relations and manifold forms of oppression along class, gender, race and North-South divides, nor the exploitative societal relations to nature, because this would imply a practical critique of power and domination. Instead, the authoritarian right shifts the blame on migrants and refugees, as well as those who do not want to be submitted to white, heterosexual and male-dominated *dispositifs*. This is functional to capitalism, to the extent that exploitation in and beyond the labour market requires competition among the ruled.

Capitalism has nothing to offer the masses, a fact that becomes crystal clear in this volume. Even the ambitious strategies of the economic and political power elites and the neoliberal mainstream to "decarbonize" the economy are a false promise and, in fact, a nightmare. The supposed "greening" of capitalism will occur at high social, economic and ecological costs and takes place in a mode that Antonio Gramsci — an author often cited in this book — called "passive revolution." That is, to transform societies in order to deal with threatening problems and crises — but in a way that largely maintains or even reinforces existing power relations.

Political ecology is a vivid and convincing approach that helps to understand these multiple crises, particularly their ecological dimension. It shows why and how ecological struggles are at the core of any contestation of the capitalist-imperial mode of production and living. Many chapters of this volume apply — or are consistent with — a Gramscian version of political ecology with a strong reference to (counter)hegemony as an analytical and normative-strategic frame. This is a highly topical and desperately needed approach.

The book also shows that one of the most important tasks of scientific work is supporting reflections of the manifold experiences of societies, social groups and political actors, particularly emancipatory movements. The latter need to be put into a broader context and dialogue about what happens and what should happen in this enormously complex and power-laden world. Why is it so difficult to realize radical emancipatory transformations? Why are emancipatory movements successful? Why do they fail?

The contributions in this book insist that systemic change needs strategizing, as well as the creation of strategic unity. But to achieve this, the very concrete repertoire of struggles and experiences needs to be understood. *Insurgent Ecologies* does not portray a master plan, but wants to understand *insurgent practices* — the strategies, actions, alliances, comradeship, solidarity and visons of those movements that struggle for emancipatory transformations.

The book is fascinating because most contributions have a clear analytical and politico-strategic compass; the text also refers to decolonial, Indigenous, feminist, queer and antiracist perspectives and experiences, and presents the enormous wealth of concrete experiences of the respective social movements. It challenges our common academic practices, which are so often separated from societal actors, particularly from social movements. In this sense, the book is a treasure of transdisciplinary research, or, in the words of the editors: engaged and militant research.

The novelist James Baldwin wrote sixty years ago in *The Fire Next Time*: "I know I'm asking for the impossible. But in our time, as in every time, the impossible is the least you can ask for." In this sense, *Insurgent Ecologies* is an inspiration for activists, scholars and people interested in emancipatory change. I congratulate the editors and authors on this important book. I wish you a broad audience and I hope that it will contribute to understanding, learning and transforming our world in emancipatory ways.

INTRODUCTION

*Diego Andreucci, Gustavo García-López
and Rita Calvário*

This book starts from the belief that the panoply of subaltern environmental struggles taking place across the Global North and South are today a necessary component of a broader transformation beyond capitalism. Nothing is more necessary and urgent. We are in a moment of multiple and intersecting crises. Planetary ecological devastation and the climate crisis are created by — and exacerbate — other social crises: of inequality and precariousness, gender, racial and colonial violence, crumbling democracy and rising neo-fascist populism (Fraser 2022). The solutions cannot come from those who created these crises. Capital responds through false technological and managerial "fixes" — ranging from "green" products and recycling, to electric cars and planes and fantasies of "renewable everything," to massive tree-planting schemes and huge carbon sucking and sequestering machines — which do little to stop ecological degradation, while displacing environmental damages onto poorer regions or turning them into economic opportunities for corporations. This deepens inequalities and environmental injustices and prevents the emergence of real solutions.

We need to look beyond. It is crucial that we direct our focus to the root causes of such intersecting crises. We must reject not only reactionary explanations, such as racist and Malthusian narratives of overpopulation, but also seemingly progressive ones, pointing to individual overconsumption, or paying exclusive attention to the excess extraction and burning of fossil fuels. The latter is certainly part of the problem, perhaps the central problem when analyzed superficially, with a narrow focus on CO_2 emissions. However, what is commonly presented as a "fossil fuel addiction" of a classless "humanity" is itself a consequence of the core political economic logic that underpins it: namely capital accumulation and its ingrained compulsion to expand indefinitely, sustained by colonial-imperial, racist and patriarchal hierarchies and institutions, which organize, justify and reinforce uneven geographies of exploitation of peoples and nonhuman natures, rendered expendable and valueless (Patel and Moore 2018).

If capital "lit this fire" (Malm 2016), doing away with capital accumulation as a structuring logic of global socioecological relations is necessary in our struggle for a livable planet. However, this is a daunting task, as capitalist class power is deeply entrenched within the command of coercion and ideological apparatuses. Who, then, will put out the fire, and how?

Political ecology for a planet on fire

This book critically engages with, and contributes to, longstanding conversations in both academic and movement-based political ecology around systemic change for advancing environmental and climate justice — in, against and beyond capitalism. We are inspired in important ways by critical academic research and theorizing. The title itself is an explicit gesture to position this book in the tradition of radical political ecology collections, such as *Liberation Ecologies* by Marxist geographers Richard Peet and Michael Watts (2004), a pioneering text in its attention to diverse movements fighting for environmental justice in the Global South. However, despite long grappling with the question of how to be "engaged" and move from theory to action, academic political ecology is still focused mainly on critique, and often characterized by inaccessible language, abstract theorization, and lack of organic involvement in specific social struggles.

This is not to say that theory and action are mutually exclusive — on the contrary, they need to be woven together. Moreover, in the massively growing scholarship on the topic, the field continues to be dominated by Northern academic positions, with limited engagement with the diversity of decolonial, Indigenous, feminist, queer and antiracist perspectives emerging from the margins (Sultana 2021). Add to this the problematic of scholars "representing" or "speaking for" movements and the marginalized actors they seek to "empower" (Asher 2014).

Another motivation for this book is to move beyond documenting resistance against environmental destruction and violence, towards interrogating possibilities of radical change that may emerge from such resistance. Giving visibility to the ubiquitous environmental mobilizations taking place globally is extremely worthwhile. An instance of this line of work is the Environmental Justice Atlas project, a platform created by researchers at Autonomous University of Barcelona that allows engaged scholars and activists all over the world to document, connect and compare thousands of environmental conflicts. The project is motivated by the thesis that, by stopping harmful projects and demanding more ecologically sound policies, environmental justice movements are "forces for sustainability" (Temper et al. 2018). However, such focused attention to the moment of resistance and conflict has at times sidelined broader political questions relating to strategy, and to the potentialities and limitations such movements have for engendering deeper — revolutionary or counterhegemonic — transformations.

The issue of systemic change, and of strategic organizing to implement such a change, has long been something of a blind spot of academic political ecology, which this book aspires to redress. We are not alone in this. In the current conjuncture of multiple and intersecting crises, radical environmental movements have forced the question of "system change" to the centre of the political agenda, shaking academic researchers out of the comfort zone of abstract critique. Despite the enormous differences that remain, there is today an unprecedented consensus — ranging from feminist activists to Indigenous organizations, from Maoist guerrillas to the IPCC scientists — that capitalism is leading humanity into a social and ecological blind alley, and that everything needs to change, swiftly.

In recent years, this has animated daring proposals and ample debates centring on the long-neglected question: *What is to be done, by whom, and how?* Two central concerns have (re)gained centrality to a broadly defined ecosocialist debate, with which political ecologists are beginning to engage. First, that of imagining a more just alternative to the current predicament. In this category, we can signal the popularity of a paradigm such as that of "degrowth," which, at least in the imperial Global North, is emerging as one of the liveliest terrains of discussion and experimentation (Barlow et al. 2022). The degrowth critique — at first ignoring but increasingly building on longer standing anticapitalist, anticolonial and feminist traditions — has revitalized ecosocialism, denouncing the impossibility of a Left "ecomodernism" and contributing to a broader and much-needed synthesis between a renewed Marxist tradition and communalist, anti-imperialist and antiproductivist political ecologies (Saito 2023).

Second, we find an important re-centring of questions of strategic, revolutionary change. For instance, think of the intense debates around climate movement tactics generated by Andreas Malm's (2021) provocative defence of direct action in *How to Blow up a Pipeline*. More broadly — after decades of remaining within the comfort zone of anti-neoliberal critique, while leaving racial-patriarchal capitalism off the hook — political ecology is rediscovering the work of revolutionary and radical anticolonial thinkers and organizers from Lenin to Fanon, Luxemburg and Cabral, Mariátegui and Césaire, Rodney and Sankara (Heron and Dean 2022).

Among such rediscoveries are the ideas of Gramsci on rebellion and radical politics (Ekers et al. 2013), revitalized by a critical engagement with anticolonial, antiracist, and feminist thinking. We find these concepts are of particular relevance to this book, specifically, for thinking about how environmental movements take part in what is often referred to as "counterhegemony" — that is, the struggle of a multiplicity of oppressed (or "subaltern") classes and social groupings against the dominance of the ruling classes and their conceptions of the world (Fraser 2022). But more than an act or moment of resistance, such a position implies the adoption of an "understanding of [counter]hegemony as a modality of convergence among a plurality of self-organized political forces" (Kipfer and Hart 2013: 338).[1] Building counterhegemonic articulations, then, has to do with allyship — but also, ideally, transcends it, as Jodi Dean (2019) has argued, to become *comradeship*. This means not just a temporary and extrinsic agreement between groups with fundamentally different identities and goals, but the construction of a common horizon of struggle, a unity across difference of identity, vision and priorities, and their mutual transformation around shared emancipatory goals and world views.

An important aspect of this Gramscian political ecology approach is that it helps us to understand how a radical, unified, revolutionary politics can emerge from place-based, often disconnected environmental struggles — and how these are able to move from the sphere of immediate self-defence to a more universal and encompassing form of interest, a more purely political interest in Gramsci's terms (1971: 181-182). This includes a connection between place-based struggles and internationalism, but also an understanding of the possibilities for convergence between feminist, anticolonial, antiracist, queer, and ecological movements through reciprocal relationship with class struggle.

Practices of self-organization, solidarity from below, comradeship and popular pedagogy to rework "common sense" are crucial to seeing the interconnectedness of multiple oppressions and their common root in racial-patriarchal capitalism — and the actors, ideas and institutions that support it — and therefore the need for an all-encompassing struggle beyond isolated issues (Calvário, Desmarais and Azkarraga 2020; Andreucci 2019; García-López et al. 2017; Karriem 2009).

This is emphatically *not* to argue that only movements that build successful and politically incisive coalitions, or that develop a universal, revolutionary ambition, are worthy of our support. In many cases, a struggle of self-defence is all that the circumstances and correlation of forces allow for, particularly in extremely violent environments, such as typically in settler colonial contexts. Indeed, not all authors and movements in this collection embrace a Gramscian analytic, nor would they share such a universalistic political vision. However, we posit counter-hegemony as an open framework with which to interrogate the diverse stories of struggle shared in this book, for readers themselves to reflect on how and why some movements come to aspire to and are able to move in this direction, and on what hinders others from doing so.

Insurgent universality

We argued that the global panoply of environmental movements studied by political ecology is a seed for systemic transformation. But seeds need fertile ground and tending in order to flourish. What makes it possible for environmental struggles to become catalysts of broader revolutionary change? In the last years, critical researchers and activists alike have argued that the current climate crisis offers an unprecedented opportunity for a mass transformative movement to emerge out of the defence of land, territory and the commons, favouring alliances between "frontline communities" and a host of others class-based and emancipatory political struggles (Klein 2014). Such diverse movements are faced today with the question that has long preoccupied revolutionary thinking: How to turn necessity into possibility, while taking contingency into account?

Our book can be seen as an exploration of this question. We posit that resistance against exploitation and dispossession, and for the defence of life in territories and neighbourhoods against the assault of extractive capitalism in its multiple manifestations, as a key moment — necessary but not sufficient — in a universal political struggle for undoing capitalist class hegemony and making way for a just and livable world. Yet, many activists and researchers today, particularly those most influenced by decolonial theory or by anarchist or autonomist politics, would disagree with the Gramscian call for a *universal* horizon of struggle. As mentioned above, many movements simply cannot think beyond resistance and self-defence due to adverse material conditions and structural power imbalances; other would choose consciously to prioritize localized and autonomous struggle. The types of movements that political ecologists research and support typically centre place, territory, and ethno-cultural, gender or racial injustices as the core axes of struggle. To capitalist universalization, decolonial theorists and movements oppose the "pluriverse" — a panoply of ways of organizing society and ecology "otherwise" — for restoring non-exploitative, horizontal, culturally and spiritually rich ways of relating within human societies and between humans and nonhumans (Kothari et al. 2019).

We agree that recognizing and valuing such a plural constitution of the global subaltern classes is important and necessary. However, consistent with our Gramscian political ecology-inspired framing, we suggest that finding a degree of strategic unity across such a plurality — through the articulation of diverse struggles, practices of solidarity, comradeship, and mutual transformation of identities, ideas and practices — remains nonetheless necessary to emancipatory politics (Hesketh 2019). Capitalism is, after all, universalizing in its destruction and violence, in imposing its extractivist logic of exchange value — a single drive that is ecocidal and destructive of different ways of relating to others and to more-than-human nature. In this sense, there is no doubt that the horizon of struggle of twenty-first-century ecosocialism should be pluriversal — allowing for the coexistence of multiple sovereignties and modes of existence, "a world where many worlds fit" in the well-known Zapatista formulation. Such a pluriverse is ontologically, structurally incompatible with capitalism. To defeat the latter, we need the recognition of: a universality or common condition of class exploitation and dispossession; the ways in which this condition is organized around, bonded upon, and entwined with structural oppressions such as racism, sexism, ableism; and the fluidity of the boundary between commodified and non-commodified spheres in the process of accumulation — all necessary components for the reproduction of capitalism as a mode of social organization (Fraser 2022).

Some recent interventions offer us insights to think through such a dialectic of unity and diversity. Critical geographer Japhy Wilson, for instance, proposes the notion of *"insurgent universality"* as a way of dialectically reconciling the organic and particularistic decolonial critique of universality as Eurocentric modernity, with the necessary universal character of a disparate and culturally grounded pluriverse of insurgencies against the destructive forces of capital, the common enemy of emancipatory politics. The source of this insurgent universality is not in theory, Wilson suggests (2022: 155), but "in the spaces of struggle, the moments of revolt, and the experiences of comradeship, in which the universal dimension emerges like a flash of lightening, simultaneously exposing false universals and transcending closed identities."

Engaging insurgent ecologies

The overall aim of the book then is to understand subaltern ecological movements from the point of view of their transformative visions, struggles and strategies for building "unity in diversity." Before presenting the contents of the book, we want to spend a few words on the term "insurgent ecologies." The reasons why we consider *ecological* struggles as fundamental for systemic transformation should be clear by now. First, every political project is also necessarily ecological: a way of organizing social reproduction within and against nature. The organization of the metabolic relations between humans and nature constitutes the grounds on which all politics takes place. In this sense, within ecological struggles we find resources to inform a broader counterhegemonic project of emancipation that keeps into focus the intertwinement of natural processes and social struggles, taking the responsibility of driving the mutual transformation of society and nature. Second, as argued above, the climate/ecological crisis is deeply imbricated with multiple political, economic and social reproduction crises, and therefore is becoming a catalyst for multiple movements to potentially come together and recognize common sources of exploitation, dispossession, oppression and violence.

In what sense, however, do we deploy a language of *insurgency*? Juris and Khasnabish (2013: 7-8), in their own account of the politics of transnational activism, explain two important reasons for adopting the term, which we also share. First, to refer to the radical character of the movement studied:

Although we realize the language of insurgency is freighted with masculinist and militaristic overtones, we deploy it here because it suggests the clearing of a path for new forms of sociopolitical imagination and construction. An insurgency is always a provocation, a forceful intervention that aims not to constitute a singular new order from whole cloth but to radically destabilize authorized forms of power, knowledge, and organization and, in so doing, to create the space necessary for new acts of constitution.

Therefore, this book focuses on the "insurgent practices" of diverse subaltern ecological movements across the world, out of which counterhegemonic strategies may be articulated. Radical urban geographer Melissa García-Lamarca (2017: 41), defines insurgent practices as "a collective socio-spatial and political nexus of actions, consisting of both doings and sayings that enact equality and disrupt the dominant production of space, creating possibilities to generate new ... meanings and relations contrary to institutionalized ones and against the interests of dominant powers."

Furthermore, insurgencies are a key moment in the dialectic of universality and particularity sketched above, precisely because they are catalysts of multiple experiences and struggles coming together as one. As Asad Haider (in Wilson 2022: 161, our emphasis), puts it:

> Universality does not exist in the abstract, as a prescriptive principle which is mechanically applied to different circumstances. It is recreated in the act of insurgency, which *does not demand emancipation solely for those who share my identity but for everyone* ... This is a universality that necessarily confronts and opposes capitalism.

Building on this understanding of insurgency — as disrupting dominant configurations, enacting equality, fighting for universal emancipation — we moreover explicitly interrogate such movements' insurgent practices from the perspective of their counterhegemonic transformative strategy.

In concrete terms, this means that each story of socioecological struggle presented in this collection entails, to varying degrees, an element of reflection on the question of how to build counterhegemonic articulations through practices of alliance, solidarity and comradeship across diverse struggles, against entangled forms of exploitation, oppression and dispossession. And how, through such articulations, new political subjects and transformative collective projects are created, aiming to build alternatives to the dominant modes of socioecological organization and development.

Unsettling academic research practices

Going back to the text by Juris and Khasnabish cited above, the second motivation for adopting the term "insurgent" is to capture the militant nature of the research methodology itself. They write (2013: 8):

> But we also employ the language and imaginary of insurgency because we believe the engaged ethnographies collected here [in their book, *Insurgent Encounters*] represent a form of critical social research that can contribute in multiple ways to social change as opposed to simply archiving, commenting on, or dissecting the efforts of grassroots social movements.

Critical, engaged research — what others also refer to as "militant research" — is "the place where activism and academia meet"; it "works in and with the movements it is concerned with," committed to advancing systemic changes (Bookchin et al. 2013).[2] Its main focus is on "the capacity for struggles to read themselves and, consequently, to recapture and disseminate the advances and productions of other social practices" (Colectivo Situaciones 2003, in Russell 2014: 2). It involves identifying contradictions within a political milieu and seeking to solve them, "a combination of thought and action oriented towards understanding and changing collective praxis, identifying and surpassing the limits of our existing selves" (Russell 2014: 223). It is an orientation and a process committed to strengthening the movements of which we are part. In the context of radical climate justice movements, for instance, it brings up difficult questions such as:

> What constitutes "us" as "politically" different? How do we act? How do we affect change? How do we talk and think about the world around us in a way that doesn't reiterate the conditions of the present? How do we produce ourselves as an empowered collective subject rather than reactive individuals? (Russell 2014: 2).

Addressing these questions involves shifting methods, from the "participant-observant" study of radical movements to long-term involvement, mutual commitment and trust within these movements. It also implies putting into question academic analyses that superimpose what the movement vision and strategies "should be" or whether the movement "was successful" based on predetermined theories about what radical transformation implies, recognizing that the "success of a movement, movement goals and people's desires come from those people, those social actors, not those studying them or politically desiring to lead them" (Bookchin et al. 2013: 12).

Our book shares this commitment to critical, engaged, militant research — and wishes to push it further. The book emerged from Undisciplined Environments, a collective of researchers that has been working together since 2014 in curating a blog (undisciplinedenvironments.org) with the aim to enrich, interconnect and disseminate radical political ecology thought and practice across movements and other non-academic audiences. All the contributions in our collection are authored by, or in close conversation with, members of the environmental movements they discuss, and primarily from the places they narrate about. In this way, the strategic reflections that each chapter proposes is, to an important extent, "organic" to the movements and place of struggles themselves. This is not only a gesture towards disrupting the "coloniality of knowledge;" for too long we have learned about subaltern struggles across the colonized world primarily via the accounts of Northern social scientists. We also see it as an attempt to build, to some extent at least, a theory from below — conceptualizing socioecological transformation from the point of view of its political protagonists, who, as Paulo Freire exhorted us, we must consider as thinkers of the revolutions, not its mere doers.

Plan of the book

In this book, we pursue such boundary thinking between plurality and universality — decolonial and counterhegemonic — by setting the overall ecosocialist framework sketched above into dialogue with key conceptual conversations and with the unique lessons learned from each struggle in its cultural, geographic, political and historical specificity. Concretely, we structure the book into five parts, each one bringing together conceptual reflections and empirical insight on a different set of movements, namely around sovereignty, land, climate, feminisms and labour.

The first part centres on how resistance against colonialism and its contemporary manifestations — variously identified as neocolonialism, (neo-)imperialism, or coloniality — intersect with struggles for building more socioecologically just futures. It posits the idea of *sovereignty* as a way of capturing such a decolonizing ambition of diverse movements. These include the fight for self-determination by stateless nations living under colonial occupation; radical movements in formerly colonized states to reassert control over their democracy and resources, against pillage by transnational corporations and Northern states; and Indigenous and peasant peoples in settler colonial spaces or internal peripheries, to reclaim control over their ways of seeing, knowing, and being in the world. The chapters in this part show that, far from being residues from the past, and an exception from the normal functioning of capitalism, contemporary colonial practices are essential to its functioning, creating and exploiting racial hierarchies to sustain capital accumulation on a planetary scale. And that in their diversity, anticolonial struggles are crucial for imagining and enacting radical alternatives to the deadly intersection of coloniality and capitalism.

Part two sheds light on the enduring centrality of the "land question" today. It explores how diverse and plural insurgent movements fighting against agrarian, forestry and fisheries dispossession, land-based working class exploitation, commodification of natural resources and privatization of landscapes are engaging in, and strategizing towards, counterhegemonic politics. The chapters in this part exemplify some of the specific ways in which engaged, political actors come together and find common ground on which to strengthen their struggles, in and across place, space and scale: urban and rural people joining forces for recovering livable rural commons against tree monocultures; migrants, farmers and food activists building comradeship relations in struggles for labour rights in agriculture and food systems; and peasants and fisherfolks using food sovereignty as a unifying concept in struggles, through which they empower and transform activists and strengthen their mobilizations. The cases presented display how land politics is about considering land as a social relationship and acting upon the terrain of power relations, involving issues of ecology, labour, and the commons, as well as fights against patriarchy, colonialism and racism.

Part three argues that "Climate Justice" and "Just Transition" have become central unifying claims of transnational movements confronting fossil capitalism and inequitable low-carbon transitions. These movements call for "system change, not climate change" — a transformation from an extractive to a regenerative economy, which involves the democratic self-management of the basic means of social reproduction, of life, and the replacement of top-down hierarchical domination with decentralized bottom-up systems. Fossil companies are making record profits and plan to continue investing in new fossil infrastructures, while the new "renewable energy" rush is leading to a significant expansion of extraction of "green" minerals. The chapters in this part explore how climate justice organizations and movements are deploying a variety of strategies and tactics to disrupt the current (im)balance of forces, including direct action and grassroots organizing by and with frontline communities. Convergence in Climate Justice and Just Transition movements confronts the challenges of overcoming unequal Global North and South relations, as well as relations between newer yet whiter youth climate movements, and more longstanding environmental justice and anti-extractivist organizations from frontline communities. These contributions point to the importance of networking between local and trans/national movements, guided by shared visions and action tools.

Part four explores how environmental movements coevolve and bridge with feminist, decolonial and queer movements' theories, activism and praxis in multiple ways. Recognizing how environmental degradation, climate change and extractivism relate to gender-based injustices, the de-valuing of the work of socioecological reproduction and to health issues, the part shows how feminist action has been — and still is — crucial to resisting and confronting heteropatriarchy, extractive capitalism, neoliberalism, growth and modernization at all costs. The chapters illuminate some different ways in which this unfolds throughout the world, in both urban and rural contexts. They narrate how different marginalized groups, including peasant women, Indigenous people, non-binary and queer communities have mobilized against the interweaving of neocolonialism, capitalism and patriarchy to create collective strategies and subaltern alliances, spaces of refuge, and alternatives to neoliberal food and urban politics. In doing so, they emphasize the nexus between body-territory-land, suggesting an understanding of the body, especially of rural, Indigenous, Black and impoverished women and gender-nonconforming people, as a territory that is too often violated and contaminated but also as site of contestation and liberation against oppression.

Part five discusses labour environmentalism as forms of environmental activism that aim for radical transformations based on principles of mutual interdependence between production, reproduction and ecology. The central question is how to rethink ecological politics in class and labour terms today, while attempting to build a political strategy for socioecological transformation upon a more solid analysis of the social forces involved, their mutual relations and shared interests. In these terms, each chapter in the part tells a story of a historical or ongoing socioecological struggle from different parts of the world. The authors describe how communities, activists, trade unions and other organized workers build, out of their interrelated practices, counterhegemonic articulations against intersecting forms of exploitation, oppression and dispossession. In several cases, they successfully create new transformative collective projects through practices of alliance and solidarity by understanding the expropriation of natural resources and the exploitation of labour as two sides of the same coin. By doing so, all chapters put forward questions of new political subjects and organizations, beyond traditional trade unionism or environmentalism, which is at the core of any transformative potential.

Art has always been central to insurgent ecosocial movements. Thus, these parts are accompanied by illustrations from three artivists — Beehive Design Collective, Lillian Sol Cuevas and B.Y. (Earth Liberation Studio) — who, in dialogue with the book's themes, invite us to think and feel insurgent ecologies from other perspectives beyond the written form. The Beehive Collective's cutoffs from "The true cost of coal" poster, "honor the corageous history of organized resistance of communities living in the shadow of Big Coal, reflecting the complexity of these struggles for land, livelihood, and self-determination. This narrative illustration was developed after over 2 ½ years of interviews, discussions, story-tellings, and song-sharing with community organizers, activists, and folks in the Appalachian Mountains whose lives and livelihoods have been impacted by coal" (author's words). Lillian Sol Cuevas's collages, "Ecologies" and "Insurgent", are "multilayered reflections on these two words. In 'Ecologies', Lillian presents an entangled world of relations where humans, more-than-humans, and the universe converge. In "Insurgent", mushrooms, a tree, and an Indigenous girl (photo of a stencil by Valérian Lenud) depict the "radical tenderness" of insurgents and the deep roots that connect them with their territories and the land. In both works, Lillian tries to challenge the notions of big and small, North and South, close and far away" (author's words). Finally, the arts from B.Y. in the cover ("Decompose the empire") and in between each section ("What you love"), "explore the themes of climate change, late-stage capitalism, ecosocialism, communism, anarchism, and revolutionary optimism" (author's words), through images weaving together human and nonhuman insurgents.

Notes

1 The authors add: "In this latter understanding, sociopolitical forces undergo mutual transformation in convergent points of struggle or processes of organizational condensation. Yet they are not assimilated into a hierarchy of primary and secondary antagonism" (Kipfer and Hart 2013: 338).
2 As Alexandra Juhasz cautions, "militant" — much like "insurgent" — can be too close to militaristic and patriarchal meanings, which do not fit well with feminist and decolonial perspectives (Bookchin et al. 2013: 20).

References

Andreucci, Diego. 2019. "Populism, Emancipation, and Environmental Governance: Insights from Bolivia." *Annals of the American Association of Geographers* 109, 2: 624–633.

Asher, Kiran. 2014. "The Doers and the Done For: Interrogating the Subjects and Objects of Engaged Political Ecology." *ACME: An International Journal for Critical Geographies* 13, 4: 489–496.

Barlow, Nathan, Livia Regen, Noémie Cadiou, Ekaterina Chertkovskaya, Max Hollweg, Christina Plank, Merle Schulken, and Verena Wolf (eds.). 2022. *Degrowth & Strategy: How to Bring about Social-Ecological Transformation*. MayFly Books. At <mayflybooks.org/degrowth-strategy/>.

Bookchin, Natalie, Pamela Brown, Suzahn Ebrahimian, Colectivo Enmedio, Alexandra Juhasz, Leónidas Martin, Nicholas Mirzoeff, Andrew Ross, A. Joan Saab, and Marina Sitrin. 2013. *The Militant Research Handbook*. New York: New York University. At <visualculturenow.org/wp-content/uploads/2013/09/MRH_Web.pdf>.

Calvário, Rita, Annette Aurélie Desmarais, and Joseba Azkarraga. 2020. "Solidarities from below in the making of emancipatory rural politics: Insights from food sovereignty struggles in the Basque Country." *Sociologia Ruralis* 60, 4: 857–879.

Dean, Jodi. 2019. *Comrade: An Essay on Political Belonging*. London: Verso.

Ekers, Michael, Gillian Hart, Stefan Kipfer, and Alex Loftus (eds.). 2013. *Gramsci: Space, Nature, Politics*. Malden, MA: John Wiley & Sons.

Fraser, Nancy. 2022. *Cannibal Capitalism: How Our System Is Devouring Democracy, Care, and the Planet — and What We Can Do about It*. London: Verso.

García-Lamarca, Melissa. 2017. "From Occupying Plazas to Recuperating Housing: Insurgent Practices in Spain." *International Journal of Urban and Regional Research* 41, 1: 37–53.

García-López, Gustavo, Irina Velicu, and Giacomo D'Alisa. 2017. "Performing counter-hegemonic common(s) senses: Rearticulating democracy, community and forests in Puerto Rico." *Capitalism Nature Socialism* 28, 3: 88–107.

Gramsci, Antonio. 1971. *Selections from the Prison Notebooks* (Hoare, Quentin, and Geoffrey Nowell Smith, eds.). London: Lawrence and Wishart.

Heron, Kai, and Jodi Dean. 2022. "Climate Leninism and Revolutionary Transition: Organization and Anti-Imperialism in Catastrophic Times." *Spectre* (June 26).

Hesketh, Chris. 2019. "A Gramscian conjuncture in Latin America? Reflections on violence, hegemony, and geographical difference." *Antipode* 51, 5: 1474–1494.

Juris, Jeffrey S., and Alex Khasnabish (eds.). 2013. *Insurgent Encounters: Transnational Activism, Ethnography, and the Political.* Durham and London: Duke University Press.

Karriem, Abdurazack. 2009. "The rise and transformation of the Brazilian landless movement into a counter-hegemonic political actor: A Gramscian analysis." *Geoforum* 40, 3: 316–325.

Kipfer, Stefan and Gillian Hart. 2013. "Translating Gramsci in the Current Conjuncture." In Ekers, Michael, Gillian Hart, Stefan Kipfer, and Alex Loftus (eds.). *Gramsci: Space, Nature, Politics*. Malden, MA: John Wiley & Sons, 323–343.

Klein, Naomi. 2014. *This Changes Everything: Capitalism vs. the Climate*. New York: Simon & Schuster.

Kothari, Ashish, Ariel Salleh, Arturo Escobar, Federico Demaria, and Alberto Acosta (eds.). 2019. *Pluriverse: A Post-Development Dictionary*. New Delhi: Tulika Books.

Malm, Andreas. 2016. "Who lit this fire? Approaching the history of the fossil economy." *Critical Historical Studies* 3, 2: 215–248.

_____. 2021. *How to Blow Up a Pipeline*. London: Verso.

Patel, Raj, and Jason W. Moore. 2018. *A History of the World in Seven Cheap Things: A Guide to Capitalism, Nature, and the Future of the Planet*. London: Verso.

Peet, Richard, and Michael Watts (eds.). 2004. *Liberation Ecologies: Environment, Development and Social Movements*, second edition. London: Routledge.

Russell, Bertie. 2014. "Beyond Activism/Academia: Militant Research and the Radical Climate and Climate Justice Movement(s)." *Area* 47, 3.

Saito, Kohei. 2023. *Marx in the Anthropocene: Towards the Idea of Degrowth Communism*. Cambridge, UK: Cambridge University Press.

Sultana, Farhana. 2021. "Political Ecology 1: From Margins to Center." *Progress in Human Geography* 45, 1: 156-165.

Temper, Leah, Federico Demaria, Arnim Scheidel, Daniela Del Bene, and Joan Martinez-Alier. 2018. "The Global Environmental Justice Atlas (EJAtlas): Ecological Distribution Conflicts as Forces for Sustainability." *Sustainability Science* 13: 573–584.

Wilson, Japhy. 2022. "The Insurgent Universal: Between Eurocentric Universalism and the Pluriverse." *Nordia Geographical Publications* 51, 2.

PART ONE

SOVEREIGNTY

INTRODUCTION TO PART ONE

*Diego Andreucci, Rita Calvário
and Gustavo García-López*

Colonialism has been, from its inception, an ecological project — an institutionalized strategy that enforces racial hierarchies for controlling, appropriating, remaking, and destroying natures and societies in colonized spaces, to the benefit of settler colonists and of ruling classes in the metropole (Patel and Moore 2017). Today, such a colonial project — variously identified as neocolonialism, (neo-)imperialism, or coloniality — is manifested in a host of institutionalized discourses, tactics and interventions that allow dominant powers to plunder valuable material and immaterial resources, typically at the expense of marginalized and racialized social groups, Indigenous and peasant communities. Far from being residues from the past, and an exception to the normal functioning of capitalism, these contemporary colonial practices are essential to its functioning, supplementing an ever greater need to sustain capital accumulation on a planetary scale. It follows that the interlinking of anticolonial and ecological struggles, in their diversity, are crucial for imagining and enacting radical, decolonial alternatives to capitalism (Ferdinand 2022).

Among several different terms used to refer to struggles against colonialism, past and present, in its diverse manifestations, we find the notion of "sovereignty" to express such a decolonizing ambition in the most affirmative way. As a political concept, sovereignty originated in early European modernity, asserting the absolute power of the monarch over a conquered territory and its people (Bonilla 2017) — precisely at the time that the colonial project was being articulated into the largest act of plunder and genocide in human history. Yet, despite such reactionary roots, sovereignty was later to turn into a dangerous, seditious idea. The principle of "popular sovereignty" was first enunciated in the course of the 1789 French Revolution, asserting that the nation — *the people* — was the only legitimate source of state authority (Russell 2021). However, only a few years after, it was the "Black Jacobins" of Haiti — former plantation slaves turned revolutionaries who expelled the French from the island of Saint-Domingue — who realized the revolutionary anticolonial promise of popular sovereignty, creating history's first decolonized republic. While the French continued to assert their imperial control over the island by other means (Alcenat 2017), the Haitian Revolution inspired a vision not of a bourgeois government seeking legitimacy *in* the people, but of a *self*-government *of* the people, the dispossessed — an emancipatory, insurgent sovereignty.

The reactionary horizon of sovereignty never disappeared from the worldview and actions of imperial powers and colonial states. At the same time, there exists today an array of insurgent struggles that embody radical anticolonial ambitions and develop alternative forms of "sovereignty from below," within-against-and-beyond the nation-state. These are typically rooted in reclaiming political and economic control over ancestral or stolen/dispossessed land/territory. Land is broadly understood here as comprising not just the ground, but also natural resources, socioecological relations and cultural-spiritual values bonded in particular places, and being shaped by spatial relations (see Part Two in this book). Land/territorial reclamations at different scales are therefore key to decolonization (Tuck and Yang 2012; Tapia 2014), as well as to asserting dispossessed people's autonomy over their own social and ecological reproduction — their bodies, minds, and lives. Irrespective of their diverse self-identification, we use the term "sovereignty" to describe and understand the anticolonial and emancipatory horizon of such struggles.

These struggles revolve around three main themes (see also Ferdinand 2022). First, there are the fights for self-determination by stateless nations and Indigenous communities living under colonial occupation, or in regions with a history of settler colonialism. This includes areas like the Caribbean and Pacific islands under the governance of the USA and European powers, as well as regions like Kurdistan and Palestine. Additionally, these struggles extend to numerous Indigenous, peasant, and Afrodescendant peoples across Latin America, as well as the Aboriginal nations in what is now known as Australia. In North America, Indigenous-led movements like Land Back are working to reclaim ancestral lands, echoing similar struggles worldwide to re-establish Indigenous authority over their native territories (Longman et al. 2020). Second, these movements encompass typically racialized subaltern groups and political movements in formerly colonized countries seeking to regain control over their democracy and resources — asserting political and economic sovereignty at the national level against the exploitation of their resources by transnational corporations, which often benefit imperial core nations. Third, these struggles serve as a source of inspiration for — and intersect with — various insurgent socioecological movements across the Global South and North, who are fighting for sovereignty over food, water, forests and other means of social reproduction (see Part Two for more details on these movements).

In sum, struggles for sovereignty constitute a key pillar for building socioecologically just alternatives to the deadly intersection of coloniality and capitalism. This is the central focus of the four contributions in this section.

The chapter by Omar Jabary Salamanca illustrates the socioecological dimensions of colonial dispossession and anticolonial resistance in Palestine. The author shows how Israeli settler statecraft is predicated on depleting Indigenous social reproduction, and how Palestinians respond to the systematic destruction of their livelihood infrastructures by autonomously building and rebuilding them, reasserting their presence on the land — their sovereignty — against the settler imaginary of ethnic cleansing. Moreover, the chapter shows the ways this resistance articulates with a multitude of strategies and actors, at multiple scales, towards building a sustained countermovement.

Ercan Ayboga and Anselm Schindler elaborate further on how anticolonial resistance articulates with visions of an alternative socioecological future by providing a grounded, activist perspective on the Kurdish Freedom Movement's (KFM) visions and practices in Turkish-occupied Bakûr (Northern Kurdistan). Deeply inspired by Murray Bookchin's "social ecology" framework, the KFM articulated its anticolonial struggle with a comprehensive critique of capitalism and the capitalist state, and a transformative vision based on radical democracy, autonomy, ecology and women's liberation. For the authors, the experience of the KFM holds key lessons for environmental and climate justice movements in the Global North by showing the importance of thinking beyond state reformism, and taking neighbourhoods, communities and workplaces as the "sovereign" starting point for building revolutionary solidarity and organizing.

Diana Vela Almeida and her co-authors shift our attention to the relationship between decolonizing ambitions and socioecological movements in Ecuador and Bolivia. The focus of the chapter is on the diverging and at times conflicting visions of sovereignty put forward —by progressive political parties and their popular-class constituents on the one hand, and by dispossessed Indigenous-peasant communities on the other. The chapter shows how, in both countries, the convergence between these different sovereignty aspirations has been a key driver of anticolonial and anti-neoliberal struggles; and how these different ways of understanding sovereignty have often caused tension and conflict between the political left and dissident Indigenous-peasant organizations.

Lastly, Gustavo García-López's essay reflects on how the praxes of environmental justice movements seed and weave decolonization and sovereignty from below in the Caribbean islands of Puerto Rico, in the context of climate colonialism. Drawing on personal and collective experiences of environmental justice mobilizing, communal autogestion (autonomous organizing and self-management), and (trans)national encounters, he identifies different elements of "decolonial ecologies," which build multiple sovereignties in food, energy, land, and culture to defend and remake life. These ecologies are based on nurturing deep relationality between people and their territories, through commitment to intersectional organizing, transgressive methodologies linking research and action, and slow-but-persistent practices of deep listening, witnessing, care and healing, from the inside out.

References

Alcenat, Westenley. 2017. "The Case for Haitian Reparations." *Jacobin*. At <jacobin.com/2017/01/haiti-reparations-france-slavery-colonialism-debt/> January 14.

Bonilla, Yarimar. 2017. "Unsettling sovereignty." *Cultural Anthropology* 32, 3: 330–339.

Ferdinand, Malcom. 2022. "Decolonial ecologies: beyond environmentalism." In Pellizzoni, Luigi, Emanuele Leonardi, and Viviana Asara (eds.). *Handbook of Critical Environmental Politics*. Northampton, MA: Edward Elgar, 40–57.

Longman, Nickita, Emily Riddle, Alex Wilson, and Saima Desai (eds.). 2020. *Briarpatch, The Land Back issue*. At <briarpatchmagazine.com/issues/view/september-october-2020> September/October.

Patel, Raj, and Jason W. Moore. 2017. *History of the World in Seven Cheap Things: A Guide to Capitalism, Nature, and the Future of The Planet.* London: Verso.

Russell, Peter H. 2021. *Sovereignty: The Biography of a Claim.* Toronto: University of Toronto Press.Tapia, Luís. 2014. *Dialéctica del Colonialismo Interno.* La Paz: Autodeterminación.

Tuck, Eve, and K. Wayne Yang. 2012. "Decolonization Is Not a Metaphor." *Decolonization: Indigeneity, Education & Society* 1, 1: 1–40.

"BECAUSE OF THE LAND"

Insurgent Infrastructures of Social Reproduction in Palestine

Omar Jabary Salamanca

On the first day of 2021, an Israeli army patrol with officers from the Civil Administration raided the Palestinian hamlet of Khirbet a-Rakeez and attempted to seize an electricity generator. Home to nine families, a-Rakeez is part of Masafer Yatta, a community of two thousand sheepherders and farmers living in the South Hebron hills under constant threat of colonial displacement. When residents rushed to stop the army from confiscating the only generator in the village, a scuffle ensued and the young Harun Abu Aram was shot by a soldier at point-blank range, leaving him paralyzed until his death on February 14, 2023. As in similar instances of settler violence, the soldier was not indicted, nor did he go on trial (JLAC 2014). Harun was using the generator to rebuild a friend's barn that had been demolished by the Israeli authorities. His own family home was razed two months earlier (Aqel and El-Kurd 2021). The generator also served to power electrical devices of various families in the hamlet; it was an essential community infrastructure.

In Masafer Yatta and other frontier regions like the Jordan Valley and the Naqab, the Israeli state systematically prevents Palestinians from developing and connecting to existing energy, sanitation, and transport networks, all while providing these very infrastructures to Jewish settlements as precondition for their existence. From the lands of a-Rakeez one can easily spot the electricity poles that connect the infamous hilltop outposts of Havat Ma'on and Avigayil to the Israeli state-run national grid. It is from these and nearby settlements that settler mobs, protected by the army and border police, regularly descend to a-Rakeez and other hamlets in the area to attack residents, burn crops, chop trees, kill sheep and vandalize solar panels and water tanks. What the army does not demolish and confiscate, settlers scorch and wreak havoc.

I begin with this gruesome episode to illustrate the lengths at which the Israeli state goes to police and hamper indigenous infrastructures in Palestine's frontiers. Like the demolition of homes, clinics and schools, settler attacks on electricity, water and roads are a regular occurrence. Local and international civil society and human rights organizations, as well as residents, activists, journalists and scholars, have documented this form of infrastructural violence for decades through exhaustive written and visual reports.[1] There is an eerie, infuriating quality to this repository of ethnic cleansing that records military convoys debarking in isolated communities to suppress resistance and protect subcontracted workers while they methodically cut electricity wires and wooden pylons, unearth and damage water pipes, demolish solar panels and rainwater harvesting tanks, and rip roads apart. These overt acts of violence betray the enduring predicament of indigenous life in the frontier.

In this chapter, I want to think of Khirbet a-Rakeez and other frontier communities in Palestine as places that convey an insurgent geography of social reproduction in the margins. Their struggles for infrastructure are distinct from accounts where the denial and failed provision of essential services is either the result of state disinvestment due to neoliberalism, urban warfare strategies confined to war time, or a lack of funding and political will to extend national development across peripheral regions. Instead, what can be learned from this context is a more insidious history of the way indigenous infrastructures are constitutive of the depleting logics of settler colonial capitalism, but also an existential terrain for land-based practices of anticolonial resistance.

Matters of reproduction

Settler colonial capitalism is fundamentally haunted by the question of indigenous social reproduction. That is, the practices, spaces and ecologies that support the biological and social reproduction of colonized bodies, households, communities, and societies on a daily and intergenerational basis. This anxiety for the "messy, fleshy, stuff" (Katz 2001) that sustains indigenous life and work fundamentally stems from the imperatives of settler statecraft. For these formations are structurally defined by a voracious determination for indigenous land theft, political conquest, economic exploitation, environmental degradation, and population removal to make space for an exclusive settler polity (Wolfe 2006). Put differently, the material presence of indigenous communities

— their ways of living, working, and relating to each other and to nature — stand in the way of settler aspirations for territorialization, accumulation and sovereignty. In this winner-takes-all model, the expansion and normalization of settler colonialism can only take place at the expense of devaluing and depleting indigenous worlds. This parasitic relation not only attaches revolutionary character to indigenous social reproduction, it also places social reproduction as an essential yet often underrecognized terrain of dispossession in existential struggles for life and land.

As feminist, anticolonial and Black scholars and activists have long stressed, the intimate, private and domestic sphere of indigenous social reproduction has been a critical site of intervention for the racialized, sexualized, and gendered violence of the settler colonial state — from the forced sterilization of women's bodies and the separation of children from their families, to the stratified regulation of fertility, marriages and family life (Jacobs 2009; Arvin et al. 2013; Roberts 2014; Vertommen et al. 2022). A more expansive understanding of social reproduction, however, must contend with the built environment that enables the conditions for indigenous reproduction, in ways that both include and exceed the body and the domestic sphere (Peake et al. 2021). Essential infrastructures such as electricity, water and roads are in this sense critical insofar as they provide the ability to reproduce ways of being in place and to sustain material livelihoods. Connecting the intimate scale of the body to the global, large and small infrastructures facilitate biological reproduction, the reproduction of the labour force as well as social relations. The availability or lack of these material supports conditions thus the tight interlinkages between productive and reproductive activities. Wires, pipes and ribbons of concrete are not just purely technical matters, but structural and intimate necessities of the body politic; without them the possibilities of living a productive and dignified life become compromised. In this sense, the social in social reproduction is decisively a socio-material relation.

In Palestine, such infrastructures, and the indigenous architectures of social reproduction they sustain over time and space, have been historically a matter of concern for Zionism's double logic of primitive accumulation and elimination (Jabary Salamanca 2014; Jabary Salamanca and Silver 2022). Take, for instance, concessions granted to Jewish settlers for monopolizing water and electricity development during British imperial rule, the Israeli dismantlement of energy production in territories occupied after the 1967 war, and the gradual appropriation and segregation of ancient trails and road systems that tie Palestinian communities on the mountain range to the rest of the country in the wake of the Oslo Accords. These acts of infrastructural theft, undoing, and replacement do not just tell a story in the abstract about an impervious drive to govern indigenous metabolic ecologies. Rather, they signal a more fundamental, coercive and radical form of dispossession. One that is premised on seizing the material means of social and biological reproduction to dissolve the indigenous bond between land and life. Infrastructures are, after all, about the "in-between" (Simone 2012) territory and population that enables communities to biologically and socially reproduce but also to be held in place, to exert a physical presence that concretizes and makes possible forms of nationhood, knowledge, development and self-determination. In other words, the availability of essential infrastructures determines material presence on the land.

This idea is most clearly expressed by Rasmi, Harun's father. In a news report featured on Channel 12, an Israeli reporter asked why Harun was willing to fight the soldiers for a generator. Rasmi soberly responded: "To you it looks like Harun was fighting for a generator. We live here. It is because of the land."[2] Whereas Harun's resolve to protect the family's generator speaks to our modern attachment to technical supports for the most vital aspects of life, Rasmi reminds us that behind settler exclusions there is more than an effort to condemn frontier communities to a condition of rudimentary existence and survivability. His concise but powerful rejoinder reminds us about the centrality of reproductive infrastructures to indigenous struggles for land.

Parasitic accumulations

The assault on the Palestinian fabric of life is most severe today in places like Masafer Yatta, the Jordan Valley and the Naqab. It is in these frontier regions, where enduring assertions of indigenous autonomy and sovereignty prevent settler territorial expansion and control, that the attack on the edifice of social reproduction manifests itself in all its cruelty. This is particularly the case in dispersed, and thus more vulnerable, communities of Bedouin sheepherders and farmers who live off the land and refuse to give up their ways of life and be forcibly transferred into dense and segregated urban enclaves and townships. As explained by Riya Al-Sanah, a feminist scholar and activist from the Naqab:

We don't want to live in cities and towns. We are agricultural communities that have an intimate relationship to the land, and they want to keep that, and they will fight to keep that. And for Israel, that is really scary because it means that it has lost the ability to exert complete and total control. (Al-Shabaka 2022)

Despite being governed by different jurisdictional and citizenship regimes, in Masafer Yatta and the Jordan Valley, where indigenous populations are considered subjects of occupation and military law, or in the Naqab, where they are nominal citizens subject to state law, the racialized and depleting logics of social reproduction are in full force all the same. Here, in the margins of the state, where indigenous geographies are unrecognized, rendered invisible and denied existence on official maps, successive Israeli governments have long used brute force as well as legal, planning and financial mechanisms to reduce Palestinians into trespassers on their own lands. These illegitimate practices make impossible for communities to legally build homes and develop essential infrastructures to accommodate natural population growth (Amnesty 2022).

The Israeli state not only denies frontier communities the possibility of developing small scale and decentralized infrastructures such as solar panels and windmills, it also bans the connection to readily available water, electricity, and road networks while foreclosing ancient and rudimentary infrastructures like dirt paths, springs, cisterns, and natural water sources (Who Profits 2018). Having access to water for human and animal consumption, roads to reach nearby urban centres with their markets and schools, and electricity for communication and small-scale production is vital to preserve kinship relationships, communal life, and to sustain indigenous modes of production. Without these urban supports, communities are relegated to unpaved, dangerous, and lengthy travel routes, forced to walk long distances, required to pay high costs for trucked water, and hampered from using electricity to build and maintain homes, conserve and process food, and to care for those in need of medical attention. These infrastructure exclusions moreover are happening in areas which already suffer from desertification, lack of rainwater, the drying up of water springs, droughts, and extreme weather conditions. The denial of reproductive infrastructures thus has a direct bearing on the health, welfare and environment of indigenous communities which have, among other revealing indicators, an average life expectancy of about ten years lower than settler populations with whom they live side by side across segregated Palestine (Amnesty International 2022).

These geographies of alienated social reproduction and environmental harm, however, need to be situated in a larger, state-sanctioned political economy that fundamentally serves Jewish settler supremacy. For indigenous and settler social reproduction do not sit opposite one another along imaginary frontier lines. Rather, they constitute a dialectical, parasitic formation whereby settlers occupy indigenous host ecologies to extract and dispossess in ways that are productive of racialized, classed, and gendered relations (see Whitener 2020). Indeed, the attack on the edifice of Palestinian social reproduction has a disproportionate impact on women, who are often forced to compensate for the absence, disruption and destruction of infrastructures with their labour (Al-Butmeh 2021). Compounded with continuous settler encroachment on farm and grazing lands, lack of access to essential infrastructures drives many rural Palestinian families into relations of debt, the abandonment of livelihoods and communal life, and their gradual incorporation as cheap and precarious workers into the Israeli economy, particularly in the construction sector (B'tselem 2016; Hackl 2023). This historical and evolving process of wearing down, harming and depleting is central to a vast territorial and

Protesters march in a-Rakeez, Masafer Yatta area, South of Hebron, towards the Avigayil outpost, one week after 24-year-old Harun Abu Aram was shot. January 8, 2021. Image © Activestills. Reproduced with permission.

racialized reordering of populations that ultimately seeks to force communities out of their lands and into dense urban enclaves to make space for an ever-expanding settler state.

Thus, settler colonialism can only thrive and be sustained at the expense of the massive resource transfer resulting from devaluating and exhausting indigenous life worlds. In the West Bank alone, since 2009, the Israeli state has forcibly impoverished and displaced more than twelve thousand Palestinians by demolishing about eight thousand structures — including homes, shops, animal shelters, and warehouses as well as water, road and electricity infrastructures (OCHA 2022). Furthermore, since 1967, the state has declared more than 60 percent of the West Bank as state land, allocating the following: forty thousand hectares to the World Zionist Organization for outpost and settlement construction; approximately 10,300 hectares to settlement councils and Israeli mobile phone companies; about sixteen thousand hectares to government ministries and utility companies such as the Bezeq telephone company, the Israeli Electric Corporation and Mekorot, Israel's national water company; and more than sixteen thousand hectares for the construction of settler-only roads by Netivei, the National Roads Company of Israel (ACRI 2013; MA'AN 2008). In the Naqab the situation is no different; in 2020 alone, during the global pandemic, more than 2,568 structures were demolished, the highest number ever recorded. At the same time, thousands of hectares are regularly deep ploughed and aerially sprayed with chemicals by the Israeli authorities to damage and destroy Bedouin lands and crops (NCF 2021). Moreover, while the Israeli government refuses to recognize Palestinian Bedouin villages and provide their residents with the basic services to live in dignity, the government continues to financially support and provide services to over a hundred Jewish rural towns and family farms while advancing plans for afforestation, urbanization, and industrialization to settle hundreds of thousands of settlers, changing the demography of the region (Nasasra 2017). It is out of this primordial act of theft and subsidy that Israel can dispose of sufficient land, capital, resources, and labour to expand and develop the very infrastructures of extraction, production and circulation that sustain its very existence. The denial of Palestinian reproductive autonomy effectively subsidies Jewish reproduction and expansion. In other words, settler spaces of excess and life are indigenous spaces of scarcity and depletion (see McIntyre and Nast 2011).

Insurgent infrastructures

The late Deborah Bird Rose once wrote that "to get in the way of settler colonization, all the native has to do is stay at home" (in Wolfe 2006: 388). What happens, however, when homes and the technical supports that sustain indigenous households and livelihoods become the very target of frontier violence? In other words, how do indigenous communities build and sustain infrastructures of biological and social reproduction when the settler state remains determined to banish them? What forms of political organization and material support are put in place to defend the land when everyday life is conditioned by denied access to the most basic of needs, but also by broken livelihoods, settler violence, and constant threats of house demolition and displacement? And how are coalitions of resistance developed across and beyond the fragmented and captive geographies of Palestine to confront settler rituals of ethnic cleansing — which are met by national governments and international institutions, at best, with silence and indifference and, at worst, with complicity and acquiescence?

To return to my original proposition, the matter of social reproduction offers a compelling entry point to grapple with the logics of settler colonial capitalism, yet it also provides fertile ground to explore land-based practices of anticolonial resistance. When biological and social reproduction are at stake, no political project escapes the primacy of rebuilding and maintaining essential infrastructures to fulfil people's most basic needs. In Palestine's frontiers, this form of existential materialism has been the most immediate and instinctive political task for the past many decades. This ethos is best articulated by Rasmiya Mohmmad, the grandmother of Harun Abu Aran, who insists that families won't leave despite settler attempts at erasure: "they destroy, we build" (Aqel and El-Kurd 2021). In the same vein, Aziz Al-Turi, from the Committee for the Defence of Al Araqib, a village in the Naqab, recently asserted that "the people will rebuild their village" after it was demolished for the 208th time (MEMO 2022). Echoing this sentiment, grassroots movements across Palestine's frontiers such as the Popular Committee for the Defence and Steadfastness in Masafer Yatta and the Jordan Valley Solidarity campaign maintain that "to exist is to resist." To confront the everyday threats posed to indigenous lives and the environments they inhabit and protect implies not simply to stay put, but also to continuously develop insurgent infrastructures of reproduction. As Rema

Hammami (2016: 172) argues, it is "persistent acts that make home and livelihoods, of going out to plant and harvest wheat, of herding sheep in the hills, collecting water in cisterns, planting trees and harvesting olives, of children walking miles to the closest schools, of men and women continuing to marry, of women to give birth and raise children."

The rebuilding and maintenance of frontier infrastructures of reproduction, which always takes place outside the legal framework of the settler state, is achieved at great costs and labour through resourceful indigenous initiatives that mobilize a multitude of strategies and actors — including localized family and community organizing, mutual aid and voluntary work campaigns, support from national civil society organizations, and interventions from international organizations. For instance, in Masafer Yatta and the Jordan Valley, the Union of Agricultural Work Committees (UAWC) has been supporting frontier communities through the development of agricultural roads, piped water, irrigation systems, and land reclamation programs, often under the cover of the night to escape the settler state's gaze (Al-Butmeh et al. 2019). In the Naqab, Palestinian communities living in so-called unrecognized villages continue to challenge state restrictions, policing, and policies of dispossession through insurgent forms of development, planning and litigation initiatives to politicize infrastructures in ways that actualize struggles for preserving lands and livelihoods (Jabareen and Switat 2019). Moreover, across the West Bank, local chapters of the Popular Struggle Coordination Committee have been organizing the "Faz3a" campaign to help frontier communities defend their villages to halt infrastructure demolition and confiscation, to protect school children on their way to school, and to shield shepherds and farmers from settler violence. Faz3a is a community-led mobilization to support, aid and resist based on voluntary work and organizing, which is at the core of the Palestine Resistance Committees.[3] These Palestinian village-and-town-based groups, which include youth activists and elders, were first formed in the aftermath of the second intifada and draw from a long history of community struggle (Hanbali 2022). Their strategy and tactics include organizing demonstrations and direct actions, popular education initiatives, as well as mobilizing international support and solidarity to strengthen the struggle for reproduction and liberation. As Palestinian anthropologist Ala Alazzeh (2011: 10) notes, "although the work of these committees is irregular, territorially disconnected or locally based, and often issue oriented, they have become arguably the most important in the current struggle against Israel's colonial practices."

However, these and other forms of collective action to halt settler encroachments on indigenous lives and lands are fraught with risk, both for dwellers and front-line activists who are regularly beaten up, arrested, and imprisoned, and for the organizations involved in supporting frontier communities. An example of the latter is the recent move by the Israeli state to arbitrarily designate six Palestinian civil society organizations as terrorist groups without providing any concrete proof — including human rights group Al-Haq, prisoners' rights group Addameer, Defense for Children International Palestine, the Bisan Center for Research and Development, the Union of Palestinian Women's Committees, and the UAWC (OHCHR 2022). These groups provide critical material support and document human rights violations of communities at risk across the West Bank. Among the immediate impacts of the designation were the decisions by the Dutch government and the European Commission to suspend funding for UAWC's frontier infrastructure projects. Even though these European measures were eventually cancelled due to lack of evidence and international outcry, these forms of criminalization — which have led to the arrest of several Palestinian organizers — speak to Israel's attempt to both undermine the work of those documenting and resisting ethnic cleansing and to isolate Palestinian civil society from the global community.

The political significance of material struggles to build and sustain insurgent infrastructures ultimately stems from the necessity to consolidate a reproductive attachment to life and land but also to create the conditions of a respite, a form of suspending the time of frontier displacement (Stop the Wall 2017). Yet it is only when these efforts are transformed into a collective and national political endeavour that such force can significantly contribute to the path of liberation. The Palestinian uprising of May 2021 — known as the Unity Intifada — is a clear manifestation of such national, mass mobilization against dispossession and displacement. Led by a new generation of activist youth groups and a new grammar of struggle, the Unity Intifada forced a rupture with decades of forced geographical fragmentation and political division by bringing together struggles across Palestine's urban and rural regions. Central to the uprising was an effective general strike that saw the widespread closure of businesses and workplaces from the Gaza Strip to the Galilee.[4]

In the coming years, bringing worker participation to the heart of the struggle will be critical to develop a cross-class, cross-geographical alliance committed to disrupting the parasitic accumulations of settler colonialism. However, this anticolonial alliance must step up mobilizations to defend frontier communities across Palestine in ways that recognize the centrality of strengthening reproductive infrastructures. As we have seen in this chapter, infrastructures are not only central to the "hidden abode of production" (Marx 2004) that sustains indigenous and settler economies; they are essential in mediating relations between land and life in ways that can contribute to both sever and affirm this bond. The cases outlined in this chapter further suggest how frontier communities relate to infrastructure and the built environment in more complex ways than as mere passive subjects at the other end of systemic practices of violence. This not only contributes to acknowledging the lasting indigenous investments in the social, economic and political promises of infrastructure. It also accounts for the often-neglected conditions and mechanisms that shape the production of indigenous built environments and spaces beyond architectures of settler colonial occupation. In this sense, the interest here is not just on settler but also indigenous facts on the ground, not only acts of negation and erasure, but also practices of affirmation and rehabilitation. Despite unimaginable vagrancies, even when the settler state successfully reduces the aspirations of frontier communities to an electricity generator or a pirate water connection through a rickety plastic pipe, modern infrastructures, large or small, have long been indigenous means of imagining and advancing forms of sovereignty, economic development and material presence on the land, from the river to the sea.

Notes

1. For comprehensive and regular reports on settler violence in the West Bank, see for instance: United Nations Office for the Coordination of Humanitarian Affairs (ochaopt.org/page/publications/demolitions); The Israeli Information Center for Human Rights in the Occupied Territories (btselem.org/settler_violence_updates_list#); and POICA (poica.org).
2. The interview can be found at <youtube.com/watch?v=Lkd9rO-yhc0>.
3. To see some of the activities organized by the Popular Struggle Coordination Committees, go to: <facebook.com/PopularStruggle>.
4. See the "Call for Dignity and Hope," which was published in Palestine in concertation between the different actors who worked for the success of May 18th's strike call: <assafirarabi.com/en/37888/2021/05/20/the-declaration-of-dignity-and-hope/>.

References

ACRI (Association for Civil Rights in Israel). 2013. "Allocation of State Land in OPT." At <law.acri.org.il/en/2013/04/23/info-sheet-state-land-opt> April 23.

Aqel, Ryah and Mohammed El-Kurd. 2021. "The Israeli Military Shot My Cousin — and the US Bears Part of the Blame." *The Nation*. At <thenation.com/article/world/us-military-israel/> March 2.

Alazzeh, Ala. 2011. "Non-Violent Popular Resistance in the West Bank. The Case of the Popular Struggle Committees." Center for Development Studies, Birzeit Univeristy. At <docslib.org/doc/3616139/non-violent-popular-resistance-in-the-west-bank-the-case-of-the>.

Al-Butmeh, Abeer. 2021. "Palestine Women Defending Water, Land, and Life from the Israeli Occupation." *Capire*. At <capiremov.org/en/analysis/palestine-women-defending-water-land-and-life-from-the-israeli-occupation> November 8.

Al-Butmeh, Abeer, Zayneb al-Shalalfeh, Mahmoud Zwahre, and Eurig Scandrett. 2019. "The Environment as a Site of Struggle against Settler-Colonisation in Palestine." In Anne Harley and Eurig Scandrett (eds.). *Environmental Justice, Popular Struggle and Community Development*. Bristol: Bristol University Press, 153–172.

Al-Shabaka. 2022. "Ongoing Resistance in the Naqab with Riya Al-Sanah." At <al-shabaka.org/podcasts/ongoing-resistance-in-the-naqab-with-riya-al-sanah/> January 27.

Amnesty International. 2022. "Israel's Apartheid against Palestinians. Cruel System of Domination and Crime against Humanity." London. At <amnesty.org/en/documents/mde15/5141/2022/en/> February 1.

Arvin, Maile, Eve Tuck, and Angie Morrill. 2013. "Decolonizing feminism: Challenging connections between settler colonialism and heteropatriarchy." *Feminist Formations* 25, 1: 8–34.

B'tselem. 2016. "Expel and Exploit: The Israeli Practice of Taking over Rural Palestinian Land." At <btselem.org/publications/summaries/201612_expel_and_exploit>.

Hackl, Andreas. 2023. "Occupied labour: dispossession through incorporation among Palestinian workers in Israel." *Settler Colonial Studies* 13: 96–114.

Hammami, Rema. 2016. "Precarious Politics: The Activism of 'Bodies That Count' (Aligning with Those That Don't) in Palestine's Colonial Frontier." In J. Butler, Z. Gambetti, and L. Sabsay (eds.). *Vulnerability in Resistance*. Durham, NC: Duke University Press, 167–190.

Hanbali, Layth. 2022. "Reimagining Liberation through the Popular Committees." *Al-Shabaka*. At <al-shabaka.org/briefs/reimagining-liberation-through-the-palestinian-popular-committees/> February 16.

Jabareen, Yosef, and Orwa Switat. 2019. "Insurgent informality: The struggle over space production between the Israeli state and its Palestinian Bedouin communities." *Space and Polity* 23, 1: 92–113.

Jabary Salamanca, Omar. 2014. "Fabric of Life: The Infrastructure of Settler Colonialism and Uneven Development in Palestine." PhD thesis, Ghent University.

Jabary Salamanca, Omar, and Jonathan Silver. 2022. "In the Excess of Splintering Urbanism: The Racialized Political Economy of Infrastructure." *Journal of Urban Technology* 29, 1: 117–125.

Jacobs, Margaret D. 2009. *White Mother to a Dark Race: Settler Colonialism, Maternalism, and the Removal of Indigenous Children in the American West and Australia, 1880–1940*. Lincoln, NE: University of Nebraska Press.

JLAC (Jerusalem Legal Aid and Human Rights Center). 2014. "Settler Violence and Impunity in the Occupied Palestinian Territory." At <ecoi.net/en/file/local/1114943/1930_1413359544_int-ccpr-css-isr-18146-e.pdf>.

Katz, Cindi. 2001. "Vagabond Capitalism and the Necessity of Social Reproduction." *Antipode* 33, 4: 709–728.

MA'AN Development Center. 2008. "Apartheid Roads: Promoting Settlements, Punishing Palestinians." At <maan-ctr.org/old/pdfs/Apartheid%20Roads.pdf >.

Marx, Karl. 2004. *Capital: Volume I*. London: Penguin.

McIntyre, Michael, and Heidi J. Nast. 2011. "Bio(necro)polis: Marx, Surplus Populations, and the Spatial Dialectics of Reproduction and 'Race.'" *Antipode* 43, 5: 1465–1488.

MEMO. 2022. "Israel demolishes Palestinian village of Al-Araqib for 208th time." At <middleeastmonitor.com/20221024-israel-demolishes-palestinian-village-of-al-araqib-for-208th-time/> October 24.

Nasasra, Mansour. 2017. *The Naqab Bedouins: A Century of Politics and Resistance*. New York: Columbia University Press.

NCF (Negev Coexistence Forum for Civil Equality). 2021. "No Shelter in Place: State Demolitions in the Naqab Arab Bedouin Communities and its Impact on Children." At <dukium.org/wp-content/uploads/2021/07/HDR-2021-Data-on-2020-Eng-5.pdf>.

OCHA (United Nations Office for the Coordination of Humanitarian Affairs). 2022. "Data on demolition and displacement in the West Bank." At <ochaopt.org/data/demolition>.

OHCHR (United Nations Office of the High Commissioner for Human Rights). 2022. "Israel/Palestine: UN experts call on governments to resume funding for six Palestinian CSOs designated by Israel as 'terrorist organizations.'" At <ohchr.org/en/press-releases/2022/04/israelpalestine-un-experts-call-governments-resume-funding-six-palestinian> April 25.

Peake, Linda, Elsa Koleth, Gökbörü Sarp Tanyildiz, Rajyashree N. Reddy, darren patrick/dp (eds.). 2021. *A Feminist Urban Theory for Our Time: Rethinking Social Reproduction and the Urban*. New York: John Wiley & Sons.

Roberts, Dorothy. 2014. *Killing the Black Body: Race, Reproduction, and the Meaning of Liberty*. New York: Vintage.

Simone, AbdouMaliq. 2012. "Infrastructure: Commentary by AbdouMaliq Simone." *Cultural Anthropology*. At <journal.culanth.org/index.php/ca/infrastructure-abdoumaliq-simone>.

Stop the Wall. 2017. "The Palestinian Periphery. Home Demolitions and Settler Colonialism in the Jordan Valley and the South Hebron Hills." At <issuu.com/stopthewall/docs/periphery_final_issuu> February 22.

Vertommen, Sigrid, Vincenzo Pavone, and Michal Nahman. 2022. "Global fertility chains: An integrative political economy approach to understanding the reproductive bioeconomy." *Science, Technology, & Human Values* 47, 1: 112–145.

Whitener, Brian. 2020. "Detroit's Water Wars: Race, Failing Social Reproduction, and Infrastructure." *CLCWeb: Comparative Literature and Culture* 22, 2: 8.

Who Profits. 2018. "Plundering the Sun: The Israeli Solar Energy Industry and Palestinian Forced Displacement." At <whoprofits.org/publications/report/40>.

Wolfe, Patrick. 2006. "Settler Colonialism and the Elimination of the Native." *Journal of Genocide Research* 8, 4: 387–409.

ECOLOGICAL THOUGHT AND PRACTICE IN THE KURDISH FREEDOM MOVEMENT

The Case of Bakûr

Ercan Ayboga and Anselm Schindler

This chapter details the evolution of the ecological principles of the Kurdish Freedom Movement, and how they have been turned into practice in Turkish-occupied Northern Kurdistan. This is the northernmost part of the majority Kurdish areas and is therefore referred to by many Kurds as Bakûr (Kurdish for "north").

Kurdistan is a territory divided and occupied by the four colonial states of Turkey, Iran, Iraq and Syria. The widespread introduction of capitalist economy and relations in the 1950s was accompanied by a systemic and destructive exploitation of the region's people and nature. The economic policies and investments, which led to the displacement of hundreds of thousands of rural people to the fast-growing cities, aimed also at benefiting from a cheap labour force to be exploited and a deepening of people's ongoing cultural assimilation. Through colonialism and the penetration of capitalist relations, Kurdistan has become fully part of the "national markets" of each of the four colonial states. This meant, on one side, rural exodus and the destruction of self-sufficiency in the countryside and, on the other side, that agriculture became more and more subject to colonial exploitation that made the surplus product flow off to the capitalist centres of the colonial states.

Among the many Kurdish political resistance organizations of recent decades, the most revolutionary, emancipatory and broad-based is the Kurdistan Workers' Party (PKK), which was assembled in 1978 in Lice, in Northern Kurdistan (the part of Kurdistan occupied by the Turkish state). In the 1980s, the PKK organized armed resistance against the Turkish state, and gained support from other parts of Kurdistan. The PKK influenced the emergence of novel social and political organizations, out of which a substantial movement developed, known as the Kurdish Freedom Movement (KFM). The movement initially focused on the Turkish-occupied areas, but later spread to other parts of Kurdistan.

In the 1990s, the KFM, and particularly its leader Abdullah Öcalan, introduced an important political debate on the ecological question within the movement. The leitmotif for this debate was the systematic destruction of Kurdish people's livelihoods through the Turkish state's war on Kurds — including the bombing of mountains, the torching of thousands of hectares of natural forest, and the displacement of more than two million civilians from villages, as well as the construction of hundreds of dams, agricultural schemes, mining facilities, and other infrastructural projects, causing dramatic physical changes to the landscape and harm to the population. Öcalan examined and elaborated theoretically how these transformations, responsible for causing negative social, cultural, ecological and political impacts to the Kurdish population and territories, were linked to the development of neoliberal capitalism in Kurdistan, and globally (see Make Rojava Green Again 2020). Next, we detail the KFM's approach to ecology and how it helped to radically shift the movement's politics towards the notion and practice of Democratic Confederalism.

The radical ecological thought of the Kurdish Freedom Movement

Öcalan's ecological thinking is summarized in diverse works. His prison writings, collected in different books, had a major impact on thousands of political activists in the KFM, and on KFM's internal politics. In his analyses, he raises the question of humans' growing alienation from nature and developed ideas how to overcome it. These ideas often refer to the concepts of social ecology and to thinkers like Murray Bookchin, with whom Öcalan exchanged letters. One of the most important ideas that Öcalan takes over from Bookchin is that the ecological question can only be solved by decentralizing power structures. Bookchin (1982) explains this connection most vividly along the lines of energy supply, where communal self-determination through small-scale energy production, such as solar or wind energy, go hand-in-hand with sustainability. At the same time, however, Öcalan agrees with Bookchin on the point that the solution to the ecological question cannot be a purely technical one, but that it also requires other social structures and greater awareness among the people. Bookchin distinguishes between "environmentalism" and "ecology," the former being the misguided attempt to solve the ecological question in a purely technical way, the latter a holistic approach. Öcalan also ties in with this thinking his critique of positivism, not least criticizing some Marxist approaches for their fixation on technological progress and science (Çiçek 2021).

Öcalan also addresses industry in his discussion of ecology. He criticizes the centralization of production, because this often also has to do with the intensification of the exploitation of people and nature. This is exemplified by large dams, agricultural corporations and coal-fired power plants. As a solution, Öcalan proposes decentralization, although he does not oppose any form of industry, but only advocates for its transformation; at this point he uses the term "Ecological Industry." A transformation of energy supply, combining efficient technology and decentralization, could lead to a more sustainable production. One could deduce from Öcalan's ideas, energy supply needs to be freed from the chains of capitalist profit pressure.

This ecological thought set the stage for important shifts in KFM politics, especially after Öcalan's abduction in 1999 — through an international plot orchestrated by Turkish intelligence and the CIA — and his imprisonment on İmralı Island. This major event catalyzed a broad discussion within the KFM. Two major consequences unfolded from this debate. First, following Öcalan's proposal, the PKK decided to end the armed struggle as strategic priority was given to political-civil struggle. Second, the KFM transformed its theory of revolution and its practice away from earlier Marxist-Leninist influences, no longer focusing on building socialism through the capture of state power but through the creation of radical democratic communes and institutions. This debate, also inspired by the new ecological perspective within the movement, led to the introduction of a new political concept called "Democratic Confederalism." Initially proposed by Öcalan and the PKK in 2005, this concept is based on three pillars: radical democracy, ecology, and women's liberation (Ayboga n.d.).

In developing this concept, Öcalan opposes the idea of Capitalist Modernity to the notion of Democratic Modernity (Kurban 2016). In his view, Capitalist and Democratic Modernity are not separate stages; they exist in parallel and in struggle. The question is which way of living will prevail. To realize radical democracy, different regions aim to organize themselves as strong autonomous structures. Consequently, the objective of a Kurdish national state has been given up, as it is considered as a legacy of colonialism. That does not mean that the Kurdish identity or the preservation of cultural diversity are abandoned. Yet, attempts are being made to create a new concept of nation that is not defined by ethnicity but by shared radical democratic organization and common values. Öcalan calls this concept the Democratic Nation. With this process, the KFM points far beyond its original goal of liberating Kurdistan. Its aspirations are universalist. The attempt to represent the diversity of society and to resist its homogenization by nationalism fits well with the struggle for preserving ecological diversity. Just as capitalist monoculture leads to ecocide, the attempt to uniform society through nationalism destroys society itself: both must be prevented.

In KFM's ecological thought, nature is the realm of all living beings, including humans, and thus should not be reduced to a source of profit. In this perspective, humans do not stand over nature or other species. Nature is regarded as alive and animated, and all living beings are part of one common ecosystem that offers everyone enough opportunities to live. Nature was and is the source of food, housing, and all other material needs of life. Throughout history, most human communities have had a strong connection with nature in daily life. Despite everyone experiencing the impacts of grave ecological damage in recent decades, the destruction of nature continues and is even accelerating. Following this assumption, KFM argues that the economy must be "decoupled" from the capitalist profit and growth pressure. Instead of following the dictates of the market, the economy should be subject to the democratic decision-making processes of the communes. In Rojava, this is already being put into practice in parts, where the communes are building cooperatives that also focus on sustainable production.

In this approach, the oppression of women is equated with the exploitation of nature. As nature is objectified as inert resources to be exploited by humanity — thus separating society and nature — so too, under capitalism, are women subordinated to and exploited for men's privilege. In result, Öcalan argues that the struggle for an environmentally sustainable society necessarily includes the struggle against patriarchy. In Öcalan's thought, and for the KFM, patriarchy is identified as a key facet of social domination, currently and historically. Moreover, it is considered that fighting women's oppression and patriarchy is central to tackling many other forms of oppression. For the movement, nationalism and authoritarianism are reinforced by being intersected with patriarchal dynamics. Consequently, superseding the idea and form of the nation-state is only possible with a fight against sexism. The women's liberation movement is thus considered to be at the forefront of the struggle for building a "new world." Thus far, however, a broader debate on gender that includes queer struggles has still to unfold.

Turning ecological radical thought into practice in Bakûr: From ecology to Democratic Confederalism

Ecology in KFM's municipal governments: 1999–2005

The successes of the KFM's legal party structures in Turkish Kurdistan in the 1999 elections made it possible to put at least some of its principles into practice. Around fifteen million people live in Northern Kurdistan — also known as Bakûr — and the KFM has a lot of support there, which is shown in the elections. In 1999, the legal parliamentarian party structures of the KFM, known as HADEP (Halkın Demokrasi Partisi / Party of People's Democracy) — which later merged into the HDP (Hakların Demokratik Partisi / People's Democratic Party) alliance — won three dozen municipalities (out of 1389) in the local elections. These municipalities — among them the large cities of Amed, Batman, and Wan — became essential territories for putting into practice the renewed KFM ecological thought and politics.

Where the KFM achieved mayoral offices through elections, there were repeated attempts to break new ground. In the process, gender-quota-based dual leaderships were used, and local administrations were not meant to administer from above, but also served to build radically democratic structures. The success of the KFM in the election happened in parallel to a reduction in the repression of the Turkish state, mainly because of the halt in the armed struggle. This facilitated more space for the municipalities and other KFM organizations to spread their political ideas and to develop more contact with less politically organized parts of society. The KFM's democratic, social and ecological principles could then be implemented at the local level through the municipal governments. Indeed, the KFM-ruled municipalities have been successful in finding solutions to many immediate practical challenges such as poor-quality drinking water, the lack of facilities for wastewater treatment, garbage mismanagement, the lack of green areas in cities, the absence of city planning, poor street conditions and chaotic traffic, limited sport opportunities, non-existent social services (particularly for women and children) and the conservation of cultural heritage. Within a few years the situation improved significantly. Corruption decreased, and gentrification processes and large infrastructure projects that benefited only the few could be largely stopped.

With the end of the war in 1999, the first ecological campaigns and movements emerged in Bakûr. The two most well-known campaigns are those that have targeted destructive dams at the Munzur River in Dersim, and the Ilısu Dam on the Tigris River, which threatened the 12,000-year-old town of Hasankeyf. Local initiatives quickly raised awareness of these issues and gained broad public support. There was substantial support from organizations and media close to the KFM, but also from other parts of society. Thousands of people protested these dams during the following years. Furthermore, with some partial success in delaying these dam projects, these campaigns generated public debates that have strongly influenced ecological consciousness among Kurdish communities. In the following years, there was a steady increase of groups working on issues concerning nature conservation, environmental health, the negative impacts of big infrastructure and energy projects, and of industrial food production. Some of these groups have been initiated by those with a strong political commitment, while others have been developed by people concerned about the grave impacts of governmental policies on their livelihoods and on nature.

Despite the increased ecological awareness and the novel politics of KFM local administrations, the comprehensive steps necessary to bring about radical democratic, ecological and solidarity municipalities were mainly missing until the end of the 2000s. For the municipal administration, the notion of ecological improvement primarily meant issues like more parks, clean drinking water and clean streets — developments seen in a few Turkish cities and more broadly in Europe. One reason for this was a weak political vision and lack of experience regarding local governing. A second reason was that although the Turkish state's approach was less directly oppressive towards the KFM than in the 1990s, in the context of neoliberalism, other strategies were used against the KFM-controlled municipalities. Imposed austerity policies, including limited support by national state bodies, and administrative centralism, sought to bring the municipalities to a point where they would weaken the KFM's standing among the people in the middle term.

After Turkey's economic crisis in 2001 and with the new conservative Justice and Development Party (AKP) in government, the neoliberal capitalist economy spread to all areas of society in Bakûr. Capitalist Modernity unfolded its most destructive forces, as the government did everything to enable private investments in Turkey, including in the occupied territories of Bakûr. There was much more capital available, mostly foreign investment, resulting in a construction boom in urban and rural areas, which had severe impacts on people and local environments. Beginning in 2005, this is also the time in which KFM advances the concept of Democratic Centralism. A broad discussion was then held across the KFM on how this line could be implemented in Bakûr given its social conditions.

Advancing Democratic Centralism on the ground: 2005 onwards

As a result of the discussions, the Democratic Society Congress (KCD) was founded in 2007 with the aim to build a grassroots organization for pushing forward Democratic Confederalism in Kurdistan and Turkey (Egret and Anderson 2016). Since then, the first steps have been taken to set up people's assemblies (councils) at the neighbourhood level, in areas where the KFM had a significant basis. At higher levels, delegates from these people's assemblies meet social movements (like women's, education, youth and economy movements), NGOs, political parties, municipalities, unions and other organizations.

The first level is the district, the next the province, with the highest being the general assembly of Bakûr. The KCD's general assembly meets regularly — usually every six months — and has 501 members. At these higher levels, usually 60 percent of all delegates come from the neighbourhood assemblies and 40 percent from social and political organizations. The inclusion of all supporting organizations and actors in the councils above the neighbourhood level is a crucial element of the new political project. With this inclusive approach, each constituency, whether social, political, cultural, or gender, has a voice in the discussion process and should be included in the decisions. Where possible, particularly in the neighbourhood assemblies, decisions are made by consensus. Unlike parliamentarian systems, the principle is that no group should rule over the others.

As members discussed ways to more deeply connect women's liberation, radical democracy, and ecology within the KCD's local self-governance structures, they realized that it was necessary to consider how to better confront existing and new challenges. In 2010, many participants took part in the First Conference on Ecology and Local Administrations, which focused on debating social relations and issues of development. Within this approach, one crucial focus was the cities, considering that most people now lived in urban areas, and migration to the cities was accelerated by the state's economic politics.

In the KCD's early years, ecological policy was positioned within its municipal committees. In January 2011, the first Ecology Forum was organized in Amed. Activists and researchers from across Turkey and the Middle East also joined this unique event. For the first time in Kurdistan's history, ecological challenges, struggles and approaches were debated in a broad and organized way. There were detailed discussions about dams, mining, energy policies, industrial agriculture, urbanization, transport, health, nature conservation, climate crises and other issues. Because of this event, a group of activists from up to eight ecology-related struggles regularly convened. A year later this group announced the formation of the Mesopotamia Ecology Movement (MEM).

At first, the MEM was a network of local groups and interested people rather than a social movement. Activists met and discussed topics within the MEM, releasing common statements. It was a gradual process for the MEM to gain wider social recognition and became part of the KCD with its own delegates. Just at this time — summer 2011 — a new wave of state war on Kurds began, which has not only attacked the guerrillas, but also social and political organizations (nine thousand political activists were arrested). In 2013, a ceasefire between the Turkish state and the PKK saw an easing of the political situation, and in this context two events contributed to the strengthening of social awareness of ecological issues. Students at Amed's Dicle University organized a protest camp at the university site against the destruction of a small forest in the Tigris Valley. With the support of many civil society organizations, they successfully stopped the project. Also in 2013, the MEM organized a demonstration in which hundreds of people protested against controversial plans for a huge housing project on a hill, also in the Tigris Valley at Amed. This campaign against a project for which the

HDP municipality had given permission, despite broad criticism, was almost unique, as the HDP is part of the KCD. This protest, which could not stop the housing construction, was therefore significant in raising critical objections to aspects of the HDP's city development. Following this and other conflicts, the HDP began to take stronger notice of the MEM's views and became more cautious in its response to applications from private developers.

Since 2013, ecology activists have initiated or joined with others in new struggles. Prominent among them were campaigns against the construction of many small hydroelectric dams, with active opposition to those at Amed City, Pasur/Amed, Zilan/Wan, and Dersim. Another important issue was hydraulic fracturing or "fracking," since the Turkish government planned to expand operations in Bakûr, where it assumed lay the largest reserves and so began test drillings in 2013. Another increasing cause of public concern was the health and water quality of the large Wan Lake. The struggle against a huge coal plant in Sîlopî/Şirnex saw thousands of people take to the streets to protest. For several years there were also protests against the site of the largest cement factory in Turkey, in Marash Province.

Protest of several hundred people organized by the Mesopotamian Ecology Movement against the Ilisu Dam in the town Kerboran (Dargeçit) in the province of Mêrdîn, where the construction of the dam had started. The hand sign carried by the women reads: "Defend your nature yourself." April 13, 2015. Photo credit: Mesopotamian Ecology Movement, reproduced with permission.

Protest action in Hasankeyf by the Initiative to Keep Hasankeyf Alive and the Mesopotamia Ecology Movement against the Ilisu Dam on the international action day called Big Jump. July 12, 2015. Photo credit: Mesopotamia Ecology Movement, reproduced with permission.

The ecology struggles, however, were not limited to rural areas, and many younger people living in urban areas also became motivated to engage with ecological groups and projects. A major contributing factor for this was the fast growth of poorly planned cities, developed with little consideration for social and ecological wellbeing. There was growing criticism of the new neighbourhoods with partly gated communities, which largely facilitated the individualization of people. Another cause for discontent was the appearance of large shopping malls, which were destroying the businesses of many small shop owners. While the capital investment behind these malls came from Istanbul, they were developed with the permission of the HDP municipalities. In the face of rising criticism, this ended in 2014, but several of these malls have already been established in all the larger cities.

Nevertheless, there are many more state-driven projects for large constructions such as housing schemes and entertainment complexes, or to redevelop existing public areas. The municipalities now usually resist such changes — particularly, given the expression of criticism by the KCD's ecology, economy, women, and youth movements. The Turkish government often overrides local decisions in order to implement the contested projects. However, the HDP municipalities were often able to prevent the destruction of neighbourhoods through gentrification to protect low-income people. Therefore, many such neighbourhoods remain close to city centres or in nice locations to this day. This is a significant difference to cities ruled by other political parties.

In 2015 the MEM restructured itself with the aim to become a broad and more effective social movement. After wide-ranging discussions, councils in each province of Bakûr were established, offering space to political activists already working on ecology and in civil society organizations, as well as to any interested parties. Within a few months several hundred people joined the assemblies of these councils, set up in some of Bakûr's twenty provinces. Each provincial council formed according to their local needs, with working committees where activists could focus on the issues that are priorities for their provinces. Typical were the committees on energy, water, food and agriculture, biodiversity, urban development and transport, and legal issues; specific and of special interest were committees on animal rights, eco-technology, forests and ecological economics. For each provincial council, a coordinating committee was created consisting of two co-chairs, one woman and one man, together with the two co-speakers, one woman and one man, who are elected directly in the assemblies, usually for every six months. The provincial coordinators send their delegates to the Bakûr MEM assembly, where a general coordinating committee is elected. Women's participation and discussions on gender issues as they relate to women in each MEM structure are a fundamental part of the KCD; it is a requirement that every organization includes this approach on their agenda.

From the outset, the MEM also sought to build strategic relations with anticapitalist and antinationalist ecologists in Turkey. After years of political collaboration, relationships between Kurdish and Turkish ecologists have become much stronger. A critical step in this direction was the creation of the HDK's (Peoples' Democratic Congress) Ecology Commission with twenty-four groups in 2013 (the HDK is a congress organized across Turkey in collaboration with the KCD). The next step was the foundation of the umbrella network "Ecology Union" in 2018, which has fifty-two organizations, including almost all ecological organizations. In recent years, several common campaigns, calls for action, public meetings, and educational activities have been achieved. However, the Ecology Union has yet to develop sufficient power to influence the political agenda.

But the cooperation goes beyond Turkey: the MEM also works with ecological groups in the Middle East, particularly in Kurdish parts of Iraq, Iran, and in Rojava. As the rivers connect these regions geographically, the search for just, free and ecological societies brings activists with different cultural backgrounds together. One example is the First Mesopotamian Water Forum in April 2019 in Silêmanî (South Kurdistan/Northern Iraq). The MEM has also built relationships with European, American and Asian ecologists. There are aspirations to join international networks as is the case with water, agriculture, fracking and energy, and to exchange ideas, perspectives and practice. Considering the growing climate and ecological crisis, this is an urgent necessity as long-term solutions must be regional and global.

What can be learned from the experience of the Kurdish Freedom Movement?

While many revolutionary, national liberation movements collapsed in the 1970s, '80s and '90s, KFM managed to survive. This is because it has proven itself capable of self-criticism and change. It has overcome many crises, especially in the conflict with the Turkish state. KFM has transformed itself from a Kurdistan-based, male-dominated organization into a transnational and feminist movement. This process is not complete and probably never will be. This constant process of becoming and evolving that constitutes KFM testifies to a deep and intuitive understanding of the dialectics of life and society. From this understanding it is unavoidable to deal with the relationship between humans and the environment.

Globally, environmental movements can draw important lessons from the Kurdish freedom movement. Many environmental and climate movements in the capitalist centres of the Global North are caught in a false dichotomy between appeals to the state as an expression of reformism on the one hand, and a radicalism decoupled from society, on the other. While most environmental NGOs and mainstream climate justice movements such as Fridays for Future dutifully appeal to governments, other apparently more radical groups like Extinction Rebellion have turned to civil disobedience with street blockades and other actions. Both forms of activism, however, do not lead far: the first continues to fuel illusions in a wrong system and the second is hardly relatable to broad sections of society. The methods of Democratic Confederalism show a way out of this dead end: they take the grassroots of society like neighbourhoods or workplaces as the starting point for building a more solidary and ecological world. It is precisely from where people live, work and learn that a new world can be built. At the same time, the capitalist state is being heckled from two sides; while trying to support the scope of radical democratic organizations by running its own candidates at the parliamentary level, KFM is fighting at the grassroots level to overcome the state.

The long process of learning and fighting would not be possible without the Kurdistan Workers' Party (PKK), which is the backbone of the construction of progressive social approaches and prevents them from being crushed militarily by the state forces. All the elements of the KFM would not work without the others and, above all, they are not contradictory. The KFM shows that participation in formal elections, together with the construction of organizations that point beyond it, and of structures that defend us against it, can and should coexist. The PKK is the unifying element between these forces, preventing the many branches of the KFM from falling apart and serving as the movement's glue and brain. We have much to learn from this approach on the relevance of the political party to organize resistance and the struggle.

References

Ayboga, Ercan. n.d. "Ecology Discussions and Practices in the Kurdish Freedom Struggle." *Cooperation in Mesopotamia*. At <mesopotamia.coop/ecology-discussions-and-practices-in-the-kurdish-freedom-struggle/>.

Bookchin, Murray. 1982. *The Ecology of Freedom: The Emergence and Dissolution of Hierarchy*. Palo Alto, California: Cheshire Books.

Çiçek, Meral. 2021. "Öcalan's Paradigm: Redefining the Revolution." *ANF News*. At <anfenglish.com/features/Ocalan-s-paradigm-redefining-the-revolution-56706> December 21.

Egret, Eliza, and Tom Anderson. 2016. "Democratic Autonomy in North Kurdistan: An interview with the Democratic Society Congress." *Corporate Watch*. At <corporatewatch.org/democratic-autonomy-in-north-kurdistan-an-interview-with-the-democratic-society-congress-2/> April 28.

Kurban, Berfin. 2016. "Democratic Modernity vs. Capitalist Modernity: Rojava's Alternative Model." *Cooperation in Mesopotamia*. At <mesopotamia.coop/democratic-modernity-vs-capitalist-modernity-rojavas-alternative-model/>.

Make Rojava Green Again. 2020. "Social Ecology and Democratic Confederalism." At <makerojavagreenagain.org/wp-content/uploads/2020/10/Social-Ecology-and-Democratic-Confederalism-eng.pdf>.

ARTICULATING SOVEREIGNTIES

Convergences and Tensions between National-Popular
and Community-Territorial Struggles
in Ecuador and Bolivia

*Diana Vela Almeida, Geovanna Lasso,
Marxa Chávez León and Diego Andreucci*

In the last three decades, some of the most inspiring transformative socioecological processes in Latin America have emerged from the encounter of multiple popular movements struggling for sovereignty. Despite its absolutist origin, the idea of sovereignty has been appropriated since the twentieth century by socialist and national liberation movements, becoming a radically anticapitalist, anti-imperialist and anticolonial horizon. In twenty-first-century Latin America, this radical anticoloniality of sovereignty is expressed in two main categories of struggles that often intertwine. On the one hand, social and political movements of the subaltern classes have claimed *national-popular sovereignty* in the face of the interventionist neocolonial political-economic order of neoliberal globalization. In this way, the political left and its social bases continue to articulate socially emancipatory political projects with national liberation and anti-imperialist discourses. On the other hand, the indigenous-peasant struggles — historically a marginalized but key political actor in the region — also mobilize an anticolonial discourse, understood from the perspective of *community-territorial sovereignty*. This is centred on the reaffirmation of the capacity for self-determination of their ways of life and community control over the land or ancestral indigenous territory, as the material substratum of ecological and social reproduction.

Both transformative visions of sovereignty are linked to control over natural resources, insofar as demands for social or environmental justice — at different scales — are articulated with claims over the control of a territory and its resources (McNeish 2017). In indigenous-peasant movements this "eco-territorial" element (Svampa 2019) is more directly visible. In many contexts, such movements clearly emerge from struggles against land grabbing or mining, oil or agro-industrial extractivism; and relations with territory and its nonhuman nature have cultural-spiritual value beyond the material. But movements of the anti-imperialist left, in countries with a history of (neo)colonial extractivism, also articulate their demands for social justice with the vindication of a national-popular, anti-interventionist control over resources, claiming that oil, gas, and minerals be "for the people."

It is worth noting that this assertion of national-popular sovereignty over natural wealth has always been mediated by the state and historically expressed in demands for the *nationalization* of natural resources, the redistribution of these (as use values), or the rents derived from them. In contrast, community-territorial sovereignty movements have a more ambivalent relationship with the state, a result of the historical coloniality of the forms of the nation-state in Latin America (Tapia 2014). This relationship oscillates, according to the conjuncture, between demands directed at the state — from land titling, to the recognition of indigenous rights, to the principle of "plurinationality" — and moments of anti-state radicalization. On the one hand, strengthening the power of the state vis-à-vis transnational capital — granting the former greater "relative autonomy" from the latter — is necessary to promote social reforms or progressive environmental policies. On the other hand, the unitary state can become an agent of internal colonialism by, for example, promoting extractive projects without consent in indigenous territories. This also influences the dynamics of convergence and tension between territorial and national sovereignty movements.

In this chapter, we present a comparative analysis of these convergences and tensions in recent political processes in Ecuador and Bolivia. We argue that, in both countries, the encounter between multiple sovereignty movements has been a key driver of anticolonial and anti-neoliberal social struggles, winning important achievements in the streets, in the territories and in the state-institutional arena. At the same time, these different ways of understanding sovereignty — as a national-popular project, or as a community-territorial project — also have elements of incompatibility, which at key moments caused tension and conflict between the political left and some indigenous-peasant organizations.

These divisions played a decisive role in both the October 2019 political crisis in Bolivia, which gave way to the far-Right interim government of Jeanine Áñez (2019–2020), and in the April 2021 elections in Ecuador, where the conservative neoliberalism of Guillermo Lasso won despite a broad electoral majority for progressive parties.

We focus the chapter on three critical moments for the two countries. First, we review the struggles against neoliberalism in the 1990s and early 2000s, in which large popular, anti-imperialist, indigenous, peasant and community mobilizations converged and achieved the first major political defeat of neoliberalism in the region, opening the way for a cycle of progressive governments. Second, we explore the constituent processes that took place in the two countries in the 2000s, leading to the approval of new constitutions of a transformative nature, and reflect on the achievements and contradictions of state reform in a plurinational sense. Third, we focus on the present conjuncture: the return of neoliberalism, characterized by moments of explosion of social mobilization in Ecuador; and the protracted political crisis in Bolivia, partly related to the demobilization of community-territorial movements. We also observe in recent years a growing prominence of feminist movements, both urban and community-territorial, and reflect on their role as a mobilizing force. We conclude with some reflections on successful forms of convergence between diverse socioecological struggles, and on the dialectic of advance and retreat that has characterized progressive transformations in the region over the last two decades.

Indigenous, peasant and popular struggles against neoliberalism and neocolonialism

Latin America is one of the regions where the neoliberal shock doctrine was implemented most aggressively since the 1970s and more markedly in the 1980s. At the same time, it was at the vanguard of struggles against neoliberalism, thanks to the convergence and articulation[1] of multiple movements of workers, Indigenous peoples, peasants, environmentalists and, later, feminists. We argue that struggles for natural resource sovereignty — with both national-popular and community-territorial emphases — were a key component of these movements. At the institutional level, this gave way to a cycle of markedly progressive governments throughout the region since the late 1990s. Ecuador and Bolivia are representative of these trends.

Ecuador: From the 1990 indigenous uprising to the anti-neoliberal bloc

The moments of struggle and significant victories of social movements in Ecuador are marked by political and socioeconomic conjunctures. indigenous uprisings, since the Spanish conquest and after independence, have allowed for greater political representation and recognition of territorial sovereignty (Coronel 2011). These struggles prompted the creation of several indigenous organizations, eventually forming CONAIE (Confederation of Indigenous Nationalities of Ecuador) in 1986, which emerged from common demands around indigeneity, class, self-determination and agrarian reform (Clark 2019). Years later, these demands would be crystalized in collective rights and in the proposal of the plurinational state in the 2007 constituent assembly.

The great uprising of 1990, historic for its capacity to unite a large number of indigenous organizations, would be the convergence of two elements that we position as the driving force of counterhegemonic mobilizations: the reaction to a situation of socioeconomic crisis caused by neoliberal adjustments; and the struggle for common demands such as comprehensive agrarian reform in the Andes and the recognition of indigenous territories in the Amazon (Peña 2016). The uprising made visible a long organizational process and the power that the indigenous movement had acquired in the country.

The beginning of the twenty-first century was also marked by popular struggles confronting the "long neoliberal night" (1992–2005). This decade was characterized by processes of privatization, market liberalization, debt securitization and deregulation of the financial sector. It led to the country's most severe socioeconomic regression, resulting in the highest rates of impoverishment and emigration in its history (Acosta 2001). As a result, social uprisings pushed back the neoliberal governments on some measures and resulted in several presidential impeachments.

Key moments that achieved broad convergence of popular, indigenous, peasant and environmental sectors were the struggles against the free trade agreement with the United States (FTA) and the Free Trade Area of the Americas (FTAA), in which they managed to stop the signing of these agreements. There were also mobilizations against oil expansion in the Amazon that years later would achieve two historic sentences: (1) the ruling of the Ecuadorian Court of the Province of Sucumbíos (2012) against Chevron-Texaco for oil pollution in the Northern Amazon;

and (2) the sanctioning by the Inter-American Court of Human Rights (IACHR) (2012) against the Ecuadorian state for awarding concessions for oil exploration and exploitation without prior consultation within the Sarayaku ancestral territory.

In this context, a political bloc formed in 2006 around the criticism of the neoliberal and imperialist model, the absence of state regulation, the inequitable distribution of wealth and the exclusion of the popular sectors. Consequently, with the support of the social organizations of the popular classes, and of the indigenous, peasant and environmental movements, the leader of the political party Alianza PAÍS (Patria Altiva i Soberana), Rafael Correa, won the presidential elections in 2007 with the promise of a new progressive constitution for the country.

Bolivia: From the "Water War" to the "Indigenous-Peasant Unity Pact"

In the mid-1980s, a period of aggressive neoliberal reform began in Bolivia. Privatizations and massive layoffs of public sector workers took place and the trade union structure of the mining workers — the backbone of the popular movement — was dismantled. In the 1990s, the Bolivian state combined the promotion of extractivism and economic deregulation with the first legislations protecting environmental and indigenous rights. These changes created opportunities for indigenous and peasant movements to radicalize against neoliberalism, strengthening grassroots organizational forms and appropriating legal discourses and tools of struggle.

The greatest cycle of social explosion took place in the years 2000-2005. In 2000, the "Water War" took place in Cochabamba: a series of mobilizations that succeeded in reversing the privatization of access to water, promoted by the transnational company Bechtel and supported by the World Bank and the neoliberal government of Hugo Banzer Suárez (1997-2001). The main organizational structure of the social movements was the Coordinadora del Agua (Water Coordinator), a platform that brought together industrial sector workers, irrigators' unions, neighbourhood organizations, and environmental NGOs. This platform proposed an anti-neoliberal program against the privatization of the "common good," and claimed the deepening of popular sovereignty, against and beyond the state (Gutiérrez Aguilar 2014).

In the following years, natural gas became the central focus of contention, it being the most important natural resource in a poor country where most households did not have access to energy. Many social movements, including indigenous organizations, protested that the Bolivian people did not benefit from the exploitation of gas on their lands, which was being sold cheaply to the USA, a fact that was considered an expression of the neocolonial and racist system that harmed the indigenous popular classes. This situation catalyzed various demands from urban and rural subaltern groups. A very intense cycle of mobilizations culminated in the "Gas War" of October 2003, whose epicentre was the city of El Alto. After military repression and the murder of more than sixty people, President Gonzalo Sánchez de Lozada (2002–2003) fled Bolivia. A phase of instability and state crisis began. The nationalization of hydrocarbons — "gas for Bolivians" — became the central demand of all movements.

A new, more pluralistic constitution was another central demand of indigenous organizations and popular classes. This demand was first expressed in the Indigenous Marches organized in Bolivia since 1990; it was later taken up by the Water Coordinator and, subsequently, by the rest of the popular forces. In August 2004, the main indigenous federations and campesino (indigenous-peasant) unions formed the "Indigenous-Peasant Unity Pact," which worked intensively between 2006 and 2007 to elaborate a proposal for a constitution, articulating the peasant union project with that of the indigenous movements in a shared horizon (Garcés 2010). The Movement Towards Socialism (MAS) party, the political instrument of the peasant unions and the main political reference point of the anti-neoliberal forces, won a historic election in December 2005. The leadership of Evo Morales, a coca growers' union leader of Aymara origin, stands out. The arrival of MAS to the government broke with the racist mestizo elites of the neoliberal era. Morales adopted in his agenda the two central demands of the Gas War: the nationalization of natural resources and the promotion of the constituent process.

Constituent processes as the pinnacle of convergence between sovereignty movements

The leftist parties that came to power with the support of the subaltern classes promoted constituent processes with a plurinational horizon, in order to channel multiple struggles for sovereignty within the state institutionality. The new constitutions approved in Ecuador (2008) and Bolivia (2009) have a markedly progressive character. Both were the culmination of a cycle of intense social struggle and the product of the convergence of diverse subaltern social forces, among which the indigenous-peasant movements played a central role. At the same time, the constitutions recognized their most radical social demands only partially, subordinating the implementation of plurinationality to the interests of extractive and agro-industrial capital. This ended up marginalizing some of the indigenous-peasant organizations that were most critical of extractivism, generating conflicts among sectors of the popular camp.

Ecuador: Institutional transformations of the constituent process

The constituent process (December 2007–July 2008), made possible by the political renewal brought about by the Correa government, was built on the basis of various proposals from civil society delegations. The Ecuadorian Constitution marked a historic milestone by recognizing, for the first time, principles such as the Rights of Nature (or Pachamama), Good Living (Sumak Kawsay), and plurinationality as organizing principles of the Ecuadorian state (Acosta and Martínez 2009); it also recognized the social and solidarity economy and food sovereignty as strategic axes. The country was declared a GMO-free territory, and access to clean and abundant water and a healthy environment were recognized as fundamental human rights.

These achievements were the result of a broad and diverse space for political discussion, including popular initiative proposals. Thus, the indigenous movement, environmental and peasant organizations, agroecological movements, trade unions, feminist and other progressive organizations generated strong lobbying and direct negotiation with assembly members. Pressure from some environmental NGOs and alliances between local organizations and inhabitants of different territories affected by extractivist projects also played a key role. This convergence between various sectors of the popular classes and social organizations whose proposals were incorporated into the constituent assembly was the result of years of organizing and solidarity building rooted in the anti-neoliberal revolts of the 1990s.

By recognizing collective rights and introducing new forms of state accountability, the institutionalization of plurinationality opened up the possibility of constructing heterodox forms of planning of distinct territorialities. These advances were related to historical demands for community-territorial sovereignty, like, for example, the recognition of ancestral territories, land redistribution, self-determination and decolonization (Simbaña 2009). However, the constituent process also reflected the interests of the economic and productive elites of the country, which possessed a strong lobbying capacity in the constituent assembly, and managed to ensure that the capitalist-extractivist core of the Ecuadorian economy was not affected by the reforms (Lasso 2019). In this way, the content of the constitution and its historical milestones were the result of an internal process of social and political dispute, constraining the achievements of social movements and the institutionalization of plurinationality. Thus, subsequent governments have largely maintained the "monocultural" structures and racist institutional character of the state (Walsh 2012).

Bolivia: Achievements and limits of the constituent process

The Political Constitution of the Plurinational State of Bolivia was approved by popular referendum in January 2009. The constituent process, which began in 2006, took place in a tense political situation, with aggressive opposition from large landowning oligarchies and old mestizo elites who articulated their class project with regionalist-separatist, identitarian and racist political-ideological postures. The new constitution draws heavily on the proposals of the Unity Pact. It adopts fundamental principles, such as the plural character of Bolivian society and the Bolivian state, formal recognition of the "indigenous-original-peasant peoples" (PIOC) and their historical struggles, and of indigenous justice systems. Like Ecuador's, it includes a historical recognition of principles such as plurinationality, the Rights of Nature, Living Well (Suma Qamaña), and food sovereignty. In both countries, the proposal for a plurinational state is an unprecedented attempt to articulate national-popular sovereignty in the face of the neoliberal and neocolonial global order, with the sovereignty of indigenous and peasant peoples over their territories and natural resources.

At the same time, however, the way the constitution was approved limited the transformative character of the indigenous-peasant proposals, in two key aspects: 1) it renounced a comprehensive agrarian reform; and 2) it did not recognize the principle of indigenous "co-government," that is, that indigenous-peasant peoples have a binding right to decide how their territories and natural resources are managed (Tapia 2014). Despite

Indigenous organizations presenting their position statements at a national "social summit" against mining extractivism. La Paz, Bolivia, 2014. Photo credit: Diego Andreucci.

many advances on the symbolic, legal and wealth redistribution levels, the core of a development or accumulation strategy centred on oil, mining and agro-industrial extractivism was maintained. Transnational capital consolidated its dominant position, despite the state's emphasis on a discourse of nationalization. In the following years, the "primary-export" character of the Bolivian economy deepened, generating growing conflicts with the affected communities (Radhuber, Chávez and Andreucci 2021).

Crises and social responses in the present conjuncture

After the Constituent Assembly, the progressive governments of Correa and Morales were consolidated. However, with the deepening of the primary-export character of the Ecuadorian and Bolivian economies, the conflicts between the indigenous-peasant organizations and the national governments and their social bases became more explicit. In a global context of falling international commodity prices since 2014, both governments entered a phase of political weakening, giving greater access to neoliberal capital. In 2017, neoliberalism returned to Ecuador with the electoral victory of Lenín Moreno. In Bolivia, a period of political crisis culminated in October 2019 with the forced resignation of Morales. Despite the extremely complicated conjuncture, organizational forms from below were maintained to resist Moreno's authoritarian neoliberalism in Ecuador, and there have been attempts to reorganize indigenous-peasant territorial resistance in Bolivia.

Ecuador: The neoliberal assault of the Right and responses in the streets

During the government of Lenín Moreno (2017–2021), the agenda of the country's economic groups that impoverished the majority of Ecuadorians was promoted. Structural adjustments were promoted: reduction of state regulation and social investment, massive layoffs and labour flexibilization, privatization of profitable public companies, and tax reforms that benefited the elites and large corporations. Consequently, in October 2019, Ecuador experienced the biggest social outburst since the beginning of the century. During eleven days of massive national protests, various social sectors across the country forcefully rejected the Moreno government's neoliberal policies and its signing of agreements with the International Monetary Fund. Despite strong state repression, Moreno had to give in to the demands of the protesters. Although months later the government managed to implement the planned structural adjustments amid a state of global pandemic, October 2019 does not cease to be symbolic for social struggles (Vela Almeida et al. 2021).

Despite the political awakening in the streets, the arrival of the pandemic and the April 2021 election of the new Guillermo Lasso government — representative of the country's oligarchy — deepened an economic, social and political crisis, with social indicators and outmigration rates even worse than in the neoliberal decade of the 1990s. This, in turn, has limited the country's sovereignty vis-à-vis transnational capital, as well as its plurinational agenda. The continuation of neoliberal reforms, privatization and reduction of social investment — coupled with the disputes and prolonged rupture between the indigenous movement and Correa's party — has resulted in one of the worst moments of disarticulation of social struggles in the country.

An important response to the country's gruelling political and economic crisis came again in the streets in June 2022. It was led by the indigenous movement CONAIE under a platform of ten demands of an anti-neoliberal and anti-extractivist character. With an even higher level of grassroots popular mobilization than October 2019 and countered by greater police repression, the eighteen days of mobilizations ended with an agreement between the Lasso government and CONAIE, where the government partially ceded to the demands of the indigenous movement (though without significantly modifying its neoliberal agenda). The main achievement of social mobilizations consisted in the inclusion of partial measures of containment against neoliberal reforms and the expansion of extractivism, and just as importantly, in strengthening an anti-neoliberal common sense throughout the country.

Faced with any possibility of meaningful dialogue, the street turned out to be the only way to resist the imposed economic measures. The responses have been massive and have been woven among a plural, heterogeneous and transversal spectrum of social movements that converged in the face of governments incapable of responding to social and popular demands. Students, workers, trade unions, feminist movements, indigenous and peasant movements, supporters of Rafael Correa, part of the transport sector, city neighbourhoods and villages in rural areas have mobilized widely and have achieved strategic articulations.

In both mobilizations, a great economy of care sustained those who were on the front line of protest. Many volunteers organized collection centres to receive donations of food and clothing; collective kitchens were built; and some universities became shelters for protesters arriving from different provinces to the capital. Many volunteers took care of the children, and medical students organized themselves to treat the wounded. The voice of indigenous women leaders was permanent and several feminist mobilizations called hundreds of women from different social, indigenous and peasant organizations to lead the marches of

Ecuadorian Indigenous and campesinx peoples, workers, students and activists march together during the October 2019 uprising. Photo credit: Luis Herrera R., Cooperativa Audiovisual Coop-Docs, 2019. Reproduced with permission.

those days. The nationwide protest had the potential to become a catalyst for new and more horizontal forms of progressive politics after years of segregation and rivalries in the Ecuadorian left. The need to keep up the pressure and remain united in resistance to neoliberalism is more urgent than ever.

Bolivia: Rearticulation from feminisms

In the last decade in Bolivia, in a context of expanding extractive and infrastructure projects, grassroots indigenous-peasant organizations have begun a difficult process of reconstitution in defence of their livelihoods and territorial sovereignty. The case of Tariquía, in the southeast of the country, stands out, where hydrocarbon exploration projects within the Tariquía National Flora and Fauna Reserve were planned by the national government since 2007. In 2015, the women of Tariquía led the formation of the Defence Committee among the peasant communities living within the Reserve, to demand that their lands not be impacted by plans to exploit hydrocarbons. In April 2017, the Defence Committee called for a march "For the Dignity of Tariquía" and, months later, the anti-oil resistance won the union leadership of the Tariquía Sub-central. The march also led to the government's temporary decision to suspend hydrocarbon exploration in Tariquía.

However, exploration returned in 2018 with greater aggression. In this context, community women who held union leadership positions were attacked by government allies. Tactics of patriarchal violence, aggression and political dispossession against women and feminized bodies were consolidated alongside the imposition of extractivist violence against the territories (Chávez León and López 2018). Despite internal divisions, this community-territorial and anti-patriarchal struggle continues to appeal to women's strength and collective political capacity for autonomous participation, discussion and decision-making in defence of life (Ulloa 2016).

The feminist movement has also consolidated in the cities over the last decade. In 2013, Bolivia passed a comprehensive law to guarantee women a life free of violence (Law 348), after the brutal femicide of journalist Hanalí Huaycho. This legal reform was part of the struggle to recognize femicide as a punishable offense in the country. This struggle, which became more massive each year, was linked to various forms of accompaniment for the families of victims of femicide, which sharpened the criticism of patriarchal violence in the justice system, evidenced by the uncovering in 2022 of a large network of corruption that had set free criminals convicted of femicide and rape. Although some ruptures within feminisms appeared after the 2019 political conflict, popular feminisms in Bolivia have always positioned themselves against capitalist expansion into protected areas and indigenous territories, along with violence against the bodies of women and children, and other species.

Conclusions

In the mid-2010s — with the return of authoritarian neoliberalism in several countries in the region — there was an intense debate in Latin America about the "end of cycle" (*fin de ciclo*) of progressive experiences. Today, however, what we are seeing in the region is rather a double-movement or continued dialectic between neoliberal counter-reform and massive responses in the streets in defence of democracy and social and environmental justice. Neoliberalism continues to dominate, although permanently in dispute and navigating on the margins of social upheaval.

The convergences and articulations between diverse indigenous-peasant and popular movements, with a growing protagonist role of anti-patriarchal feminism, are the centre of the anti-neoliberal and anti-colonial responses, as shown by the great popular revolts that took place in several countries in 2019, or the recent electoral victories of the left allied to feminism and the indigenous, peasant and Afro-descendant movements in Chile and Colombia. These struggles continue in the tradition of twentieth-century Latin American anti-imperialism, but converge and in part articulate with struggles for community-territorial sovereignty, and for the sovereignty of bodies as the first territory of defence.

In our chapter we have tried to reflect on the main conditions of possibility and limits of these articulations in the last three decades in Ecuador and Bolivia. We see that the victories achieved both in the streets and during the constituent processes are linked to permanent and long-standing organizational processes, the ideological work of constructing shared visions of struggle, and the often-invisible reproductive work of building and maintaining political-organizational capacity, which at certain times explodes into mass protests and at others remains latent.

The moments of social outburst have been mainly associated with contexts of socio-economic and political crisis, and in the mid-2000s, they resulted in an ambitious attempt to institutionalize the demands of multiple social movements as part of new progressive hegemonic blocs. The constituents, in particular, were the expression of a great effort of articulation, formulation of proposals, and construction of organizational and mobilization capacity from the popular classes and indigenous, peasant, environmental and feminist movements. In both countries, this social bloc managed to institutionalize historical demands and was able to modify the legal-institutional framework in a progressive and plurinational sense. Such victories, however, were only partially institutionalized, due to the persistent power of capital and of national and transnational elites, and to the primacy of neo-developmentalist and reformist ideologies within the progressive governments and some of the movements that support them. Therefore, within the limits of the great inequalities in the correlations of forces between the subaltern and dominant classes, the horizon of change of the popular-indigenous and feminist articulations must continue aiming to transcend and dismantle — not only reform or contain — the capitalist, colonial and patriarchal core of the state.

Notes

1   In this chapter we use the notion of "articulation" and derived terms in three senses. First, to indicate the way in which a class project intersects with political-ideological referents (here reformulated as the articulation of a socio-environmental struggle with a sovereignty claim). Second, to describe a relationship between two or more social movements, in which movements intertwine, partly maintaining their vision and identity, but adapting to those of other movements. In this sense, articulation is akin to "convergence" — which indicates the different priorities of different movements aligning towards a common goal — but places more emphasis on the organizational element. An articulation is also more durable and deeper than an "alliance" — which is tactical and temporary in nature, and in which the identities of the movements remain completely distinct — but less definitive than a "confluence" — which indicates irreversible fusion (like two streams of water "flowing together," becoming one). Third, the process of structuring and developing the internal organizational capacity of a social movement; or, conversely, the process of its de-structuring and demobilization (disarticulation).

References

Acosta, Alberto. 2001. *Breve Historia Económica del Ecuador*. Quito: Corporación Editora Nacional.
Acosta, Alberto, and Esperanza Martínez (eds.). 2009. *El Buen Vivir: Una Vía para el Desarrollo*. Quito: Editorial Abya-Yala.

Chávez, Marxa, and Claudia López. 2018. "Women Rebel in Tariquía: In southern Bolivia, the fight for the dignity and against oil interests begins with women." *NACLA Report on the Americas* 50, 4: 408–410.

Clark, Patrick. 2019. "Campesino Organizations and Public Policies from Neoliberal to Post-Neoliberal Rural Development in Ecuador 2006–2016." PhD dissertation. Carleton University, Ottawa, Canada. At <repository.library.carleton.ca/downloads/1j92g8436>.

Coronel, Adriana V. 2011. "A Revolution in Stages: Subaltern Politics, Nation-State Formation, and the Origins of Social Rights in Ecuador, 1834–1943." PhD dissertation. New York University, New York, United States. At <repositorio.flacsoandes.edu.ec/bitstream/10469/6489/2/TEXTN-2011AVC.pdf>.

Garcés, Fernando. 2010. "El Pacto de Unidad y el Proceso de Construcción de una Propuesta de Constitución Política Del Estado: Sistematización de La Experiencia." La Paz: Centro Cooperativo Sueco et al.

Gutiérrez Aguilar, Raquel. 2014. *Rhythms of the Pachakuti: Indigenous Uprising and State Power in Bolivia*. Durham, NC: Duke University Press.

McNeish, John-Andrew. 2017. "A vote to derail extraction: popular consultation and resource sovereignty in Tolima, Colombia." *Third World Quarterly* 38, 5: 1128–1145.

Peña, Karla. 2016. "Social Movements, the State, and the Making of Food Sovereignty in Ecuador. *Latin American Perspectives* 43, 1: 221–237.

Radhuber, Isabella M., Marxa Chávez León, and Diego Andreucci. 2021. "Expansión extractivista, resistencia comunitaria y 'despojo político' en Bolivia." *Journal of Political Ecology* 28, 1.

Simbaña, Floresmilo. 2009. "El movimiento indígena ecuatoriano y la construcción de la plurinacionalidad." In Hoetmer, Raphael (ed.), *Repensar la política desde América Latina: Cultura, Estado y movimientos sociales*. Lima: Universidad Nacional de San Marcos, 153–168. At <democraciaglobal.org/wp-content/uploads/Repensar-pdf.pdf>.

Svampa, Maristella. 2019. *Neo-Extractivism in Latin America: Socio-Environmental Conflicts, the Territorial Turn, and New Political Narratives*. Cambridge: Cambridge University Press. At <memoria.fahce.unlp.edu.ar/libros/pm.5180/pm.5180.pdf>.

Tapia, Luís. 2014. *Dialéctica del Colonialismo Interno*. La Paz: Autodeterminación.

Ulloa, Astrid. 2016. "Feminismos territoriales en América Latina: defensas de la vida frente a los extractivismos." *Nómadas* 45.

Vela Almeida, Diana, Angus Lyall, Geovanna Lasso, and Diego Andreucci. 2021. "Resisting austerity in the era of COVID-19: Between nationwide mobilization and decentralized organising in Ecuador." In Calvário, Rita, Maria Kaika and Giorgos Velegrakis (eds.), *The Political Ecology of Austerity*. London: Routledge, 135–155.

Walsh, Catherine. 2012. *Interculturalidad, Crítica y (De)Colonialidad: Ensayos desde Abya Yala*. Quito: Abya-Yala.

4

DECOLONIAL ENCOUNTERS AND AUTOGESTION

Struggles for Life and Sovereignty in Puerto Rico and Beyond[1]

Gustavo García-López

Prelude: With love, truth and courage[2]

Dear Maia, I am here because of you. You whose name means water, mountain, magic, creativity, Spring, love, courage.[3] You who have taught me so much in so little time about what matters most in this life — heart, care, truth — and to whom I owe the responsibility to give everything I have to help build livable worlds.

I want to promise you that "no one / will come and devour you / … no one's drowning / … no one's losing / their homeland" (Jetnil-Kijiner 2014). But "If this will drown / or burn // then let us drink starlight / night under trees / sing on beaches — // … If we are dying / then let me rip open / and bleed Love, / spill it, spend it / see how much / there is // … If this is life ending / then let me begin / a new one." (Odel 2020)

Dear Maia, always remember, always dream, "… you are a seed in potent darkness / … touch the earth that is your skin / call in the magic buried in your blood / dare to break open in climax by your own hands / for our work now is to bloom beautiful in chaos" (Chilomé 2023). Let us be grateful for all who have given life so we can live, to all those with whom we walk. Let us mourn and honour all those whose future has been stolen. Let us never give up: "For everyone, everything … For us joyful rebellion … For us insurgent dignity" (EZLN 1996).

From the colonial hurricane to decolonial ecology in the Caribbean

The world-ship is in the midst of a tempest, the eye of which is in the Caribbean, where colonialism first landed. As Malcom Ferdinand

(2022: 65) argues, this storm manifests a "colonial hurricane," which shapes the ways we inhabit the world. Colonialism has always operated as a "permanent war," causing genocide and ecocide, primarily on colonized human and nonhuman populations deemed unworthy (Maldonado-Torres 2016). This coloniality, embedded in global institutions, discourses and interventions, blocks possibilities for climate action and justice (Sultana 2021). Every year, hundreds of environmental defenders are killed (Global Witness 2022), millions are displaced by climate disasters, and thousands of species become extinct. This "everywhere war" carries an enormous global climate "bootprint" (Belcher et al. 2020). Global greenwashing deceit hides trillions of annual subsidies for fossil fuels (Coady et al. 2017; Rainforest Action Network et al. 2023), from the same corrupt financiers that make a killing gambling, laundering, and defrauding highly indebted countries (Hedge Clippers 2016). In this context, global justice movements affirm that *"we do not owe, we are the creditors,"* demanding colonial and climate debt reparations (Roa Avendaño 2023).

Island nations in the Caribbean and elsewhere are amongst the most impacted by the climate crisis, despite being amongst the least responsible, and are facing enormous challenges to respond. Our islands are labelled as "remote and isolated" and "poor," while being subjected to intensive exploitation from offshore rentier capital — plantations, petrochemical industrialism, tourism, banking (Sheller 2020). Many islands remain under the control of imperial powers, subjected to the logic of "let them drown" under sea level rise and disastrous storms — the same racist logic that lets refugees drown in the Mediterranean (Klein 2016). This "discriminatory carelessness" is followed by "discriminatory redistribution," where disasters reinforce inequalities and extract profit (Ferdinand 2022).

This logic is enmeshed with imperialist militarism, turning islands into bases, war experiments and geopolitical games. As Henry Kissinger said in justifying nuclear testing in the Marshall Islands, "who gives a damn" about a place with so few inhabitants. Yet, the Caribbean's history of anticolonial and ecological struggles opens new visions of future free from the colonial hold, a "decolonial ecology" (Ferdinand 2022). *We are not drowning, we are fighting. The sea is rising, and so are we.*[4]

To counter this system's madness, we need imagination, hope and memory to "shift the narrative of struggle from trauma and violence to care and liberation," as Sundus Abdul Hadi (2020: 31) puts it. Hope is "trusting the unknown and the possible," and is rooted in memory (Solnit 2016: xix, 23). Remembering is witnessing, to see our wounds and encounter liberation (Glisch-Sánchez and Rodríguez-Villafañes 2023). Thus, memory is another word for justice (EZLN 2000). A memory not bound by narratives of defeatism and conformism (Marcos 2001), which only foresee more crises (Garriga-López 2020), but which become seeds for a limitless imagination. It is an "alive memory" — "each promise a threat, each loss, an encounter; from fears are birthed the courage/angers, from doubts, the certainties" (Galeano 2000: 110-111).

These are the fires driving movements to both stop the systems killing us and to build "collective frameworks for justice, freedom, self-determination, and interdependence" (Abolition Collective 2020). Beyond representation, redistribution and recognition, this justice is "defiant worldmaking" to create new ways of being, based on care and repair of ourselves and our life-giving systems (Glisch-Sánchez and Rodríguez-Villafañes 2023). It is a weaving of anticolonial, antiracist, feminist and ecological struggles fractured by colonial inhabitation (Ferdinand 2022) — an encounter of communities "connected … through deeply rooted ancient identities, familiar spirits, and shared experiences of resistance to white supremacy and colonialism" (Abdul Hadi 2020: 29).[5]

Decolonial maroon autogestion to make "livable worlds"[6]

Puerto Rico (Borikén in the indigenous Taino language) has been a colony since 1492, first of Spain and then, since 1898, of the United States. Climate colonialism has expanded through logics of extraction, experimentation and disposability. In the 1960s, the USA experimented with "free" industrial zones for petrochemicals to refine the most toxic fuels, for their military to test their weapons, and for birth control interventions. This "Operation Bootstrap" was designed by the Chicago Boys that later experimented in Chile's Pinochet dictatorship. Additionally, it sought to turn us into the "showcase" for the rest of Latin America to stop the advance of communism (Berman Santana 1996). They argued we were too small, poor, overpopulated to be sovereign. If fully executed, this plan would have meant genocide. Colonial institutions have continued with these plans since, a toxic legacy that has sickened us and blocked alternative life-making paths.

In the Caribbean, the "colonial hurricane" manifests in the dozens of territories controlled by imperial powers: Puerto Rico, US Virgin Islands (USA); British Virgin Islands (U.K.); Aruba, Curaçao, Bonaire, and St. Marteen (Netherlands); St. Martin, Guadeloupe, Martinique, Guiana (France), among others (see Bonilla and Hantel 2016). Source: Wikipedia.

Environmental justice struggles have been confronting these projects ever since, centring life and decolonization (Avilés-Vázquez et al. 2023). They coined the concept "environmental colonialism," denouncing its politics of extraction and murder. And they developed grassroots community initiatives, intercommunity alliances, legal and scientific support, and accessible educational materials. *Autogestion* has become a keyword naming collective, deliberative, autonomous organizing, rooted in solidarity and mutual aid, for the self-management of essential needs (energy, water, food, housing and so on). It can be considered a "coalitional counter-praxis of survival," refuge and togetherness amidst the disasters of colonialism (Vega-Soto 2019). With this grounding, these "deeply rooted" communities work against all odds to defend and remake worlds of dignity, justice and freedom.

For sixty years, the US Navy dropped an estimated trillion tons of munitions, including depleted uranium and napalm, in the eastern island-municipality of Bieké (Vieques), leading to high rates of cancer and other severe illnesses, and making it one of the country's most contaminated sites. These bombs were later used in Palestine, Iraq and Afghanistan. In the 1990s, a two-decade fisherfolk struggle turned into a (trans)national movement for "peace and justice," demanding the Navy's exit, and demilitarization, decontamination, devolution, and development. Over three years, thousands of us engaged in civil disobedience, entering the training range during live-munition trainings. Together with massive national protests uniting all political parties, and international solidarity campaigns from the US to India, Hawaii, Japan, Korea, Costa Rica and Palestine, we kicked the Navy out in 2003 (McCaffrey 2006). Yet the struggle did not end there: Vieques faces new bombardments from luxury tourism and other extractive forces, coupled with government abandonment and foot dragging on the base cleanup. In this context, a group of women, including the daughter of one of the leaders of the anti-Navy movement, created Colmena Cimarrona (Maroon Hive) to foster food sovereignty and solidarity economy. The project includes an agroecological farm and training space,[7] a network for supporting similar farms on the island, communal spaces of conviviality, popular education and healing, and food markets. The Hive is part of a broad agroecological movement that seeks to nurture food sovereignty and ecosocial justice, with a strong female leadership (Ramos-Gerena et al. 2020).

In the predominantly Black southern coastal town of Salinas, Jobos Bay, another of the most impacted by Bootstrap, "intergenerational sisterhoods" of care, mutual aid, solidarity, hope, creativity and joy have been making "livable worlds" for centuries against deadly racial-colonial regimes (Lloréns 2021; de Onís 2021). The Jobos Bay Eco-Development Initiative (IDEBAJO), a network of community organizations formed in the 1990s, builds on the region's rich cultural and environmental heritage and ancestral "maroon" practices to foster socio-productive alternatives to the "colonial blackmail." Projects including an ecotourism initiative, a community solar project, a garden, a youth camp, a *bomba* music workshop,[8] and a radio program, show that they can govern themselves without having to work in what kills them.

In the Central Mountain Range town of Adjuntas, predominantly *jíbaro* (peasant) territory, a four-decade long struggle against mining finally forced the government in the 1990s to cancel this Bootstrap-era plan. Casa Pueblo (People's House) led the last phase of the struggle, making the connection between ecological defence, national sovereignty and above all, life.[9] They developed autogestion as a form of having their own voice and initiative, breaking political and economic dependency and "self-realizing" their concrete utopia (Massol-González 2022). Casa Pueblo's organizing method of science, community and culture, grounds autogestion as making insurgency and sovereignty. Science is

Banner "We are Caribe. We don't owe, we are owed" [colonial-ecological debts]. Made by Colmena Cimarrona for an event in solidarity with Haiti, organized with other (trans)national agroecological and food sovereignty organizations. Source: Colmena Cimarrona

transdisciplinary and with a conscience, a tool for community well-being, seeding hopes and dreams. Culture grounds science with other local forms of knowing-feeling: radio, music, cinema, theatre, visual arts. Community is the point of departure and main driving force for change, joining words and action. It is grounded geographically but networked transnationally, especially with the diaspora and Latin America and the Caribbean.

These projects are rife with challenges. In a recent meeting, IDEBAJO recalled the constant assault from new extractive projects over decades: they stopped a Monsanto herbicide factory, but a few decades later came the transgenic seed fields; they stopped a nuclear plant, but then came the thermoelectric and a coal plant, and now industrial-scale solar farms on prime agricultural lands. This "permanent war" can easily be demoralizing. And it reminds us that broader political-economic shifts at national and transnational scales are urgently needed.

Resistance, hope and sovereignties in the midst of the "colonial hurricane"

In 2007, a historic year of extreme events in the Caribbean, Hurricanes Irma and Maria hit Puerto Rico. The devastation that followed lifted the veil on the "colonial hurricane": a hurricane that murdered 4,654 of us and displaced hundreds of thousands. A year before, the US government, with support of local elites, imposed a "Fiscal Supervision Board" (locally known as *La Junta*), made up of bankers, financial lawyers and vulture investors, to impose austerity to pay the $74+ billion in unaudited debt attributed to Puerto Rico. Debt became another mechanism for deepening colonial extraction (Zambrana 2021). These events added to open traumas, showing colonialism's neglect and intention to conquer, exploit and dispose.

To survive and counter the sorrow from the government's criminally neglectful response to Hurricane Maria, the Hive, IDEBAJO, Casa Pueblo, and dozens of other mutual aid initiatives emerged over our islands to provide basic needs, based on the principles of "solidarity not charity" and "only the people saves the people." I went to the mountain community of Mariana, in the eastern town of Humacao, to support my friends Luis Rodriguez and Christine Nieves to clean up their house and collaborate in the mutual aid centre they had created with the community's longstanding cultural association, ARECMA. ARECMA's large kitchen, built for their famous breadfruit (*pana*) festival,[10] had been turned into an everyday kitchen for the community, based on solidarity exchanges. The place was surrounded by signs and art exclaiming "the disaster is the colony," "our existence is resistance," and "moved by happiness." They told me it was time for action and that "community is our best chance of survival" (Nieves 2020). I could feel the joy becoming "an insurrectionary force" (Solnit 2016). I was reminded that, as put by Portnoy (2020), "in the fissures of crisis there is joy, / for without it, / there is death."

Beyond the immediate disaster response, these initiatives sought to build "popular power" as ways to create freedom and "decolonization from below," through concrete actions that delink from and transform socioecological relations of (re)production of the colony, particularly those tied to the basic needs of life: food, energy, water. Perhaps leading to a new sovereign "spirit," in a context where we have never governed our nation.

Two years after Maria, in July 2019, a leaked government chat, full of misogynistic and racist remarks as well as evidence of corruption, generated a month of daily protests along the street that lead to the governor's residence (later renamed Calle de la Resistencia, "Resistance Street"), and the largest national mobilization in our history, leading to the first-ever resignation of our country's governor. Participants danced to *perreo combativo* ("combative grinding/twerking"), affirming that without music, *perreo* and feminism, there is no revolution (Abadía-Rexach 2020).[11] Having been stripped of so much, there was a willingness to risk much more. Black, queer transfeminists led the way in a "hopeful pessimism," in which "there is little faith in the arrival of a better future, yet a great desire to create the world anew" (Bonilla 2022). This reminds us of Gramsci's old adage: "pessimism of the intellect, optimism of the will."

Encounters as worlding-in-common: Embracing and energizing each other

In January 2018, Professors in Solidarity Resistance (PAReS) — Mariolga, Fede, Bernat, Juanqui, and others[12] — together with local and transnational activists, organized an investigative visit by *The Intercept* (Klein 2018),[13] a public forum on disaster capitalism at the University of Puerto Rico,[14] and movement encounter held at the mutual aid centre of Mariana, with hundreds of participants from dozens of organizations. These events sought to connect climate and environmental justice, food sovereignty, education, debt justice, as well as feminist and national freedom struggles. We discussed strategies of resistance and building of alternatives to the disaster we were witnessing. We reflected on nurturing and networking "multiple sovereignties" beyond the colonial state (Reyes-Cruz 2018). A series of follow-up encounters led to the "Manifesto on Emergency/Emergence and Hope," which outlined demands for basic conditions of life, and calls for movement coalitions and "permanent assembly."[15] JunteGente was created to pursue this goal. Over two years, we held a series of thematic encounters, guided by the question: "What can we do together that we cannot do alone?"

While JunteGente has dispersed as seeds into several organizations, encounters have continued across various networks within Boriken and transnationally: the Peoples' Assemblies organized in the "Boricua summer" (Cabán 2020), Amigxs del MAR's series of beaches,[16] Coastal Communities Encounters,[17] and Casa Pueblo's encounters of "insurgent territories" and community energy. This experience has left valuable lessons about the tensions between the slowness of deep deliberative listening and solidarity, and the fastness of colonial and disaster-capitalist operations, exacerbated by the climate crisis. Bringing together different struggles and addressing intersecting forms of oppression is rife with barriers and contradictions, requires patience, commitment, and energies, which are often dispersed in fighting colonialism's everywhere wars.

We have continued to delve into encounters as part of diasporic networks after our post-Maria migration to Portugal. In 2021, together with a small group of *compas* (comrades/partners) from outside academia (Sebitas, Tati and Danya),[18] we started to organize another encounter that was initially focused on Just Transitions, but which we ultimately called "Post-Extractive Futures," held online for three days in February 2022. The event focused on sharing skills and tools, envisioning ways of doing things differently, and embracing each other to provide the collective energy needed to continue our struggles. The workshop included thirty-five representatives of organizations from nineteen different countries, almost all from the Global South. Practices of groundings opened every day. They were followed by different methodologies of co-learning and co-creation. A shared visioning was done through a collective altar of the future, where we identified the many elements that give fire and hope to our movements: care, radical love and intersectional solidarities, music, ceremony, joy and connection,

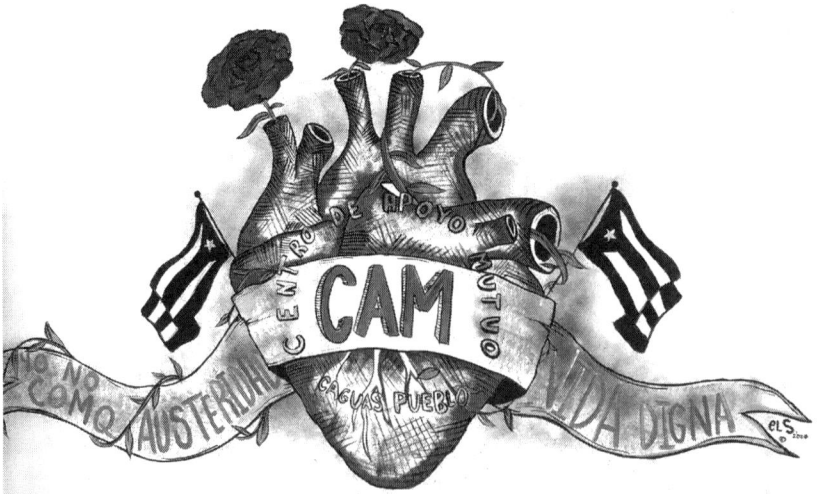

"I don't eat austerity/Dignified life" mural at the mutual aid centre in Caguas Pueblo. Source: CrimethInc.

public abundance and commons, decolonial thinking-feeling, abolition, liberation and justice, communal energies, food, water, territorial sovereignty. In the third day's sharing circle, reflecting on how to continue working together, one shared lesson from a participant, drawing on the Zapatistas, has accompanied me since: "advance slowly so as to go far," like the snail, always from the inside out.

With this intention of going deep, after the encounter, we invited participants to join our biweekly meetings. There, we continue experimenting with methodologies to foster *intimate encounters for weaving caring relations*. The Post-Extractive Futures collective grew with Delmy, Lily, and Vasna.[19] One year later, led by Teresa of Disobedient Futures (formerly Fossil Free Culture) along with Aldo and Yuchen of Weaving Realities, we organized the "Towards a Post-Extractive Culture" gathering in Amsterdam.[20] Over three days opened and closed by ceremonies, the event hosted numerous workshops and conversations around the role of artistic expressions in social transformations. Today, Post-Extractive Futures forms part of my family and are a major source of inspiration. It has taught me that "Coming together (*juntarse*) is one of the best ways to counteract monoculture, patriarchy. Coming together to make places flourish, to make healing, love and tenderness flourish" (Futuros Indígenas 2022).

Caring and healing our body-territories together

Suffering is usually a very isolating experience, but healing and transformation are "based on connection, unity, and sharing" (Abdul Hadi 2020: 19). Being hit "from everywhere," our movement spaces are often exhausted. Particularly for those suffering from the intergenerational traumas of colonial/class/race/gender exploitation, we need to do this work of care and healing if we are to reach towards self-determination and liberation as individuals, communities and nations. This requires doing the hard emotional labour to care for and heal ourselves as well (Abdul Hadi 2020). It also requires a deep solidarity, which is a "feeling of each other's pain," a struggling together, and expression of love for humanity and hope for the future.[21] Ferdinand (2022: 212-213), thinking-feeling with Fanon and deeply rooted Afro-Indigenous Caribbean experiences of world-making, centres healing of the bodily fractures of colonization by reconnecting not only across struggles, but with our mother-earths:

tending to the plot, playing the Indigenous conch and the African drums, the "melody of an encounter," which reminds us of "the sensitive powers of the body and the earthliness of existence in the world."

When I received news that my sister Isabel passed away three months ago, I was blessed to be together with my Post-Extractive Futures family in London. We had spent a week together in an intimate gathering to continue deepening our collective project, and to prepare for our facilitation of a meeting of the Climate Reparations Network. We had been sharing life stories, cooking, laughter and tears, music, literature and dance, walks, meditations, and other exercises. We had done a beautiful cartography of our collective body-territory, a methodology developed from within Delmy's collective together with feminist community struggles (see chapter 13 in this collection), to express the pains, sorrows, joys, dreams within our bodies and how they are connected to experiences from our territories. I remember the need to hold earth in my hands to connect with Isabel, the reminders to breathe while being held in loving care. Thanks to Sebas's family and their diasporic network, I was taken to a Quechua healer, Sofia, who gave me sacred *Rapé* medicine to help cleanse and calm. The next day, she offered a grieving ceremony in the magical Erpin forest, where we asked for permission to enter to ancestral trees and conversed with the *abuelo wachupa* (San Pedrito) medicine plant and *Rapé*. We made an altar to Isabel and sang to her, maracas in hand, "Isabel, Isabela, Isabel, Isabela, Vuela Libre, por la Arena."

We affirmed that these rituals connecting with our more-than-human others are central to our struggles and should be shared widely. Plants, understood not only as medicine, but as our ancestors, together with participants in a "circle of the word" (*círculo de la palabra*),[22] helped us reach into our souls. We were guided by *Ayni*, a sacred word that means reciprocity, sufficiency, and the circle of life. As I travelled to our homeland, I felt deep calm, strength, and gratitude, emotions that percolated into celebrating Isabel's life through our ceremonies. Compas from JunteGente came to help me plant trees, to reconnect with earth, community, struggle, home. Later, sharing grief and intentions, our family made an altar of the future in our garden with Isa's ashes, accompanied by one of her ceramic vases and a *Ceiba* (*pentandra*) tree, a powerful species with spines and enormous roots. Our Indigenous Tainos buried their dead underneath and later used the wood for their canoes. Remembering Isabel means remembering our childhood games in our garden-forest, our family and our ancestors. It means feeling my mom and abuelitas' hands saying: "Sana sana colita de rana, si no sana hoy sanará mañana."[23]

These encounters linking the personal and political, solidarity and healing, remembering and visioning, gave us energy to continue seeding and weaving decolonial ecologies. After returning to Portugal, I participated in one final encounter that we had been organizing with Teresa, Roberto, Hestia and Aline in the Ecology and Society Workshop (ECOSOC)[24] in Coimbra: "Un-schooling the summer." With a small group of scholar-activists from various countries and backgrounds, we walked across one hundred kilometres of the southern region of Alentejo, witnessing its intense environmental injustices and movements, and its transnational connections. We approached encounters as convivial semi-structured and emergent moments of unlearning-and-becoming in-common. Across these sites and in between, we experimented with undisciplined approaches transgressing traditional methodologies of summer/field schools: gentrification and toxic industry counter-tours, body-territory cartographies, soundscapes, political-ecology theatre of the oppressed, collaborative writing, and deep-listening conversations.[25]

One of the most special days was when we stopped in the Santo Andres Lagoon camping site to go deeper into these methodologies. After an experimental dynamic with collective music-making led by Ivo, Amigxs del Mar *compa* Eric and I cooked Puerto Rican rice and beans, remembering our abuelas' and mothers' recipes. *Soul food.* I danced and sang to Isa again with my maracas, and the wind responded. After lunch, we did a theatre dynamic, facilitated by our ECOSOC *compa* Teresa, to tell each other stories dear to us. It took me to all the trees in my house: the beach grape (*Coccoloba uvifera*) and yellow oak (R.I.P.), the breadfruit trees (*panapén*), plantains and *gandules* (Puerto Rican peas), *moralones* (*Coccoloba pubescens*), flamboyans, and malaguetas (bay-rum tree), and the *Bodhi* ("Budha's tree"), all the way to Isa's *ceiba*. We finished the day with a body-territory cartography, joined by the sea and a beautiful sunset.

"Struggle never ends, life is all struggle, for the desired freedom," to quote our national freedom-fighting poet Juan Antonio Corretjer. All struggle is also full of life, of joy, and grounded in knowing our mountains and rivers, plants and birds, smells and colours (Corretjer 1957). Struggle takes time, many forms and scales, from the personal and local community all the way to the transnational. It is full of missteps, trials and errors, and cannot be predetermined based on existing conditions. But it requires intersectional autonomous organizing, re-rooting with our body-territories, risking with memory and hope into an uncertain future, and deep commitment to collective care and healing. Overwhelmed with all it takes to "change everything," I call into memory my *abuelita*: "Take me slowly, because I am in a hurry."

Notes

1. An earlier version was presented at the seminar "What Animates and Challenges the Possibilities for Collective Action Today?" organized by the World Peace Foundation, September 21–23 at Tufts University European Center in Talloires, France; (published in the WPF blog: <sites.tufts.edu/re-inventingpeace/2023/11/08/on-environmental-justice-and-militarism>); and at the "Turning the Tide: Climate Change, Social Change, and Islandness" conference, October 23–26, at the University of Aruba and online. I'm deeply grateful to the participants for the reflections and solidarities shared during and after both events. I am fully indebted in this essay and all my work to Maia's mother, to my family — including my extended families of life, love and dignity — and to all the *compas* across diverse geographies with whom I have learned.
2. Inspired here by Johnson and Wilkinson (2020), who speak of the "truth, courage and solutions" guiding transformational women leaders confronting the climate crisis.
3. Wikipedia: <wikipedia.org/wiki/Maya_(given_name)>.
4. Slogans of Pacific Climate Warriors (in Aguon 2021) and global climate activists (Kaufman 2022), also used in the "La mar se levanta y nosotras también" encounter in Puerto Rico (García-López et al. 2019).
5. Abdul Hadi (2020: 8) uses this concept as "an empowered phrase … to replace white-centering descriptions of identity such as 'marginalized,' 'racialized' and 'colonized.'"
6. Concept from Lloréns (2021).
7. At <colmenacimarrona.org/>.
8. Bomba is an Afro-Puerto Rican music that combines drums (barriles or bombas), maracas, and dance. It was developed by slaves in plantations more than four hundred years ago, as a way of communicating and resisting, and today, continues to be part of these struggles.
9. See <casapueblo.org/>.
10. Breadfruit is one of the highest-yielding food plants in the world. A single tree produces up to two hundred or more grapefruit-sized fruits per season, requiring limited care. Originally from New Guinea, the Maluku Islands, and the Philippines, it spread to Latin America and the Caribbean during the Colonial Era. See <wikipedia.org/wiki/Breadfruit>.
11. The slogans point to feminist socialist Emma Goldman's famous maxim that "a revolution without dancing is not a revolution worth having," with a tweak to emphasize the "perreo."

12 Mariolga Reyes-Cruz, anthropologist, educator, agroecological farmer-activist, founder of the Community Agricultural Land Trust; Bernat Tort, philosopher, artist-performer, militant atheist; Federico Cintrón-Moscoso, anthropologist, educator, activist, director of El Puente–Latino Climate Action Network; Juanqui Rivera, sociologist, collaborator in community and alternative media projects.
13 Documentary: <youtube.com/watch?v=pTiZtYaB3Zo>.
14 Forum: <youtube.com/watch?v=W0S3sV-xZgU>.
15 At <juntegente.org/manifiesto/>.
16 At <amigxsdelmar.org/encuentrocomunidadescosteras>.
17 Amigxs del MAR is an intersectional, anticapitalist eco-feminist collective engaged in direct action, activist research, organizing and popular education. At <amigxsdelmar.org/encuentrocomunidadescosteras>.
18 Sebastian Ordoñez-Nuñez, currently based in London, coordinates the Global Green New Deal program at War on Want; Tatiana Garavito, organizer and facilitator, part of at the UK climate justice organization Tipping Point, collaborator in part of the UK Climate Reparations Network and the Race & Health initiative; Daniel Macmillen-Voskoboynik, freelance multi-talented artist and activist, currently with Amazon Frontlines.
19 Delmy Tania Cruz, anthropologist, communitarian feminist, co-founder of the Feminist Critical Views of Territory and the Mujeres Transformando Mundos collectives, professor at the Science and Arts University of Chiapas; Liliana Buitrago, co-founder of the Venezuelan Political Ecology Observatory, part of the Ecosocial Pact of the South; Vasna Ramasar, facilitator at the Global Tapestry of Alternatives network, professor at Lund University in Sweden.
20 Teresa Borasino, independent artist-activist, based in Amsterdam, co-founder of FFC-Fossil Free Culture NL. See <stedelijk.nl/en/events/towards-post-extractive-culture>.
21 Paraphrasing the participants in the public event of Day 3 of the first Post-Extractive Futures Encounter (2022): Bumika Muchhala, Rosa Marina Flores, Sabrina Fernandes, Asad Rehman, and Thapelo Mohapi, moderated by Harpreet Kaur Paul. See <youtube.com/watch?v=Z20DpyOhUyA&feature=youtu.be>.
22 "The circle of the word" is an ancestral Indigenous practice of meeting for reflection, where the elders of a community (in this case, Sofia) share their cultural and cosmogonic legacy and their experience, making life stories part of the circle, recovering ancestral memory, and promoting reflexivity and a shared understanding amongst participants (Hernández Rincón 2022).
23 "Heal, heal, toad tail, if it doesn't heal today, it will heal tomorrow" — a popular saying from our abuelas and mothers in Puerto Rico and across Latin America. See Glisch-Sánchez and Rodríguez-Villafañes (2023).
24 See <ces.uc.pt/pt/ces/ecosoc>. Teresa Meira, ecological economist, educator, actress and director, plant caretaker; Roberto Sciarelli, PhD student and activist on commons in Naples; Hestia Delibas, PhD student on land-grabbing and peasant resistances in Romania, ECOSOC co-coordinator; Aline Leite, PhD student, environmental analyst at the Chico Mendes Institute in Brasil.
25 See <ces.uc.pt/en/agenda-noticias/agenda-de-eventos/2023/un-schooling-the-summer>. A fanzine currently in progress will gather some of the practices, recipes, sounds, and collaborative writings developed there.

References

Abadía-Rexach, Bárbara. 2020. "Summer 2019." *Society and Space Magazine*, February 25. At <societyandspace.org/articles/summer-2019-the-great-racialized-puerto-rican-family-protesting-in-the-street-fearlessly>.

Abdul Hadi, Sundus. 2020. *Take Care of Your Self: The Art and Cultures of Care and Liberation*. Brooklyn: Common Notions Press.

Abolition Collective. 2020. "Introduction." In *Making Abolitionist Worlds*. Brooklyn: Common Notions Press, 1–6.

Aguon, Julian. 2021. "To Hell with Drowning." *The Atlantic*, November 1. At <theatlantic.com/culture/archive/2021/11/oceania-pacific-climate-change-stories/620570/>.

Avilés-Vázquez, Katia, Gustavo García-López, Carol E. Ramos Gerena et al. 2023. "Environmental justice movements as movements for life and decolonization: Experiences from Puerto Rico." In B. Bustos, S. Engel-Di Mauro, G. García-López et al. (eds.), *Routledge Handbook of Latin America and the Environment*. New York: Routledge.

Belcher, Oliver, Patrick Bigger, Ben Neimark, and Cara Kennelly. 2020. "Hidden carbon costs of the 'everywhere war.'" *Transactions of the Institute of British Geographers* 45, 1: 65–80.

Berman Santana, Debora. 1996. *Kicking off the Bootstraps*. Temple: University of Arizona Press.

Bonilla, Yarimar. 2022. "Pessimistic futurity." In M. Guerrero (ed.), *no existe un mundo poshuracán*. New York: Whitney Museum, 20–21.

Bonilla, Yarimar, and Max Hantel. 2016. "Visualizing sovereignty." *archipelagos* 1: 1–19.

Cabán, Pedro. 2020. "Puerto Rico's summer 2019 uprising and the crisis of colonialism." *Latin American Perspectives* 47, 3: 103–116.

Chilomé, Edyka. 2023. "A recommendation." In D. Glisch-Sánchez and N. Rodríguez-Villafañes (eds.), *Sana, Sana*. Brooklyn: Common Notions Press, 109.

Coady, David, Ian Parry, Louis Sears, and Baoping Shang. 2017. "How large are global fossil fuel subsidies?" *World Development* 91: 11–27.

Corretjer, Juan A. 1957. "Distancias." At <josealicea.com/uploads/4/6/9/0/46904393/distancias.pdf>.

de Onís, Catalina. 2021. *Energy Islands*. Berkeley: University of California Press.

EZLN (Ejército Zapatista de Liberación Nacional). 1996. "Cuarta Declaración de la Selva Lacandona." *Enlace Zapatista*, January 1. At <enlacezapatista.ezln.org.mx/1996/01/01/cuarta-declaracion-de-la-selva-lacandona/>.

———. 2000. "Mamá Piedra." *Enlace Zapatista,* April 18. At <enlacezapatista.ezln.org.mx/2000/04/18/mama-piedra/>.

Ferdinand, Malcom. 2022. *Decolonial Ecology*. Cambridge: Polity.

Futuros Indígenas. 2022. "Cura de la Tierra." *Milpamerica Resiste* podcast, Episode 2.

Galeano, Eduardo. 2000. "Celebración de las contradicciones I y II." In *El libro de los abrazos*. Mexico City: Siglo XXI, 110–111.

García-López, Gustavo. 2019. "La recuperación justa ante la emergencia climática." *80grados*, October 11. At <80grados.net/si-la-mar-se-levanta-nosotras-tambien/>.

Garriga-López, Adriana. 2020. "Debt, crisis, and resurgence in Puerto Rico." *Small Axe* 24, 2: 122–132.

Glisch-Sánchez, David and Nic Rodríguez-Villafañes. 2023. "Introduction." In D. Glisch-Sánchez and N. Rodríguez-Villafañes (eds.), *Sana, Sana*. Brooklyn: Common Notions Press, 1–12.

Global Witness. 2022. "Decade of Defiance." At <globalwitness.org/en/campaigns/environmental-activists/decade-defiance/>.

Hedge Clippers. 2016. "Pirates of the Caribbean." At <hedgeclippers.org/wp-content/uploads/2016/12/20161025_HedgeClippers_ReportPR_v3-3.pdf>.

Hernández Rincón, Marleny. 2022. "De la oralidad a las nuevas oralidades. Un estado del arte." *Enunciación* 27, 2: 249–264.

Jetnil-Kijiner, Kathy. 2014. "Dear Matafele Peinam." Opening ceremony at United Nations Climate Summit. At <kathyjetnilkijiner.com/united-nations-climate-summit-opening-ceremony-my-poem-to-my-daughter/>.

JunteGente and El Puente. 2023. In G. García-López and F. Cintrón-Moscoso (eds.), *Pactos Ecosociales en Puerto Rico*.

Kaufman, Cynthia. 2022. *The Sea Is Rising and So Are We*. Oakland: PM Press.

Klein, Naomi. 2016. "Let Them Drown: The Violence of Othering in a Warming World." *London Review of Books* 38, 11.

———. 2018. *The Battle for Paradise*. Chicago: Haymarket.

Lloréns, Hilda. 2021. *Making Livable Worlds: Afro-Puerto Rican Women Building Environmental Justice*. Seattle: University of Washington Press.

Maldonado-Torres, Nelson. 2016. "Outline of Ten Theses on Coloniality and Decoloniality." Frantz Fanon Foundation. At <fondation-frantzfanon.com/outline-of-ten-theses-on-coloniality-and-decoloniality/>.

Massol-González, Alexis. 2022. *Casa Pueblo*. A. Ravikumar and P. Schroeder Rodríguez (trans.). Amherst, MA: Lever Press.

McCaffrey, Katherine. 2006. "Social Struggle against the US Navy in Vieques, Puerto Rico." *Latin American Perspectives* 33, 1: 83–101.

Nieves, Christine. 2020. "Community Is Our Best Chance." In A. Johnson and K. Wilkinson (eds.), *All We Can Save: Truth, Courage, and Solutions for the Climate Crisis*. New York: One World, 363–368.

Odel, Lynna. 2020. "November." In A. Johnson and K. Wilkinson (eds.), *All We Can Save: Truth, Courage, and Solutions for the Climate Crisis*. New York: One World, 36.

Portnoy, Ana. 2020. "In the Fissure of the Crisis." *Society and Space Magazine*, February 25. At <societyandspace.org/articles/three-poems-from-the-summer-2019>.

Rainforest Action Network et al. 2023. "Banking on Climate Chaos: Fossil Fuel Finance Report 2023." At <bankingonclimatechaos.org/wp-content/uploads/2023/08/BOCC_2023_vF.pdf>.

Ramos-Gerena, Carol et al. 2020. "Desde mí, desde nosotras." *LEISA* 36, 1: 31–34.

Reyes-Cruz, Mariolga. 2018. "Por quiénes esperamos." *80grados*, February 2. At <80grados.net/por-quienes-esperamos/>.

Roa Avendaño, Tatiana. 2023. "Ecological debt and extractivism." In *Handbook of Latin America and the Environment*. New York: Routledge, 112–122.

Sheller, Mimi. 2020. *Island futures*. Durham: Duke University Press.

Solnit, Rebecca. 2016. *Hope in the Dark*. Chicago: Haymarket.

Soto-Vega, Karrieann. 2019. "Puerto Rico Weathers the Storm." *Feral Feminisms* 9: 39–55.
Subcomandante Marcos. 2001. "Flowers, Like Hope, Are Harvested." In J. Ponce de León (ed.), *Our Word Is Our Weapon*. New York: Seven Stories Press.
Zambrana, Rocío. 2021. *Colonial Debts*. Durham: Duke University Press.

PART TWO

LAND

INTRODUCTION TO PART TWO

Rita Calvário, Marien González-Hidalgo and Irmak Ertör

> So, while land is something that is constructed by humans over their daily lives, both physically and symbolically, by being invested with meaning, memory and value, land is also something that constructs humans as social beings.
> (Akram-Lodhi 2021: 73)

Struggles over land access and control continue to be relevant today for peasant and Indigenous communities making their identities and livelihoods from the land primarily in the Global South, as well as for urban people and those living and working in rural areas increasingly affected by extractivism or high-farm complexes in the Global North. Nowadays, a varied range of land conflicts exists, which expresses how life on land is crisscrossed by unequal power relations across lines of class, gender, race and other axes of domination, as well as uneven geographies.

Land politics is typically framed in relation to equitable redistribution of land and public support services to farming activities via agrarian reform. In the current context of resurfacing enclosures and violent expansion of extractive industries, affecting people's lives in rural territories and local food systems, an increasing need emerges for the recognition, protection, and democratization of land and food systems, putting it in the hands of peoples, not capital. Also, many of these extractivist capitalism trends are based upon and contribute to reinforce colonialist powers, which bring to the fore claims around the "defence of territory" and local socio-ecologies by peasants, Indigenous people, and other urban, peri-urban and rural dwellers, in many contexts. A case in point is the Land Back Movement in Canada and the US, which aims to restore Indigenous governance and land stewardship (Longman et al. 2020). Moreover, new food dynamics in rural and urban areas — such as agroecological producers, alternative food networks, communitarian forest management groups, and community gardening initiatives —seek to reestablish the commons and more just and sustainable socioecological metabolic relationships through "commoning" practices, reclaim land control, equitable access to resources, and the power to decide on their own socio-ecologies. Other rural working people, including artisanal fishers, farm and forestry workers, and landless and migrant farmworkers, also search for control over their material basis of living, including access to quality food, which links to land control issues. All these examples show how territory, land, food and ecology are interrelated, and how collective struggles for land and socioecological metabolism are daily, performative, and organized expressions of insurgent ecologies. They put at the centre key issues to consider in relation to land politics in the current context of the Anthropocene.

Presently, the "land question" is about socioecological conflicts over access to, control over, and use of natural resources, territory and landscapes. These conflicts are shaped by people's particular and situated relationships to land, such as their local ecological knowledges and practices, everyday lived experiences of violence and exclusion, feelings of belonging to a community, and collective struggles — creating "varied forms of territoriality" (Shattuck and Peluso 2021). Land politics involves struggles for wealth, resources, and power redistribution, bottom-up processes of governance, fights for collective rights vs. individual rights, and private property — as well as the recognition of people's practices, meanings and identities. In other words, it involves struggles for "land sovereignty" as a unifying concept for the diversity and plurality of land-based struggles (Borras, Franco and Monsalve Suárez 2015). The variety of the "land question" also highlights the diversity of subaltern social actors — urban, peri-urban and rural, peasants and other rural peoples, young and old, women and migrants, etc. — who are organizing, mobilizing, and making land and territorial claims. How are land conflicts and movements being brought together and contributing to build social muscle in order to challenge the hegemony of neoliberal capitalism in relation to broadly defined land issues?

This section interrogates how land can be the focal point through which convergences between insurgent socioecological movements can be forged. The three chapters draw our attention to the contingent, diverse and contested processes through which enclosures, privatization and commodification of land develop, in its links to people's everyday co-production of environments and territories. They illustrate the multiple ways in which the "land question" emerges in collective struggles, and how land (and food) sovereignty movements gain strength when building common ground between the subaltern, united in diversity in fights against extractivist capitalism on land. The everyday struggle of the different collectives presented in the chapters also shows how activism is about fighting dominant powers, as well as daily challenging, reworking and contesting powerful divides within the movements related to patriarchy, racism, closed identities and idealizations of community, among others.

Marien González-Hidalgo, Diego Cidrás and Joám Evans Pim focus on the current struggles in rural Galicia against the hegemony of tree monocultures, in its material and symbolic dimensions. They show how forest extractivism was historically enforced to rural populations through the plunder of people's commons, and the deliberate erasure of the memories, knowledges and cultures of the land and its peoples. They reveal how urban and rural people are now converging and mobilizing together to uproot eucalyptus monocultures and restore the social, ecological and political justice for the forested commons, through everyday grassroots actions that disrupt the dominant logics and open new imaginaries beyond extractivism.

Antonella Angelini, Giulio Iocco and Martina Lo Cascio look at how two different food sovereignty movements in Spain and Italy — one more rooted in rural areas, the other more urban-based — address issues of wage-labour in agriculture and support the mobilization of migrant farmworkers. They disclose both movements' different tactics and mobilization strategies, in the first one more of a unionist type linked to international solidarity, in the second the construction of a wide, and diverse, autonomous alternative food value chain. During the COVID-19 pandemic, the deteriorating living conditions of migrant farmworkers catalyzed new forms of self-organization and activism, along similar lines in both countries. The authors highlight the strategic relevance of including "labour" issues into food sovereignty struggles, and of devising strategies for migrant worker mobilization, as they are a centrepiece of the land-labour nexus of commodification in agri-food systems.

Rita Calvário, Irmak Ertör and Zoe W. Brent inquire into how well food sovereignty, born as a peasant concept, does travel into and back from the fisheries' world. They look into how the "translation" of food sovereignty contributes to potentiate fisher-peasant convergences, both at the international level and in the more localized context of Brazil. In the case of Brazil, it is around the defence of livelihoods, land/territory, and the environment that fishers engage with food sovereignty, and identify common grievances, shared identities, and mutual goals with peasants and other rural people. Food sovereignty is a powerful analytical framework for understanding the global food system, as well as a mobilizing tool for joint collective struggles, but it requires strategic and consistent two-way translation of concepts and organizational practices across sectors and between local, national, regional and international scales.

References

Akram-Lodhi, Haroon. 2021. "Land." In H. Akram-Lodhi, K. Dietz, B. Engels and B. McKay (eds.), *Handbook of Critical Agrarian Studies*. Cheltenham: Edward Elgar Publishing.

Borras Jr., Saturnino M., Jennifer C. Franco, and Sofía Monsalve Suárez. 2015. "Land and food sovereignty." *Third World Quarterly* 36, 3.

Longman, Nikita, Emily Riddle, Alex Wilson, and Saima Desai (eds.). 2020. "The Land Back Issue." *Briarpatch*, September/October.

Shattuck, Annie, and Nancy Lee Peluso. 2021. "Territoriality." In H. Akram-Lodhi, K. Dietz, B. Engels and B. McKay (eds.), *Handbook of Critical Agrarian Studies*. Cheltenham: Edward Elgar Publishing.

UPROOTING MONOCULTURES, RE-ROOTING THE COMMONS

Everyday Struggles against Eucalyptus Tree Plantations in Rural Galicia

Marien González-Hidalgo, Diego Cidrás and Joám Evans Pim

Tree plantations are monocultures for the production of industrial round wood at high growth rates, organized to supply external markets: timber, charcoal, logs and, most important of all, pulpwood, the raw material for the paper industry (Carriere and Lohman 1996). This type of land-use, focused on high-growth rates and export-oriented production, is characteristic of the "Plantationocene era," a term used to describe the current epoch in which large-scale agriculture, particularly in the form of plantations, has become a dominant force (Wolford 2021). Historically the expansion of agricultural and forest monocultures has been facilitated by European colonization processes, relying heavily on forced labour to produce commodities for global markets.

Tree monocultures are therefore a form of extractivism: they are large-scale, intensively managed, plantations of mostly non-native trees like fast-growing eucalyptus, pine and acacia species, destined for industrial processes usually under control of multinational corporations for selling in globalized markets. A large number of conflicts between forest corporations, the state and local populations have been reported worldwide, mainly related to the large-scale occupation of state land customarily used by local inhabitants, who report power concentration, displacements, water shortage and impact of their local uses of natural resources (Gerber 2011). In terms of governance, this forest model has historically been — and it is currently — associated with dictatorial processes, violence, and socio-environmental and territorial inequalities, affecting especially those who count less for the interests of capitalism, such as Indigenous populations and peasants, landless communities, and women and children (Arora-Jonsson et al. 2021).

The worldwide expansion of tree monocultures has been recently justified under the green capitalism rationale, since some — like the Food and Agriculture Organization of the United Nations (FAO) — name tree monocultures as "forests" or "planted forests." This is justified based on the capacity of trees to capture CO_2, and therefore are promoted as a green or climate-friendly industry, masking the polluting and conflicting aspects of the forest extractivist industry under climate change compensation discourses. Therefore, "tree plantations" and "tree monocultures" are critical terms to refer to what others would simply call "forests," as explained by international environmental activists such as World Rainforest Movement under the campaign "Plantations are not forests!" (Rainforest Rescue n.d.).

In regions and countries with a well-established forest-extractivist sector, forestry plays an important role in the rural economy, generating employment and income for local communities. Nevertheless, as the International Labour Organization states, the sector faces important deficits in decent work. These include low wages and productivity, widespread informality, significant gender equality gaps, low unionization rates and highly hazardous work (ILO 2019). The sector is also in the spotlight due to widespread cases of forced labour (Montague 2019) as well as corruption and illegal logging, estimated by the UN Environment Program at 15–30 percent of all logging (UN 2014). Local and Indigenous communities, environmentalists and peasants, especially in the Global South, have for decades opposed this model and pushed for alternatives based on local biodiversity and ancestral knowledge and local governance for sustainable forest management. However, uprooting the logic of tree monocultures is not at all easy, since, as according to Vandana Shiva (1993), monocultures are associated to a culture based in capital's interests, as well as Western colonial knowledge and technologies, which constitute "monocultures of the mind": a culture whose roots are sometimes deeper than the roots of pines or eucalyptus, and which destroy non-capitalist lives and imaginaries in rural areas.

In this chapter, we engage with a particular rural initiative in the periphery of the Global North: the daily struggle of some communities in rural Galicia, in north-western Spain, to uproot the eucalyptus and acacia trees that grow and expand in their communal lands. First, we will briefly describe how tree plantations expanded at the expense of the forest commons in rural Galicia; next, we introduce how the recent grassroots experience of the "De-eucalyptising Brigades" (Brigadas Deseucaliptizadoras in Galician language) is seeking to uproot both physically and symbolically the culture associated with the tree monocultures in the area.

Tree monocultures in Galicia at the expense of the commons

Since the mid-twentieth century, Galicia has experienced a significant process of de-agrarianization. A substantial portion of the rural population migrated to urban areas, while abandoned agricultural lands have gradually been replaced by shrubs and other forms of vegetation (Vadell et al. 2016). This shift in land use has paved the way for the rapid expansion of tree plantations, especially in coastal areas where they are well suited. The promotion of these plantations dates back to the origins of modern silviculture in Spain, which emerged around 1877. However, it especially gained momentum during Franco's dictatorship. Initially, pine trees, primarily *Pinus pinaster*, were the favoured choice for plantations. Later on, eucalyptus trees, mainly *Eucalyptus globulus*, became increasingly popular. Eucalyptus plantations were seen as a convenient source of income, especially for landowners who were no longer engaged in agricultural production (Evans Pim 2020). The expansion of these plantations was remarkable, growing from 28 thousand hectares in 1973 to 388 thousand in 2009.

Such a process of expansion is more intense in this region than in the neighbouring territories of Asturias, Spain (about 60,000 hectares) and the Região do Norte (Northern Region), Portugal (about 165,000 hectares). Currently, eucalyptus plantations supply a good part of the raw materials that the paper pulp industry demands. ENCE (Energía y Celulosa S.A.) is the Spanish enterprise (with headquarters in Madrid) that centralizes the pulping process in the region, being now the biggest "producer"[1] of eucalyptus pulp in Europe. By September 2022, ENCE reported a net benefit of 67 million euros. More than 96 percent of the cellulose ENCE processes is exported to countries in Northern Europe. However, in Galicia, many of these plantations are usually abandoned, until it is time to harvest. This has implied an abandonment of rural areas and a disconnection between everyday rural politics, "*o monte*"

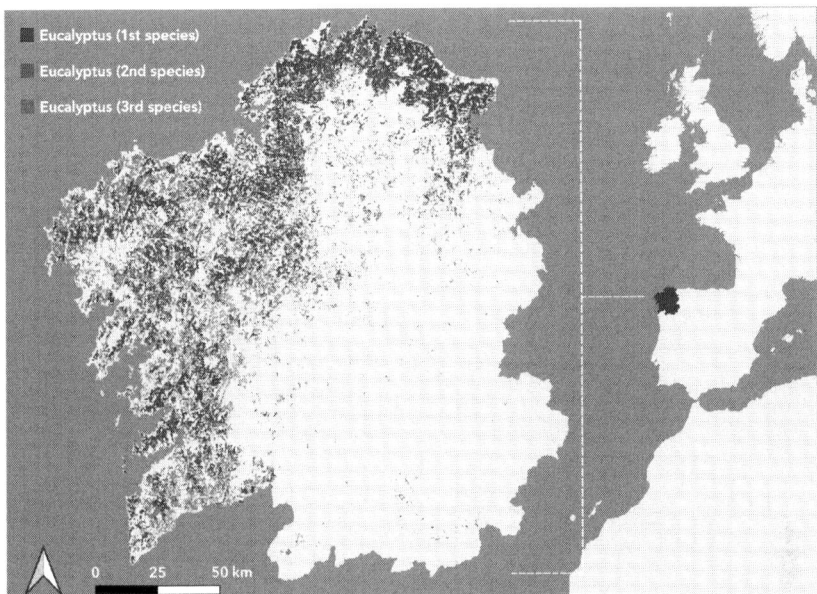

Map of Galicia, representing the current degree of predominance of eucalyptus types, indicating the first (1st), second (2nd), or third (3rd) most widespread species. Elaboration by Diego Cidrás. Data by Spanish Forestry Map & Xunta de Galicia.

[the (common) forest] and people, beyond timely moments such as the felling of trees and harvesting of wood.

As mentioned before, tree plantations increased in Galicia in the renewed plunder of the commons initiated by Franco's regime. Extinguishing centuries of community rights over the land became a prime target of the State Forest Services (Patrimonio Forestal del Estado). With an aging and dying population, in many places the erasure of documented history in the 1940s–1960s was followed by the erasure of the oral memory of the land and its peoples. Nowadays, about one quarter of Galicia's total land mass (29,574 km^2) is officially classified as Common Land that belongs to 3,300 Common Land Communities (Comunidades de Montes Vecinhais). Commons vary in size from a few hectares to several thousand — the average being around two hundred hectares — and from just one or two "open houses" (*casa aberta*) with people living in them to hundreds or even thousands — the average being around forty houses. All in all, approximately 15 percent of the Galician population lives in commons "open houses." There are also considerable differences in terms of how "alive" communities are.

While formal property rights were reasserted in most of the common lands that had been seized during the dictatorship, tree monocultures indicated a shift from intergenerational solidarity and land stewardship to quick cash gains, transforming the lands seized in the 1940s into a very different cultural landscape. Not only did State Forestry engineers direct the plantation of thousands of hectares of usurped forest lands with pines and eucalyptus, but also struggled to cram the "eucalyptus = progress" association into rural mentality — in conunction with its "oak = backwardness" counterpart. Eucalyptus plantations, with their long straight trunks in parallel lines, stood out in sharp contrast with the randomness of shapes and distribution of oak forests, becoming a visual outcropping of a radically different mind-set and relationship with the environment. The same can be applied to the radical transformations of agriculture through the forced introduction of agrochemicals and industrialized processes that created critical dependencies and impoverished the land; or it can apply to the proliferation of dams and mines destroying rivers, valleys, mountains and whole communities, which literally disappeared from maps (Evans Pim 2021).

The rapid expansion of forest plantations has positioned eucalyptus trees at the crossroads of a complex interplay of land and environmental conflicts. These conflicts, which have evolved over time, encompass various dimensions. Starting as far back as the 1980s, agrarian peasants staged rebellions against the encroachment of new plantations on their private lands. Their acts of resistance included uprooting trees from their own properties (López and González 2002) and setting fire to the plantations (Cabana 2007). These actions vividly underscore the deep-rooted opposition to the expansion of eucalyptus plantations.

In recent years, a series of initiatives have emerged to counteract the proliferation of tree plantations and to foster rural alternatives. These efforts represent a departure from decades of rural development primarily centred around forest extractivism. For instance, numerous local governments have come together and collectively declared themselves as "Eucalypt-Free-Zone" municipalities (Cidrás 2020). This united front reflects the increasing resistance to the spread of eucalyptus plantations. Moreover, protests have arisen in response to the socio-environmental consequences stemming from plantation expansion. These include protesing wildfires (Calviño-Cancela and Cañizo-Novelle 2018), concerns about biodiversity loss (Deus et al. 2018), and opposition to the presence of an environmentally controversial pulp factory in southwest Galicia (Masa 2016).

In the next section, we briefly present the experience of the "De-eucalyptizing Brigades,"[2] which seek to mobilize people in order to eradicate eucalyptus and acacia trees and substitute them with native species. Their activism attempts to increase biodiversity, prevent the expansion of disasters, and reclaim communal forest management (see also Cidrás and González-Hidalgo 2022). By doing so, the Brigades, we argue, help to slowly transform the "monocultures of the mind" into engaged cultures for the rural commons.

The "De-eucalyptizing Brigades"

On May 1, 2016, the Froxán commons, in the municipality of Lousame, faced a forest fire that was presumably started intentionally by unknown individuals, in the context of an ongoing land dispute with the Spanish mining company Sacyr, whose operations encroached the village's lands (today, the project has been taken over by the Australian firm "Pivotal Metals"). The fire failed to reach the houses because of a green oak firebreak and was quickly extinguished by the community. However, it once again revealed the community's vulnerability caused by exposure to monocultures, which are more subject to severe fire damage compared to multi-aged and biodiverse forests. In the following months, the community — made up of just five households — started to organize "*rogas*" (calls for communal work) and "*albaroques*" (the feast that followed these works), rescuing these traditional practices to try and engage more people beyond Froxán. Dozens of such actions were organized with the aim to help commoners in Froxán reduce eucalyptus plantations, bring back native forests, and create a more diverse landscape less prone to fire (Evans Pim 2021; Grove et al. 2020).

Just about a year later, a horrific wave of forest fires affected large swaths of land in Galicia and Portugal, accounting for over one hundred deaths. At this point people in Froxán reached out to a Galician environmental NGO, Verdegaia, with a proposal to scale up the model they had been experimenting with into a larger national initiative, aiming to mobilize volunteers and communities into a collective effort to improve the situation of communal forested lands. The "Brigadas Deseucaliptizadoras" were launched in April 2018 in Froxán with just a few dozen volunteers. Four years later, the Brigades have more than a thousand registered volunteers (*brigadistas*) and have done hundreds of actions throughout Galicia. The project is mostly self-funded and self-managed with local common land communities that direct actions in the frontlines. In this context, we have been engaged in several Brigadas working days, as co-organizers (Joám), or as recurrent (Diego) and sporadic participants (Marien). The information that we provide here is a summary of some of our insights as part of our participatory research, which has included interviews, surveys and focus groups with the participants of the Brigades.

The profile of activists participating in the Brigades is diverse and can change from one event to the other (Cidrás and González-Hidalgo 2022). Generally speaking, young adults participate in the Brigades and there is gender parity. Also, although most of Common Lands are located in rural areas of Galicia, participants mostly come from urban or peri-urban areas. Typically, self-organized "de-eucalyptizing" working days (*rogas*) consist of a variety of tasks such as felling and cutting up large eucalyptus trees, the uprooting of small eucalyptus sprouts, hacking away at eucalyptus stumps, peeling eucalyptus bark, and collectively transporting cut logs. During the *rogas*, *brigadistas* can also plant local species such as oak and chestnut, consolidating natural regrowth of native trees through selective clearing. Also, these working days allow people to exchange scientific information about local species, discuss current challenges of forests in rural areas and local particularities, meet and network with others to assess the effectiveness of these actions. This engagement in direct action is explained by activists as: "we organize ourselves because we believe there is another (forestry) system that is possible, and because there is no adequate response from authorities."

Performing most of these tasks is physically demanding, especially for people who do not work in the fields daily. Removing the eucalyptus trees requires strength; often it takes more than two people to be able to remove some larger ones. "Uprooters" do not see the physical demand of these activities as negative, but rather as the opposite, as a way of "exercising, unloading the stress of the week and also the anger of seeing so many eucalyptuses planted" (interview). In these embodied actions, women are as visible, active and engaged as men. While this is not outstanding *per se*, it does mark a difference regarding the usually over-shadowed labour of women in both the everyday commoning labour and collective mobilization in rural Galicia (Cabana 2017). Female

Spring working day of the *brigadas* in Froxán. Photo credit: Brigadas Deseucaliptizadoras. Reprinted with permission.

brigadistas can be in charge of the caring activities for the preparation of the shared meals or "*albaroques*," as well as also publicly expressing their strength and anger while grasping an axe or chainsaw and hacking at a eucalyptus root.

While the act of uprooting is a manifestation of (physical) strength or capability, some participants easily acknowledge the limitations of their actions amidst an extensive expansion of monocultures: "We have to consider that this type of forest [eucalypt monoculture] has been established with a lot of propaganda, subsidies from the *Xunta* [Galician government] for planting, in order to impose only one use of the forest ... it is difficult to change all that discourse imposed over 35 years" (interview).

However, participants highlight how their engagement is awakening a new culture:

> [In the Brigades,] in addition to the physical work of uprooting eucalypts, we are forming a community, ... eating together, debating, ... and depending on the day ..., one day we can visit a Castro [Iron Age hill forest], another day we go to a

book presentation ...; we have a good time, we learn things that you would not learn anywhere else, ... and all of that gives you a bit of a historical perspective. (interview)

In doing so, the Brigades result in a movement that combines conservationist aims (planting native trees to increase biodiversity and reduce vulnerability to fire), engaged and radical embodied actions (uprooting eucalyptus), moments of community work, and critical thought and mobilization. Since the first experience developed in Froxán in April 2018, over one hundred working days have taken place by the Brigades (as of January 2023), as well as recently in Portugal, in collaboration with local associations. The experience has also inspired local associations around Galicia beyond the scope of Verdegaia, who have self-organized similar actions under similar formats. From an initial group of a few dozen activists, the Brigades have now enrolled over 1,200 volunteers.

Undoing monocultures, re-doing the commons

The De-eucalyptizing Brigades in rural Galicia is one of several movements globally that organize to undo the impacts of monoculture tree plantations in the everyday life of Indigenous, peasant and rural dwellers. Their work is trying to slowly restore the social, ecological and political justice of the forested commons, as a culture that was destroyed and undervalued during Franco's dictatorship, and continued by means of Spanish and Galician policies based in forest extractivism. Through the Brigades, the forest commons are revived by urban-rural connections, expanding the scope of the "circle of concern" beyond just the local community. They offer a gathering place for peoples — with room for those usually undervalued regarding the rural commons, i.e., women, children, urban and young individuals — from throughout Galicia to engage in non-extractive and regenerative activities. That is, the Brigades re-root the rural commons not merely as related to a physical, delimited space associated to a communitarian property, but the commons as an action that is performed and disputed on an everyday basis by means of collective actions among peoples and territories.

This of course does not happen without challenges. For example, some *brigadistas* living in urban areas recognize they would not like to return to the land beyond sporadic visits, while some commoners feel uncomfortable with a lot of people coming, suddenly, from outside. Also, some *brigadistas* would acknowledge that the task of manually uprooting hectares and hectares of expanding eucalyptus looks overwhelming. Nevertheless, they also know it is not their individual or collective task to do it, since that would need specific commitments by the public and private authorities in the area. However, their role in breaking the "monocultures of the mind" and opening new imaginaries for the rural areas in Galicia is clear and slowly advancing. As a matter of fact, the term *Deseucaliptización* was chosen word of the year 2018 in an initiative of the Royal Galician Academy (RAG) and the Barrié Foundation. According to the RAG, the victory of "de-eucalyptization" reflects "an outstanding aspect in the growing social concern for the management of the Galician forest" (RAG 2018).

Given the huge expansion of tree plantations in Galicia, it is obvious that initiatives like this one do not imply an immediate transformation of the rural areas as a whole. But they do have an impact: by increasing the biodiversity of certain areas, the work of the Brigades helps to have a territory better prepared to cope with and resist the dynamics of present and future global environmental change, especially regarding forest fires. And probably more importantly, with their everyday grassroots work, these movements help to articulate imaginaries beyond extractivism, mobilizing and venting activists' anger into action to uproot monocultures, while also planting seeds of hope and futures of socioecological restoration.

Notes

1   ENCE does not "produce" the pulp as they claim. Trees are grown by the action of nature; what ENCE and subcontracted enterprises do is to "extract" (cut, transport, process and make money from) planted trees.
2   See <brigadas.gal> and <brigadas.pt>.

References

Arora-Jonsson, Seema, Carol J. Pierce Colfer, and Marien González-Hidalgo. 2021. "Seeing the Quiet Politics in Unquiet Woods: A different vantage point for a future forest agenda." *Human Ecology* 49, 3.
Cabana Ana. 2007. "Los incendios en el monte comunal gallego: Lugo durante el primer franquismo." *Historia agraria: Revista de agricultura e historia rural* 43.
_____. 2017. "Mulleres diante. Rostros femininos e acción colectiva no rural galego." *Boletín galego de literatura* 50.

Calviño-Cancela, María, and Nuria Cañizo-Novelle. 2018. "Human dimensions of wildfires in NW Spain: Causes, value of the burned vegetation and administrative measures." *PeerJ* 6.

Carriere, Ricardo, and Larry Lohmann. 1996. *Pulping the South: Industrial Tree Plantations and the World Paper Economy*. London and New Jersey: Zed Books Ltd.

Cidrás, Diego. 2020. "Municipios 'libres de eucaliptos': análisis de los actores políticos locales en Galicia." *Boletín de la Asociación de Geógrafos Españoles* 84.

Cidrás, Diego, and Marien González-Hidalgo. 2022. "Defining invasive alien species from the roots up: Lessons from the 'De-eucalyptising Brigades' in Galicia, Spain." *Political Geography* 99.

Deus, Ernesto et al. 2018. "Are post-dispersed seeds of *Eucalyptus globulus* predated in the introduced range? Evidence from an experiment in Portugal." *Web Ecology* 18, 1.

Evans Pim, Joám. 2020. "Indigenous and Community Conserved Areas (ICCAs) in Galiza: Indigeneity or Peasanthood?" In R. Colbourne, R. Anderson (eds.), *Indigenous Wellbeing and Enterprise: Self-Determination and Sustainable Economic Development*. London: Routledge.

———. 2021. "'Galiza is (not) a mine': rural responses to pro-extractivist policies." *Araucaria* 23, 48.

Gerber, Julien-François. 2011. "Conflicts over industrial tree plantations in the South: Who, how and why?" *Global Environmental Change* 21, 1.

Grove, Richard et al. 2020. "Pastoral Stone Enclosures as Biological Cultural Heritage: Galician and Cornish Examples of Community Conservation." *Land* 9.

ILO (International Labour Organization). 2019. "Promoting decent work and safety and health in forestry." Report for discussion at the Sectoral Meeting on Promoting Decent Work and Safety and Health in Forestry (Geneva, May 6–10, 2019), International Labour Office, Sectoral Policies Department, Geneva.

López, José A., and Marta I. González. 2002. *Políticas del bosque. Expertos, políticos y ciudadanos en la polémica del eucalipto en Asturias*. Madrid: Ediciones Akal.

Masa, Antón. 2016. "A prórroga de ENCE: corrupción e contaminación ambiental na ría de Pontevedra." *Cerna* 75.

Montague, Brendan. 2019. "Forestry sector 'failing' to combat forced labour." *The Ecologist*, November 13, 2019. At <theecologist.org/2019/nov/13/forestry-sector-failing-combat-forced-labour>.

Rainforest Rescue, Campaign "Plantations are not forests," n.d. At <rainforest-rescue.org/petitions/772/plantations-are-not-forests>.

RAG (Royal Galician Academy). 2018. "'Deseucaliptización,' elixida Palabra do Ano 2018." At <academia.gal/-/deseucaliptizacion-elixida-palabra-do-ano-2018>.

Shiva, Vandana. 1993. *Monocultures of the Mind: Perspectives on Biodiversity and Biotechnology*. London and New York: Zed Books Ltd.

UN (United Nations). 2014. "Illegal Trade in Wildlife and Timber Products Finances Criminal and Militia Groups, Threatening Security and Sustainable Development."

United Nations Environment Programme, June 24, 2014. At <unep.org/news-and-stories/press-release/illegal-trade-wildlife-and-timber-products-finances-criminal-and>.

Vadell, Enric, Sergio de-Miguel, and Jesús Pemán. 2016. "Large-scale reforestation and afforestation policy in Spain: A historical review of its underlying ecological, socioeconomic and political dynamics." *Land use policy* 55: 37–48.

Wolford, Wendy. 2021. "The Plantationocene: A Lusotropical Contribution to the Theory." *Annals of the American Association of Geographers* 111, 6.

MIGRANT AGRICULTURAL WORKERS, RADICAL FOOD ACTIVISM, AND THE STRUGGLE FOR EMANCIPATORY RURAL CHANGE IN SOUTHERN EUROPE

Antonella Angelini, Giulio Iocco and Martina Lo Cascio

Perhaps nowhere more than around food production and consumption has the neoliberal model come into contestation over the past three decades. Beyond their radical critique of the industrial agri-food model and its devastating impacts on humans and the environment, food movements and alternative food networks have offered fertile ground for new food practices reclaiming the ideals of mutualism, social justice and ecological sustainability (Sage et al. 2021). In Europe, initiatives inspired by the principles of solidarity economy have aimed to integrate environmental, economic and social concerns, while developing new food systems, principally at the local level, as spaces of self-organization, and of horizontal, equal participation and deliberation, alternative to the dominant model of food production, distribution and consumption (Rossi et al. 2021).

In this context, the aspirations and needs of farmers have always featured centrally to the project of building food sovereignty, intended as peoples' right to healthy and culturally appropriate food produced through ecologically sound and sustainable methods, and their right to define their own food and agriculture systems (Declaration of the International Forum for Agroecology 2015). At the same time, most initiatives under the solidarity economy and food sovereignty umbrella have been less attentive to the role of other rural working classes, namely farmworkers and food workers. This is all the more relevant considering the ever-growing reliance on waged labour in Southern Europe agricultures, where, albeit the average size of enterprises varies across regions, small-scale farming and its accompanying model of self-employment and family farms has largely been displaced by the consolidation of larger producers.

Migrant farmworkers have constituted the bulk of these industrial agri-food supply chains since the early 2000s (Corrado et al. 2016). The precariousness of their employment relations is notorious: discontinuous daily employment, informal contracts without social security entitlements, and indirect hiring through intermediaries (Iocco et al. 2019). To be sure, leading movements, such as the worldwide peasant network La Vía Campesina, have developed a discourse against the discrimination of wage workers and migrant rural workers. But the initiatives developed on the ground by organizations that are part of or close to these movements remain less known and discussed. At the same time, few solidarity economy initiatives have developed specific strategies and campaigns to tackle the living and working conditions of migrant agricultural workers.

We contribute to this important emerging conversation by focusing on two food sovereignty movements: the SAT–Sindicato Andaluz de Trabajadores/as (Andalusian Workers' Union) in Spain; and FuoriMercato (which roughly translates as Outside the Market) in Italy. Both organizations work extensively with migrant workers in two of Europe's most important strongholds of intensive agriculture. They do it from radical perspectives oriented at promoting social and ecological transformation. Both are connected to La Vía Campesina (though FuoriMercato's position within the network is somewhat more marginal).

Our reflection tries to understand how these two organizations have integrated the protection of waged labour, particularly of migrant farmworkers, in their practices of food sovereignty. We then try to capture the tactics that have been developed to support the unionization and mobilization of migrant farmworkers. The conjoint emphasis on environmental, food and social justice concerns, with special focus on migrant worker rights, is fairly unique to these organizations in the Southern European context. Each organization has developed a distinct array of tactics for (migrant) farmworker mobilization. Differences exist in how the struggle against the mainstream, retail-based, food regime is organized. A comparative analysis of the two organizations can yield fruitful exchange and mutual learning between the two experiences.

Most importantly, it shows how both movements articulate struggles against food commodification and labour exploitation with antiracist activism for migrants' rights. We see in the convergence of these multiple struggles the connection with the notion of an insurgent ecology.

Our choice to focus on these two organizations also reflects our position as participants in social movement activism. As members of FuoriMercato, we have first-hand experience of the forms of power that activists encounter as they articulate claims. The exchange with SAT offered an occasion for self-reflection on our practices and engagement. We feel that, from an activist perspective, coupling a dialogue with an analytical reflection on the similarities and differences between the SAT and FuoriMercato fosters the objectives of our organizations.

The study relies on interviews with senior SAT members between 2015 and 2022. The first round of interviews, in 2015, formed part of a dialogue between the freshly established FuoriMercato and other European organizations active in the food sovereignty movement. It was part of a learning process, as FuoriMercato was embracing the food sovereignty agenda. The most recent exchanges emerged out of the need to assess how other organizations addressed the pandemic and its implications on farmworkers and rural work more broadly. As active participants in FuoriMercato, we also draw on the daily exchanges within our respective regional hubs and regular meetings at a national level.

Origin and organizational structures

The Andalusian Workers' Union

Established in 1976, the Rural Workers' Union (SOC–Sindicato de Obreros del Campo) was originally a farmworker union with eclectic underpinnings, including Marxism-Maoism, Christian syndicalism, Andalusian nationalism and anarchism. Its agenda revolved around three core axes: syndicalism, land struggles and occupations, and political advocacy. In 2007, the change of name to SAT–Sindicato Andaluz de Trabajadores/as coincided with a partial reorganization as a more urban union and the intent to expand its base beyond farmworkers.

Land struggles have historically played (and continue to play) a central role in the organization's work. Moreover, since the late 1990s, within a broader reorientation towards ecology, peace and other new issues of social mobilization, SOC/SAT has also embraced the food sovereignty project. In 1986, SOC was one of the founding members of the European Farmers Coordination, the European organization set up by farmers' associations demanding alternatives to the EU's neoliberal policy framework for agriculture (known as the Common Agricultural Policy). In 1993, SOC was among the co-promoters of the establishment of La Vía Campesina, the transnational agrarian movement that later launched the food sovereignty project at the global level in 1996.

Since then, SOC/SAT has proactively participated in the development of the organization and its broader political project as a member of the European Coordination of La Vía Campesina and in the launch of a "European movement for food sovereignty and another Common Agricultural Policy" in March 2009 (e.g., the Nyeleni Europe Movement).

In these fora, SOC/SAT has always played the crucial role of giving voice to the perspective of farmworkers. Over years, the organization has acquired a major coordinating role within the Rural Workers and Migration Working Group of the European Coordination of La Vía Campesina.

In SOC/SAT's vision, the critique of the mainstream food regime and the quest for an alternative model based on agroecology, biodiversity and agrarian reform go together with a worker rights agenda. As Federico Pacheco, a long-time SOC/SAT staff member, put it, "Our nature is not only trade-unionist but also revolutionary, that is, for radical transformation" (Pacheco 2020). Strategically, these two fronts are related to different time horizons. In the short term, the priority is to meet workers' basic needs. But having radical change as the long-term objective is crucial to avoid reproducing patterns of exploitation built into the agro-industrial system.

As Andalusian agriculture has increasingly shifted toward relying on a migrant workforce, SOC/SAT has expanded and adapted its activities accordingly over the past fifteen years. Most migrant workers employed in Andalusia come from Morocco, sub-Saharan Africa and Eastern Europe. Typically, they spend the harvesting season huddled in uninhabitable buildings, often with no water supply, in shantytowns periodically razed by the local councils. Dispersion and isolation are serious hurdles against mobilization. So too are violence and volatile working conditions, especially since the global financial crisis of 2008, which increased precariousness in purchaser-producer relationships and, in turn, led producers to rely on short-term, often informal, contracts for farmworkers.

Mobilization has proved particularly difficult in three key areas: Almería, which hosts about 100,000 workers, mostly employed in greenhouses; Huelva, a key hub for strawberry production, which has recently been in the spotlight thanks to the fight of women migrants against exploitation and sexual violence; and Jaén, a high-concentration area for olive, orange and asparagus production by a mostly domestic workforce.

SAT activities range from providing legal advice in local offices to organizing protest marches and strikes. Conflict, training and organization are the key ingredients in SAT's action, coupled with a broader fight against discrimination and violence. Racist attacks are not uncommon in Spain. One outstanding example is the El Ejido riots of February 6–9, 2000, in which local Spanish residents rose against Moroccan workers, torching their homes and shops. These infamous episodes of violence, which represented the culmination of a long series of attacks against workers from the Maghreb, encouraged the inception of SOC's organizing and solidarity work with migrants in Almería. They also raised an alarm at the European level, leading to information and advocacy activities by European civil society networks within and outside the food sovereignty movement.

In the specific context of migrant trade unionism, SAT also engages in broader social issues like health and education, legal assistance with residence permits, appeals against expulsions, and family reunification. Direct work with migrant labourers is challenging and potentially delicate, which is why SAT always makes sure that the persons they collaborate with are truly representative of the community and come from the workplace, which is not only companies but also shared flats or shacks, all spaces that are relevant for a grassroots trade union action.

Another important aspect is for SAT to provide a space where workers, particularly immigrant workers, and members of SAT can meet for the first time or where they can discuss things. Although it is still important to go to companies to make it clear that there is a possibility to organize, the office is a place for offering legal and social assistance or other training and information sharing activities.

This approach reflects the broader philosophy that the union is an instrument for migrant workers' self-organization. Part of this work includes slow and painstaking unionization work through assemblies in public spaces where people can come and share their individual problems. When addressing these problems, the attempt is to try and bring out their collective dimension, their class dimension, in a way, and hence the need for solutions beyond individual fixes.

The collectivization of responses and the plural construction of the union itself are also very important elements in light of the strong union-busting activities by private companies, of which SAT has been the target. Such activities include lawsuits and legal actions, but also violence against SAT activists.

The FuoriMercato network in Italy

Established in 2016 in the Milan urban area, FuoriMercato is a collective, participatory, nationwide network that includes, among other things, occupied lands, reclaimed factories, popular kitchens, mutual care activities, and "off-market" events. Within these spaces and practices, activists attempt to redesign urban and rural areas according to the needs of cohesive and solidarity-based communities, while also respecting the earth and living beings, and pursuing social justice.

This urban/rural hybridity is inscribed in FuoriMercato's genesis, which saw the coming together of the former workers of an automotive factory near Milan with members of the alternative food landscape — particularly, small farmers from the autonomist food network Genuino Clandestino (Genuinely Clandestine) and consumers from some of Milan's solidarity-based purchase groups (Orlando 2018). This is an unusual mix. But when the factory closed in 2012 and the workers decided to occupy it, they realized that they needed to gain support for their action from the local community and, more concretely, to generate income. It was then that the workers started collaborating with a local shop — which purchased its products directly from local farmers — by setting up a delivery point at the factory warehouse.

The real take-off happened when the workers liaised with SOS Rosarno, an association of small-scale farmers working with migrant workers in the southern Italian region of Calabria. Due to the insufficient local demand, SOS Rosarno had come in contact with several purchase groups in Milan, but it struggled to cope with the monetary and time costs of sending small parcels of its citrus products to each group. SOS Rosarno and the workers then agreed that the farmers would send the whole shipment to the warehouse, where the workers would divide it up and deliver it to families in Milan.

Eager to further tap into the potential of this form of intermediation, the workers started to expand their network to local farmers and thus diversify their food offerings. Part of this expansion effort saw the involvement of the Genuino Clandestino network, which helped the workers connect with small-scale producers and farmers across the Italian peninsula. Since 2015, these collaborations have grown into a nationwide network with a single governance structure and a shared vision, but it also highly decentralized and autonomous, with diverse nodes.

Some of FuoriMercato's rural nodes emerged in the wake of the shift to buyer-driven food supply chains and the ensuing squeeze on working conditions downstream. The Calabria-based SOS Rosarno, for instance, brings together two segments of the workforce typically pitted against each other: exploited migrant farmworkers, mostly employed in mid- to large-size farms; and small-scale farmers, disadvantaged in market-price determination dynamics due to the low-cost production ensured by migrant worker exploitation in larger farms. The intent is to meet their respective interests for regular contracts, fair wages, and dignified working conditions in the citrus industry. Similarly, Diritti a Sud (Rights to the South), an organization based in Apulia, the stronghold of Italian tomato production, brings together migrant workers and members of the organization, primarily young unemployed or precarious workers, in a project of self-managed tomato sauce production. Further South, in Sicily, another hub of intensive horticulture, is Contadinazioni (which roughly translates as Peasant-Actions). Born in one of the informal settlements hosting migrant workers for the harvest season, Contadinazioni brings together Sicilian precarious workers and migrant workers to create an economic alternative based on peasant and exploitation-free olive production. More broadly, Contadinazioni promotes initiatives to break migrant workers' isolation and to gradually build worker power and raise political claims.

As this cursory overview suggests, both supporting migrant workers in their immediate needs and the process of organizing are at the core of FuoriMercato's mission. Migrant workers were, and still are, only marginally represented by traditional unions in Italy. More broadly, FuoriMercato has revived the tradition of mutualism as practical self-help and as solidarity towards marginalized, latent, or emerging worker struggles.

This focus on work-related issues distinguishes FuoriMercato from most other Italian experiences challenging the mainstream food regime.

At the same time, like other initiatives of the Italian solidarity economy movement, FuoriMercato sees building alternative practices around food as an incubator and gateway to broader transformative processes. In this sense, the satisfaction of basic individual and collective needs through the construction of an alternative and autonomous value chain is the linchpin of the struggle against neoliberal and extractivist food production policies.

Mobilization strategies

SAT and migrant worker actions addressing the mainstream retail sector

In its long-standing engagement with migrant workers, SAT has deployed and developed several strategies to cope with their hurdles. Migrant workers rarely become SAT members, but they increasingly participate in its actions. SAT's approach favours direct engagement with the company management, but also includes pressuring Spanish producers by appealing to buyers in the European retail sector.

Strikes are a particularly costly strategy for migrant workers. To curb the costs for workers, SAT has relied on a mix of international solidarity and campaigning with local resistance techniques. International advocacy and campaigning, especially targeting major retailers abroad, is a crucial component of SAT's strategy. Much of the produce grown in Almería is sold to supermarkets in the UK and the rest of Northern Europe. A triangular model — i.e., activists abroad lobbying their domestic chains, which have in turn lobbied Andalusian companies to enforce workers' rights and/or claims for marketing reasons — has been implemented with the support of German, Swiss and English ethical consumer or labour rights protection organizations (see Rügemer 2021). As one SAT activist put it, insisting on the role of intermediaries, especially certification bodies, is a powerful piece of this mobilization scheme.

One good example of this strategy is the controversy with agro-industrial producer Godoy Hortalizas. In January 2019, the greenhouse workers of Godoy Hortalizas in Almería went on strike over a pay and working conditions dispute. They argued that the company was in breach of the minimum wage provisions in the sector agreement and that they were exposed to unsafe use of agricultural pesticides. This first stage of the controversy ended after only three days of strike. Crucial to its success was the wise use of consumer pressure and the media. At the time of the strike, SAT was pursuing a new campaign about working conditions in the region in collaboration with La Vía Campesina and the UK-based organization Ethical Consumer.

Thanks to the pressure from Ethical Consumer, one of the supermarkets put pressure on Godoy Hortalizas to enter negotiations with the union and the striking workers. Lamenting the persistent violation of their rights, workers went on strike again in September 2020. To support this longer action, SAT organized a resistance fund in support of forty-three workers. Other independent organizations, such as the collective of Jornaleras en Lucha, created a resistance fund, which raised funds to free up the time of a worker to promote the activities of the collective.

International solidarity also improves the organization's visibility. This is particularly the case for SAT's participation in La Vía Campesina, which provides fundamental support and communication tools. To achieve workers' objectives, it is important for supporting organizations to understand what the needs of the workers are and how to translate alliance strategies into the concrete lives of workers, whether they are organized or not.

SAT also pursues its food sovereignty agenda through its twelve cooperatives dispersed throughout Andalusia and the occupation of four hundred hectares of land for production purposes. These cooperatives emphasize the model of direct producer-consumer relations, as most agri-food European networks tend to do. Albeit circumscribed, these experiences add another chapter to the SAT's overall work, complementing its core set of activities targeted at mainstream retailers.

Sharing the construction of a solidarity economy network with migrant workers in Italy

As a decentralized and internally diverse organization, FuoriMercato has always been concerned with its internal articulation. Selling its products outside the mainstream retail system is a cornerstone of FuoriMercato's vision of how to strengthen the producer-consumer relationship. This has coincided with an emphasis on distribution: how to organize an effective, nation-wide distribution network is crucial to FuoriMercato's political project.

FuoriMercato's rural hubs, such as Sfruttazero (Zero Exploitation) in Apulia, Contadinazioni in Sicily and SOS Rosarno in Calabria, emerged as social projects against farmworkers' exploitation. Their aim is to imagine and promote farming that is tailored to the needs of communities and of those who are active in the construction of agroecological lives. These are projects based on organizational models that take their cue from peasant movements and workers' economies, aiming to be a reservoir of resources and energy to engage in struggles of resistance against the agro-industrial and extractivist model.

Recently, the need to integrate FuoriMercato's principles of agroecological production and those of decent worker conditions led them to develop a participatory guarantee system. According to this scheme, all FuoriMercato's productions are to be based on the principles of:

1. Coordination of production through co-design, carried out at the national level, between rural producers and urban distribution groups, and the creation of a national price list for all FuoriMercato's products, which helps even small producers get visibility;
2. Mutualistic support between actors in the network (at the local and national level) through various instruments such as pre-purchasing and co-production;
3. Support for the struggles of exploited workers outside the network (for instance, delivery workers).

This set of principles combines the internal sustainability of the FuoriMercato network with the support for struggles outside alternative circuits, which must be supported within a transformative logic. This approach has its roots in the international peasant movement, which sees food sovereignty as a broader project to affirm peasants' rights. The construction of new food production and, crucially, distribution practices, suggests that the core objective of the struggle against productivism and an extractivist approach to the land and people is in the construction of a complex and articulated, alternative value chain.

Organizing in the face of the COVID-19 crisis

While the target and the tactics developed by the SAT and FuoriMercato differ, for both organizations the COVID-19 pandemic has opened unprecedented or previously underused spaces of action along very similar lines. Early into the pandemic, the Spanish and the Italian governments, like many others worldwide, qualified farmworkers as essential workers. At the time, workers lacked any protective gear, but companies were concerned about keeping up with their usual production levels. This entailed increased exploitation, as many workers could not go to work, and so those who had the means to do so had to compensate for it.

The hurdles faced by workers in this phase were numerous. A SAT activist we interviewed told us about the case of a group of Moroccan women who remained stuck at the border and could not reach Andalusia in 2020. No social security or work alternative was offered to them and for those already in place, more intensive work was offered without any advantage. The figures of the red fruits harvest of 2020 were unaffected by the pandemic, and the housing conditions in worker settlements were as poor as always.

At the same time, the pandemic spurred an increase in worker mobilizations. In Almería, for example, in October 2020, migrant farmworkers employed by a horticultural company of the Godoy group promoted a thirty-day strike to protest the violation of the fundamental rights of forty-three workers, including unpaid wages. The participation in the strike was incredibly high among the workers, which was also able to last for such a long period of time thanks to the financial support received by the strikers from a mutual aid fund promoted by the SAT. The mobilization eventually culminated in the negotiation of a satisfactory agreement between workers and the ownership of the company. Also in Almería, in March 2021, a similar protest erupted animated by farmworkers employed by Haciendas Bio. The company responded by firing twenty workers, who were eventually readmitted at work after one year of mobilization, following a court order. In this case, Haciendas Bio was also condemned to pay the wages to the workers made redundant to cover the entire period they were not allowed to work. The same year, in the nearby area of San Isidro, at Campo Hermoso, a group of workers launched a protest to demand the full respect of their rights. Here, as in many other labour conflicts that occurred in Andalusia, workers denounced contracts that did not respect national regulations of minimum wage and overtime payments, as well as racial discrimination. In San Isidro, protests reached a new momentum in March 2022 when a twenty-kilometre-long march took place to voice workers' demands and to kick-start an indefinite strike against a local horticultural company named Hortigada. A few months later, a new march was organized by SAT in El Ejido, one of the main urban centres of the region.

While in Almería, the union played a major role in workers' protests. In Huelva, autonomous collectives established by workers during the pandemic took the driver's seat. The most important among them were the collective Jornaleras de Huelva en Lucha and the collective of African workers who organized the defence and protection of the basic needs of workers living in the local shantytowns (*chabolas*). Another important element was the space taken by women in highly masculinized contexts, such as the informal settlements.

Direct migrant worker mobilizations sparked by living conditions in informal settings can also be seen in Italy, particularly in Sicily. FuoriMercato has long been active in the Campobello di Mazara ghetto, a crowded shantytown in one of the region's most important enclaves for olive production. From May 2020 to October 2021, FuoriMercato increased its activities and presence in the ghetto by organizing legal support activities, including the implementation of health regulations and special work permits for migrant workers. A crucial phase was the implementation of the "Let's bring water to the ghetto" campaign, which ensured a regular water supply for the settlement at the peak of the health crisis.

But the turning point towards self-organization was in the midst of the 2021 harvest season, when the migrant workers living in Campobello di Mazara organized themselves as Braccianti FuoriMercato (*braccianti* means farmworkers) and confronted the local authorities, first asking

Protest following a deadly fire in the Campobello di Mazara ghetto. The banners on the sides read "NO MORE WORKPLACE DEATHS" and "PAPERS FOR ALL." In the middle, the FuoriMercato banner with the slogan "Food self-determination and mutual aid." Photo credit: FuoriMercato.

for the removal of the piles of rubbish that surrounded the ghetto, and then denouncing that this inaction had contributed to a deadly fire that destroyed the camp on September 30. The refusal to abide by the relocation to an institutional and government-supervised camp marked a crucial moment of worker agency. Migrant workers at Campobello had formulated a list of claims based on their first-hand experience of their needs. Their requests included that the local authorities provided basic utility services to the areas where their temporary dwellings were. Implicitly, this also entailed a rejection of the government solution to establish an institutional camp, with a more formal and surveillance-based organization. By voicing their claims in public spaces, migrant workers have brought the contrast between their preferred solutions and the government one to light and opened a new space where the "politics from the margins" has gained concrete content and strength. Workers bring to the stage their own representation of what the right to life is and what the right to housing is.

Conclusions

SAT and FuoriMercato share an affiliation to the food sovereignty model and a strong focus on migrant worker rights. Their experiences show their ability to pursue radical change through different tactics and practices. SAT has mainly strengthened its capacity to pressure local producers through their embeddedness in global supply chains and vulnerability to consumer pressure abroad. This combination of local action and reliance on transnational labour alliances has allowed maximizing the gains from classical worker struggles tools, particularly strikes. FuoriMercato has instead pursued a radical challenge to the predominance of intensive agriculture and its extractivist practices by organizing a complex, internally diverse, alternative food value chain.

The example of the farm labourers of Campobello di Mazara and the stories of SAT during the pandemic open a useful window for our analysis: they resituate the sense of political and organizational innovation that SAT and FuoriMercato pose in this search for circularity between workers' rights, the right to food, and the different organizational forms of struggles towards the horizon of sovereignty. More broadly, as the agro-industrial model relies ever more strategically on migrant workers for cheap labour, challenging this system will also need devising strategies for migrant worker mobilization. Food sovereignty movements can and need to consider this dimension as a crucial component of their mission to politicize food and challenge its commodification, including the exploitation of migrant workers.

References

Corrado, Alessandra, Carlos De Castro, and Domenico Perrotta. 2016. *Migration and Agriculture: Mobility and change in the Mediterranean area.* London: Routledge.

Declaration of the International Forum for Agroecology. 2015. Nyéléni, Mali: February 27, 2015.

Iocco, Giulio, Martina Lo Cascio, and Domenico Perrotta. 2019. "Lavoro migrante, mercati nidificati e sviluppo rurale nelle aree ad agricoltura intensiva del Sud Italia: due esperienze in Calabria e Sicilia" *Mondi Migranti* 1/2019: 31-36.

Orlando, Giovanni. 2018. "Understanding Alternative Food Networks After the Crisis: Testing Four Scenarios in Italy." In A. Corsi, B. Barbera, E. Dansero, C. Peano. Cham (eds.), *Alternative Food Networks: An Interdisciplinary Assessment.* Switzerland: Palgrave Macmillan.

Pacheco, Federico. 2020. "Un sindacato di braccianti e contadini in Andalusia." In Martina Lo Cascio (trans.) FuoriMercato blog, February 7. At <fuorimercato.com/pratiche/292-un-sindacato-di-braccianti-e-contadini-in-andalusia.html>.

Rossi, Adanella, Mario Coscarello, and Davide Biolghini. 2021. "(Re)Commoning Food and Food Systems. The Contribution of Social Innovation from Solidarity Economy." *Agriculture* 11.

Rügemer, Werner. 2021. *Imperium EU: Labour Injustice, Crisis, New Resistances.* Berlin: Tredition.

Sage, Colin, Cordula Kropp, and Irene Antoni-Komar. 2021. "Grassroots initiatives in food system transformation. The role of food movements in the second 'Great Transformation.'" In C. Kropp, I. Antoni-Komar, C. Sage (eds.), *Food System Transformations: Social Movements, Local Economies, Collaborative Networks.* New York: Routledge.

FOOD SOVEREIGNTY AS TRANSLATION

Strengthening Fisherfolk's Struggles and
Cultivating Peasant-Fisher Alliances in Brazil

*Rita Calvário, Irmak Ertör and Zoe W. Brent,
in conversation with Josana Pinto*

Many of us did not feel included when people talked about peasants. ... But, we understand that artisanal fisherfolks have a very important role in food production; we produce agro-ecological food. ... For us, La Vía Campesina is a very important space. ... The strengthening of the struggle comes from being part of a larger collective.
 — Interview with Josana Pinto, fisherwoman and leader of the Movement of Artisanal Fishers in Brazil

Peasants and small-scale fisher people are both key protagonists of social struggles against neoliberal globalization and free trade in the food system in today's world. Since the mid-1990s, they have organized into powerful transnational social movements, namely, La Vía Campesina[1] and the World Forum of Fisher People.[2] In the past fifteen years, both peasants' and fishers' movements have started to meet at diverse political spaces and moments, mostly internationally, and have been slowly converging under the umbrella framework of food sovereignty — "the right of people to healthy and culturally appropriate food produced through ecologically sound and sustainable methods, and their right to define their own food and agriculture systems" (Nyéléni 2007).

In December 2015, after days of COP21 side events, internal meetings, late-night debates, and strategy sessions exploring the convergence of land and water struggles, the trust between the diverse group of fishers and peasants from all continents, members of the World Forum of Fisher People and La Vía Campesina, seemed to stretch like an invisible web keeping in step as they marched through the chilly streets of Paris. As these groups began chanting protest slogans in unison, exchanging flags and bandanas, and demanding food sovereignty, one of the authors of this chapter, Zoe Brent, who was at the event, could not help but feel like she was witnessing an important step in international alliance building. Especially for the very same fishers who had only months before, at the World Forum of Fisher People International Coordinating Committee meeting in Pondicherry, India, expressed frustration that engaging with peasant politics and its call for food sovereignty made them feel like their issues were not well understood and somehow subordinate. Were the events that took place at the COP21 evidence that food sovereignty as a concept and a movement might just be big enough to make space for a more horizontal fisher-peasant convergence? And importantly, how relevant is food sovereignty for fisher movements in more localized contexts?

In this chapter, we engage with these questions in two ways: first, we look into the international convergences between fisher-peasant movements; second, we examine how the Movimento dos Pescadores e das Pescadoras Artesanais–MPP (Artisanal Fisherfolks Movement),

La Vía Campesina and World Forum of Fisher People members at the COP21 march in the streets of Paris, December 2015. Photo credit: Zoe Brent.

a nation-wide movement of artisanal fisher people in Brazil, and one of the few artisanal fisherfolk movements that are members of both World Forum of Fisher People and La Vía Campesina, engages with food sovereignty. We draw our analysis from an interview with Josana Pinto, fisherwoman and leader of the MPP, who usually participates in both World Forum of Fisher People and La Vía Campesina international gatherings. The interview was conducted online by Rita Calvário, in early March 2022, in Portuguese and then translated into English. Our goal was to understand MPP's view and politics of food sovereignty and how this potentially shapes a fisher-peasant convergence in socio-political struggles. Drawing on the work of Antonio Gramsci, we shed light on what we call the process of "translation," by which food sovereignty feeds into and is fed by fishers' struggles. By translation we broadly mean the process of transforming theory into practice, and vice-versa, with attention to particularities, in order to extend and unify social struggles against hegemonic powers.[3] We then discuss the potential of food sovereignty in building fisher-peasant convergences for a counterhegemonic struggle.

The power of translating food sovereignty as a unifying concept

> To have these international spaces function better, with our representation of fisher people, it is necessary to have adequate translation into our language …. I want to be there to understand and to try to collaborate. But if there is no translation, we miss the opportunity to understand, and we will not be able to contribute. The biggest difficulty of our participation in La Vía Campesina has been the lack of an interpreter for our language: to be able to feel more secure in these spaces and make contributions, make our denunciations.
> — Josana Pinto

As the phrase authors have heard repeated many times in international food sovereignty gathering spaces goes: "Without translation, there is no revolution."[4] The words of both this slogan and that of Brazilian fisherwoman and movement leader, Josana Pinto, are very literal calls to value, recognize and politicize the work of translation. As in Antonio Gramsci's theory of language and power relations, translation is to be seen as more than just a means of transmission and communication.

Translation is at the core of Gramsci's understanding of politics.[5] For him, politics involves a process of translation through which we learn, become self-aware, develop critical thinking, and better understand others and the world that surrounds us, enabling us to struggle to transform the world in which we live. In turn, it is through acting upon the world, and learning from processes of struggle, that we can better understand the world and how to change it. In all of this, attention to the specificities and interrelationships are crucial (Kipfer and Hart 2013).

The idea of "politics as translation" offers a relational view of power, which is relevant to food sovereignty as well. This view brings an "approach to power [that] is vastly different from politics as circumscribed to struggle for the reigns of state power or narrowly defined policy change — it locates power in multiple spaces and histories, reaching deep into everyday life, identity and history, and simultaneously focusing on institutional … and civil society" (Shattuck et al. 2015: 426).

Thus, translating food sovereignty on the ground involves a practice of "elaborating, modifying, and transforming meaning from context to context" (Kipfer and Hart 2013: 326), so that it stimulates a two-way process of social struggle and theoretical elaboration, in local contexts but also at upper scales. In order to build counterhegemony, the convergence between local and seemingly different struggles involves a capacity to embrace diversity while finding a common ground, central to which is translation. Born as a peasant concept, how well does food sovereignty travel into, and back from, the fisheries' world?

Food sovereignty was introduced in 1996 by La Vía Campesina as a radical critique and alternative to neoliberal approaches in food politics and rural development. Over the years, the peasant notion of food sovereignty has evolved to respond to shifting terrain of struggle; La Vía Campesina's constituency has enlarged to include fisherfolks, Indigenous peoples, pastoralists and landless workers, all key actors in the food system. Most of La Vía Campesina member organizations are peasants and small farmers from around the world. The Brazilian Artisanal Fisherfolks Movement (MPP) is one of the few fisher organizations that is a member of La Vía Campesina. At the national and regional levels, however, fisherfolks' organizations and initiatives are putting into practice the key pillars of food sovereignty,[6] without necessarily using that terminology (TNI 2020). Internationally, the World Forum of Fisher People representatives were present at the landmark Nyéléni gathering for food sovereignty in Mali, 2007. And, since the formation of a working group on agroecology and food sovereignty in 2015, the World Forum of Fisher People has begun to deliberately "translate" the concept of food sovereignty into the context of fisheries. We now look closely at how this politics of translation has occurred at the international level and how it continues to potentiate fisher-peasant convergences.

Food sovereignty as an analytical and mobilizing tool for fisher movements and fisher-peasant alliances

In approaching food sovereignty, the World Forum of Fisher People has highlighted the similarities between small-scale fishers' struggles and struggles of other small-scale producers such as peasants, beekeepers and pastoralists around food systems and territory (TNI 2020). This is in line with La Vía Campesina discourses and its calls for unity in diversity. Moreover, the framing of political agendas and discourses of both fisher and peasant movements increasingly share significant conceptual — and practical — overlap. Seen as a strategic and important component of alliance building, this work of translation has been carried out primarily by the agroecology and food sovereignty working group of the World Forum of Fisher People, which has conducted study trips (for instance, in 2016 to Indonesia) to learn about food sovereignty and agroecology on the ground, published reports sharing their findings (WFFP 2017), and even translated these concepts into drawings.

Conceptually, like La Vía Campesina, World Forum of Fisher People mobilizes its constituency against a common threat: the capitalist-neoliberal food system that is accused of creating multiple forms of dispossession, exclusion, and marginalization of fishers, for instance by blocking access to and control over fishing grounds and natural resources. The movement has also been drawing attention to ocean and water "grabbing practices," and to how fisher communities are being affected by them — similar to La Vía Campesina approaches to land grabbing and its impacts on peasants. A striking example was the protest of the Our Ocean Conference, which took place in 2018 in Bali, Indonesia, and in 2019 in Norway. Protesting against the "blue-washing" of the industrial marine sector — which presents itself as being fair and sustainable while actually destroying local ecosystems and fishers' livelihoods — fisher people rejected this conference and instead organized an Ocean's People Conference.[7] One of the six axes of this counteraction was entitled "Food sovereignty and agroecology as an alternative to blue economy." Another axis proposed a human rights-based approach to fisheries and ocean grabbing, focusing on collective rights and de-commodification practices, in a very similar way to discussions of peasant movements as part of the food sovereignty framework.[8]

Peasants and fishers have also begun to join forces in key international political spaces and meetings such as the International Planning Committee for Food Sovereignty (IPC), the Committee on World Food Security (CFS), and the Committee on Fisheries (COFI) of FAO. On some occasions, both movements participate in such spaces in order to define and push for a common agenda, and to strengthen their voices and claims for being recognized in political debates and policy making. In other moments, they opt to establish their own alternative spaces in solidarity relationships with other movements, and adopt a more oppositional, contentious politics. Fisher and peasant movements have also participated together in collective mobilizations and protests such as a parallel civil society-led climate summit during COP21, including the second meeting of the Global Convergence of Land and Water Struggles (Mills 2021).

World Forum of Fisher People marches for food sovereignty at La Vía Campesina 7th international congress, Basque Country, 2017. Photo credit: Roberto Villar.

This was followed by a huge protest (described in the Introduction) with the participation of approximately thirty thousand people demanding climate and social justice. At the same time, after the 7th General Assembly of the World Forum of Fisher People in Delhi, India in 2017, the World Fisheries Day, November 21, coincided with farmers' protests, where a joint march took place close to the parliament building. World Forum of Fisher People leaders also participated in La Vía Campesina's 7th International Congress and subsequent protest in the streets of Bilbao in 2017.

Translating food sovereignty into the fisheries' sector at the international level has shown its power as both an analytical framework and a mobilizing tool. First, it has offered tools for a better understanding of how the capitalist-neoliberal food system works and the similarity of its impacts on peasant and fisher communities and territories. Second, it has been a catalyst of convergences — in meetings and protests — of peasants and fishers in fights for common causes and goals. However, how do fishers' movements engage with food sovereignty in local contexts? This is what we will look at next, by focusing on the case of the Artisanal Fisherfolks Movement from Brazil.

Food sovereignty in Brazil's Artisanal Fisherfolks Movement

The Artisanal Fisherfolks Movement (MPP) is a social movement that was created informally in 2009 during the 1st National Conference of Artisanal Fishing in Brazil, which brought together around one thousand fishers in Brasília. In 2010, the MPP was formalized. The movement emerged out of the fishers' frustrations with how state policies were disregarding artisanal fisheries, as they struggled for a development model and policies that could protect their livelihoods, and ways of fishing and living (Fox and Efken 2019). Currently, it is one of the few fishers' and fishworkers' movements that is both a member of La Vía Campesina and World Forum of Fisher People. According to Josana Pinto, the

Josana Pinto in the Basque Country, La Vía Campesina 7th international Congress. Photo credit: Roberto Villar.

movement is present in seventeen out of twenty-six Brazilian states with different degrees of coordination. The national level of representation is made up of one man and one woman from each state.

In this section, we examine MPP's critical engagement with food sovereignty. We first shed light on how food sovereignty offers a framework for understanding fisherfolks' everyday life experiences, grievances and struggles, and how these relate with those of peasants. We then focus on how MPP is strengthened by engaging in fisher-peasant convergences, and what that brings to food sovereignty as a concept and a practice.

Food sovereignty as a framework for understanding fishers' struggle in Brazil

In the MPP, food sovereignty is a framework that allows for a better understanding of fisher struggles and their commonalities with peasant struggles in Brazil. This builds on the understanding that increased extractivism in agriculture, energy and mineral resources, catalyzed by capital and state power, are violating the rights of local people who make their living out of the land, ocean and waters. As Josana explained, "the expansion of hydro-, agro- and mineral-business is affecting us all." MPP is thus aware that fisherfolks' specific problems relate not only to the fisheries' sector or particular fishing sites, but also to the global economy and its modes of governance. It is from their lived experience on the ground that this perception arises, but the concept of food sovereignty certainly helps to construct this broader understanding. With it also comes the awareness that fishers and peasants share common threats and struggles for reproducing their lives. Josana gave the example of the overflow of large dams in their territories, affecting both peasants and fisher communities along the watershed. She also mentioned how peasant and fisher activities influence each other, for instance, through pollution. In addition, many fishers are peasants, and vice-versa — the division by sector of activity is often dismissive of the multiple livelihood strategies of peasant-fisher people. For the MPP, food sovereignty is a framework that translates and illuminates peasants' and fishers' common grievances, as well as their interconnections and inclusively shared identities as experienced in everyday life. Moreover, it offers tools — for instance, an understanding of how the capitalist-neoliberal food system works — to grasp the underlying structures and ideologies that engender those shared experiences. It is precisely from these translation efforts that the potential for peasant-fisher convergence arises. In Josana's words:

> In the MPP, we are aware of the need to have a broad understanding of the world in which we live. This insight is already present in Vía Campesina. In the fishers' movements also, but it's more recent. Through it, we are called to be conscious of the necessity to strengthen and unify our struggles, to form a collective, in order to defend us from, and fight against these violations [of our rights as small-scale producers].

Attached to the defence of fishers' and peasants' livelihoods is the idea of the "defence of territory," as Josana mentioned. For the MPP, the territory is more than the specific locales where people live and make a living. It also includes an understanding of those places as interconnected by the violations of rights mentioned above. In fact, the formation of MPP arose from the realization that "men and women of fishing, and waters, are losing their territory to agri-business and mining, whose aggressions towards the environment and social rights we must fight against," she added.

Parallel to this livelihoods and territorial approach, environmental concerns are also at the core of the MPP's understanding of food sovereignty. The MPP rejects the industrial model of food production, in fisheries and agriculture, because it poisons local environments and food, Josana commented. Artisanal fisheries are seen as a practical manifestation of agroecology, as "fish is not farmed nor artificially fed, it comes directly from nature; our fish is healthy food," she asserted. Moreover, it is a mode of fishing that does not overexploit resources, nor "poisons our territories and bodies," she pointed out. As in La Vía Campesina, agroecology as translated into the context of fisheries fits within MPP practices and vision for building a more ecologically based food system. In turn, the MPP offers a view of food sovereignty that includes a broader vision rather than solely focusing on agriculture and peasant agroecology.

Cultivating fisher-peasant alliances and strengthening the struggle

It was after a fellow MPP activist participated in a La Vía Campesina event outside of Brazil that the MPP clearly saw the importance of joining

La Vía Campesina. Peasant and fisher movements are "partners sharing the same causes and struggles," as Josana indicated. For the MPP, a main goal of becoming a member of La Vía Campesina was to be able to learn from other struggles, "and to exchange experiences, but also to raise awareness in La Vía Campesina of the relevance of incorporating fisherfolks [and their concerns and demands] into the movement's struggles," she specified. MPP's dual membership in La Vía Campesina and World Forum of Fisher People means that MPP leaders bridge knowledge from participating in multiple organizational spaces and activities of these movements. Josana told us about her desire to bring more into the MPP debate on women's rights, gender equality and feminism — a result from her participation in the women's collective of La Vía Campesina at the international level and in Brazil. For her, "La Vía Campesina is like a second family," as the direct contact with many other movements and activists from all around the world, and the debates held there, have allowed her and the MPP to broaden their understandings of the diversity of people and struggles in the food system, and the many adversities — similar and specific — that they face. As she explained to us:

> Our movement [the MPP] is in a process of learning, for instance, on issues such as patriarchy, environmental and structural racism, homophobia, and the diverse forms of violations of rights [in rural areas and throughout the food system]. All of these are debates occurring in La Vía Campesina. We want to bring the debates we have in La Vía Campesina into the MPP and the fisher movement so that we can strengthen our struggles.

But the participation in La Vía Campesina is also a way of inserting fishing issues and proposals into food sovereignty through a process of debate and mutual understanding. Josana affirmed the importance of respect for fisher people and making fishers' voices heard. In her view, such debates are key for recognizing differences, and particularities, but also to realize what is common between fishers and peasants, all with "respect for diversity."

In Brazil, the MPP works closely with other member organizations of La Vía Campesina. Josana mentioned the "great partnership" the MPP has with the MST–Movimento dos Trabalhadores Sem Terra (Landless Workers Movement), as well as the "good relationship" it has with the MPA–Movimento dos Pequenos Agricultores (Small Farmers Movement). Both peasant movements, but especially the MST, are large and influential movements in Brazil, and internationally.

The MST supports the relatively young MPP with its long political experience, for instance in elaborating political analysis of relevance to the sector of fisheries. Also, the MPP has collaborated with the MST to make its voice heard in the Parliament and the House of Representatives, especially during the Lula (2003–2010) and Dilma (2011–2016) governments (social movements' ability to speak to formal institutions shrunk under Temer-Bolsonaro governments). Other relevant aspects of this collaboration are the activities of training and knowledge exchange. Josana considered these to be highly relevant for strengthening the MPP politics and struggles. At the time of writing this chapter, she was trying to organize a training event for fisherwomen on women's rights and gender issues, with the participation of MST and MPA. This event was also being envisioned as a space for mutual exchange and learning between peasant and fisher women, so that both groups can realize their commonalities, but also specificities. Josana gave the example of "fighting machismo" as a common threat to women, while mentioning how fisher women are much less respected and valued in fishing activities than peasant women in farming. Thus, bringing up the different lived experiences of fisher women into food sovereignty and feminist debates is also a potential contribution of a politics of translating food sovereignty into the context of fisheries.

Conclusion

How is food sovereignty significant to the fisheries' world and to building fisher-peasant alliances? In recent years, internationally, several moments of convergence between peasants and fishers seem to indicate that food sovereignty is a powerful analytical framework for understanding the global food system, as well as a mobilizing tool for joint collective struggles. In this chapter, we examined the case of Brazil's Artisanal Fisherfolks Movement (MPP) to discuss the potential of food sovereignty in strengthening fishers' politics and in building peasant-fisher convergences for counterhegemonic struggle.

For the MPP, food sovereignty provides a framework to understand the struggle of fishers not as isolated or exclusively place-based, but as the result of structural and systemic "violations of rights" led by capitalist and neoliberal policies, which also impact other rural people. This understanding emerges from fishers' lived experiences and struggles, which are interpreted with the help of the concept of food sovereignty. In this mode of interpreting the world, the territory and the environment appear central to fishers' struggles. It is precisely around the defence of livelihoods, territory and the environment that fishers engage with food sovereignty, and identify common grievances, shared identities, and mutual goals with peasants and other rural people — all of which are essential for engendering mutual convergences and alliances.

This work of fisher-peasant convergence is happening both internationally and within specific countries, as we have shown in the case of Brazil. For the MPP, La Vía Campesina provides an important space of meeting, learning, and exchange of knowledge with a wide range of collectives on topics so far less developed in the World Forum of Fisher People and in the fisher movement in the country. The collaboration with peasant movements in Brazil has also helped to consolidate MPP's own political analysis and to strengthen its struggle. At the same time, MPP's participation in these multiple spaces inserts fisheries issues and fisherfolks' concerns and demands into food sovereignty struggles. All of this generates processes of mutual learning, critical thinking, and reinforcement of convergences between movements around a common goal — that of food sovereignty.

It is precisely in this respect for difference, while finding common ground, that the potential for building a counterhegemonic movement arises. This, we have argued, involves a process of "translation" — i.e., a practice of "elaborating, modifying, and transforming meaning from context to context" (Kipfer and Hart 2013: 326). In this process, food sovereignty is not static, but a co-evolving concept and practice. As a concept, the strength of food sovereignty is found in its ability to interpret, and learn from, everyday life and the struggles of small-scale producers and rural people, and then contribute to strengthen them. As a practice, the force of food sovereignty is evident in its capability to join together a diversity of socio-political forces through developing common strategies, collective identities, and raising awareness of their common features and goals. The case of the MPP we analyzed here is illustrative of the power of translating food sovereignty in localized contexts and among similar actors of social change.

However, convergence is built on the foundation of solid alliances forged through mutual transformation of peoples, ideas and practices.

Just as Josana relies on translation into Portuguese in order to engage politically in multilingual contexts, political convergence under the umbrella of food sovereignty requires strategic and consistent two-way translation of concepts and organizational practices across sectors and between local, national, regional and international scales.

Notes

1. La Vía Campesina was founded in 1993 by peasant and small farmer organizations from different continents. Currently, it comprises 182 organizations in 81 countries from Africa, Asia, Europe and the Americas, representing about 200 million small-scale food producers. La Vía Campesina has more than 70 schools and training processes for scaling up of agroecology and strengthening processes of building food sovereignty from below, which are dynamized by its member organizations. See: La Vía Campesina, "International Peasants Voice," 2021. <viacampesina.org/en/international-peasants-voice/>.
2. The foundation of the first transnational fishers' movement dates back to 1997, which was followed by a division into two separate movements in 2001: World Forum of Fish Harvesters & Fish Workers (WFF) with members of mainly North and South American organizations and World Forum of Fisher People (WFFP) with mostly Asian, African and some European and Latin American national organizations. Currently, World Forum of Fish Harvesters & Fish Workers has 44 member organizations from 42 countries and World Forum of Fisher People has 75 member organizations from 50 countries. In this chapter, we will focus on World Forum of Fisher People because this organization has recently made more visible and deliberate efforts to engage with the politics of food sovereignty and to build convergences with La Vía Campesina. Two of the authors, Irmak Ertör and Zoe Brent, have been engaged in this process over the past eight years.
3. For developments on Gramsci's work on translation and politics see: Ives, Peter. 2004. *Language and Hegemony in Gramsci* (London: Pluto Press); Ives, Peter, and Rocco Lacorte (eds.). 2010. *Gramsci, Language and Translation* (Lanham MD: Lexington Books); Thomas, Peter. 2009. *The Gramscian Moment: Philosophy, Hegemony and Marxism* (London: Brill).
4. See also: Müller, Eline, and Alice Froidevaux. 2018. "Without translation, no hay revolución! The importance of interpretation, translation and language justice in building global counter-power." *Transnational Institute*, January 7. At <longreads.tni.org/stateofpower/without-translation-no-hay-revolucion>.
5. See endnote 3.
6. Food sovereignty has six pillars: focusing on food for people, valuing traditional knowledge, working with nature, valuing food providers, localizing food systems, and putting control locally (Nyéléni 2007).
7. Karibu Foundation. 2019. "Whose Ocean? Statement from the Ocean's People Conference," October 28. At <karibu.no/news/2019/10/whose-ocean-statement-from-the-ocean-peoples-conference/>.

8   WFFP (World Forum of Fishers People). 2018. "Fisher Peoples reject the 'Our Ocean Conference' and organize the Ocean's People Conference," October 25, 2018. At <worldfishers.org/2018/10/25/fisher-peoples-reject-ocean-conference-organize-oceans-people-conference/>.

References

Fox, Veronica, and Karl Efken. 2019. "O Discurso de Resistência do Movimento dos Pescadores e Pescadoras Artesanais do Brasil." *Policromias* 4, 2.

Kipfer, Stefan, and Gillian Hart. 2013. "Translating Gramsci in the current conjuncture." In M. Ekers, G. Hart, S. Kipfer, and A. Loftus (eds.), *Gramsci: Space, Nature, Politics*. London: John Wiley & Sons.

Mills, Elyse. 2021. "The politics of transnational fishers' movements." *The Journal of Peasant Studies* 50, 2.

Nyéléni. 2007. *Declaration of Nyéléni*. At <nyeleni.org/IMG/pdf/DeclNyeleni-en.pdf>.

Shattuck, Annie, Christina M. Schiavoni, and Zoe VanGelder. 2015. "Translating the politics of food sovereignty: Digging into contradictions, uncovering new dimensions." *Globalizations* 12, 4.

TNI (Transnational Institute). 2020. *Situating small-scale fisheries in the global struggle for agroecology and food sovereignty*. Amsterdam: Transnational Institute.

WFFP (World Forum of Fishers People). 2017. Agroecology and Food Sovereignty in Small-scale Fisheries. At <worldfishers.org/wp-content/uploads/2017/09/WFFP.Food_.Sov_.web_.pdf>.

PART THREE
CLIMATE

INTRODUCTION TO PART THREE

Salvatore Paolo De Rosa, Gustavo García-López and Amelie Huber

Climate justice and just transitions have become central unifying claims of transnational movements confronting fossil capitalism and inequitable low-carbon transitions. These movements have spearheaded calls for "system change, not climate change" — a transformation from an extractive to a regenerative economy, from profit-making to solidarity-building. Climate justice has been called a "movement of movements," since it provides a platform of convergence across nations, sectors, struggles and grievances by bringing to the forefront the connections between multiple intersecting injustices and the processes leading to global warming. Indeed, the climate and ecological crises are both the direct result of centuries of colonial and capitalist resource grabbing powered by fossil fuels, as well as the justification for new rounds of accumulation and unproven capital-friendly "solutions" for mitigation and adaptation. The promise of climate justice is to take longstanding demands for transformational justice across disparate issues — from energy and water to housing and transportation, from post-disaster recovery to debt and reparations — and tie them to the existential struggle for a stable climate and a more equitable world.

There are, however, enormous challenges in climate justice movements' ability to truly intersect all these issues and categories of oppression. The state-corporate criminal machine of capital continues its destructive path of eco/genocide, to destroy and extract life from as many corners of the world as possible, while paying lip service to deepening global socio- and ecological crises, green-washing with fake solutions. While a global energy transformation is underway due to geopolitical and environmental pressures, the coal, gas and petrol interests are not subsiding easily and are resurging in some regions. Indeed, some observe we are not witnessing an energy transition, but an energy expansion (TNI 2021). This is already having significant ecological and socio-political impacts on territories across the Global South. Fossil companies are making record profits and plan to continue to invest in new fossil infrastructures, while the new "renewable" energy and "green transition" rush is leading to a significant expansion of extraction of "green" minerals (such as lithium and nickel) needed for building new energy infrastructures (solar panels, electric cars, batteries and such). Moreover, renewable energy development (e.g., hydropower and geothermal) often necessitates a large-scale transformation of landscapes, disrupting ecosystems and the livelihoods that depend on them. Renewables thus provide new avenues for accumulation by dispossession, typically, in the same regions and (Black/Indigenous/peasant/women/queer) populations already exploited by previous waves of extraction.

In reaction to such challenges, and in order to disrupt the current (im)balance of forces, climate justice organizations and movements are deploying a variety of strategies and tactics, both old and new, that support the intensification of direct actions and the grassroots organizing by and with frontline communities. The chapter by De Rosa addresses this relation between strategies of direct action and the tactics that could support a shared agenda of system-wide transformation. By focusing on existing and emerging repertoires of action that put into practice a politics of common articulation of struggles, De Rosa explores direct actions as arenas of convergence: "a conceptual and political space at the crossroad of various forms of dissent and contestation, where different lines of conflict, actors, grievances, and socio-political and ecological concerns intersect and can be harnessed through conscious political work." He identifies six tactics that may inform such political work: *connection*, *escalation*, *prefiguration*, *just transition*, *preparation* and *litigation*. For each tactic, he provides insights on shortcomings and strengths, and ways to advance their combination, in the spirit of collaboration and mutual strengthening needed to build global counter-power and to hasten solidarity-weaving and organizing.

The chapter by Turhan and Aydın explores how the ruthless sacrificing of communities, livelihoods and landscapes in Turkey's energy transition (specifically, the expansion of hydropower and geothermal power generation) has produced counterhegemonic flows, transforming and accelerating environmentalist opposition to the Erdoğan regime's hegemonic bloc. Seeing their trust in the state injured, affected communities have started fighting back with counterhegemonic arguments, questioning both the real role of the state as well as the economic model it propagates, which fails to deliver collective well-being and a higher common good. While the chapter explores two temporally and spatially distinct environmental movements, it also focuses on the commonalities and continuities in their discourses and repertoires of contention. The creation of national-level platforms in the wake of the Gezi Park protests in 2013 has especially enabled a convergence of grassroots environmental movements in Turkey, facilitating mutual learning and thus helping to produce counterhegemonic knowledge. Since then, Turkey's ecologist movements have been drawing the limits of authoritarian energy governance by politicizing their actions through a triad of popular mobilization, courtroom battles and political lobbying.

Convergences in climate justice movements also confront the challenges of overcoming unequal Global North and South relations, as well as relations between newer yet whiter youth climate movements, and more longstanding environmental justice organizations from frontline communities. Debates about the Green New Deal is an example. Coined by the youth Sunrise Movement, it was focused mainly on government investment in the renewables transition and employment potential. Later the grassroots-led climate justice movements centred more on questions of capitalism, colonialism, extractivism, and the leadership of frontline communities, connecting to the earlier concept of just transitions, coined from the intersections between environmental justice and labour movements.

The chapter by Julie Sze in conversation with Gopal Dayaneni, one of the founding members of Movement Generation: Justice and Ecology Project, discusses the development of the Just Transition (JT) framework as a vision and strategy guide for a radically transformative climate justice. This framework of Just Transition is based on the grounded historical experiences of grassroots social and environmental justice organizing, and serves as a "connective tissue" across a variety of movements. It thus centres the experiences and visions of these communities at the frontlines and fencelines of disasters. It reminds us that climate justice will be intersectional-decolonial, or it will not be. The Just Transition framework proposes a systemic transformation from an extractive to a deeply democratic and regenerative economy. An essential element is the democratic self-management of the basic means of social reproduction, of life — making energy, food, water, housing a commons — and not just for us humans, but for all life on our common home. This utopian vision is put in practice by building and supporting autonomous grassroots movements, drawn together through an alliance of values, which supplants top-down hierarchical domination systems with decentralized bottom-up systems. "Just Transitions" foster the interweaving of diverse insurgent struggles through a common vision and a networked space to share insights and build collaborations, weaving together a tapestry of diverse transformative movements: from food sovereignty, land reform movements and energy democracy to cooperative economics and commons, Indigenous sovereignty, and many more. The framework is not just a vision or a theory of revolution, but a *strategy* to navigate the contradictions in the *process* of transitions. This has allowed the framework to continue to evolve and expand in response to gaps and emergent wisdom from other movements such as disability justice and queer liberation, as well as internationalist social justice movements centring on the Global South.

Taken together, these three contributions point to the importance of different organizing frameworks, structures and tactics for promoting convergences across struggles, depending on the particularities of each context. A common element that resurfaces in all chapters is the importance of processes of networking between a diversity of local and trans/national movements, guided by shared visions and action tools.

Reference

TNI (Transnational Institute). 2021. "Energy Transition or Energy Expansion?" In J. Angel and D. Burke (eds.). At <tni.org/en/publication/energy-transition-or-energy-expansion>. October 22.

SEE YOU ON THE FRONTLINES

Direct Action Tactics of Convergence for Climate Justice

Salvatore Paolo De Rosa

Anyone concerned with the fate of life on a burning planet should have realized by now that altering the trajectory of catastrophic warming and building a more just world are not the elite's priorities. These must be accomplished through bottom-up political praxis.

Carbon concentration in the atmosphere dictates the urgency of needed transformations, but it cannot be the only horizon of climate action. Climate breakdown is the result of long-lasting political, economic and social processes intertwined with broader systemic inequalities and rooted in colonial dispossession, imperial relations and capitalist exploitation. Today, the very same dynamics inform phantasmagorias of "ecological transition," which maintain unchanged social hierarchies while deepening environmental destruction. As activists and resistant communities from the frontlines have stated, climate stability is inseparable from climate justice: true transformations can only be achieved by addressing fundamental power imbalances.

Climate justice acknowledges that oppression and exploitation are not only inextricably linked to global warming and socioecological degradation, but also persist in the governance of multiple crises. Not only does such an approach reveal the disparities in responsibility for climate breakdown and the unequal exposure to its risks; it also illuminates the continuous political relevance of (neo)colonization, dispossession and military control, and offers principles for avoiding further waves of extraction amidst more extreme conditions. Climate justice calls for "system change, not climate change": by declaring the current system unreformable, it solicits the exploration of more desirable worlds. The task is not simply avoiding global catastrophe, but to do so while nurturing a radical politics of emancipation.

The monumental challenges of reversing the warming, preventing the rise of eco-fascism, empowering people, and protecting and regenerating ecosystems, while advancing mechanisms of accountability and reparation on a global scale, impose a politics of convergence. Such a politics can be defined as the synergistic articulation of a variety of social forces and groups under a shared agenda of system-wide transformation — what was once called *revolution*. Not an easy task. Heterogeneous histories, locations and social conditions come with diverse immediate interests and contextual challenges. Nonetheless, all struggles are touched by the deterioration of planetary life support systems, just as they are intertwined with climate responses. Falling upon political subjects is the task to thread climate justice into all emancipatory battles. The question is *how*, and it can only be answered by attending to the strategies and tactics emerging on the ground.

In the following, I contribute to this task by drawing on experiences of direct action for climate justice. My emphasis is on identifying bottom-up tactics that could support a multi-scalar climate justice agenda responsive to the urgency of the moment and oriented toward the construction of global counter-power. The focus is thus on the *repertoires of action* (Tilly and Tarrow 2007) capable of putting into practice a politics of convergence.

November 30, 2019 – Open Pit Mine Scheenhain (Leipzig). After an open pit occupation near Leipzig, activists of the initiative "Ende Gelände" leave the mine in the evening. In the background is the occupied open pit excavator. Photo credit: Tim Wagner. Source: <ti-wag.de/>. Reproduced with permission.

Direct action — a range of activist practices through which a political effect is pursued without political intermediation (e.g., of elected representatives) — has a long history in social struggles. At its most basic, it is a tactic of intervention, militant and symbolic at the same time, that individuals or groups exercise to realize in practice what they believe are their rights or the rights of others, humans and nonhumans. Direct action can entail obstructing, occupying, seizing, or dismantling the institutions or infrastructures that deny those rights, or it can focus on providing services that are lacking, in defiance or regardless of the state. It is militant in the sense that it acts "as if people are already free" (Graeber 2009); it is symbolic because it also aims to change dominant narratives, to wrestle a space of autonomy, and to impose the presence of an organized resistance that cannot be ignored.

Past and present direct action campaigns, and the debates they triggered, provide insights into how to leverage specific sites and processes to advance the threading together of struggles, claims and desires. I consider direct action politics as an arena of convergence: a conceptual and political space at the crossroad of various forms of dissent and contestation, where different lines of conflict, actors, grievances, and socio-political and ecological concerns intersect and can be harnessed through conscious political work. Such spaces can foster coalitions, influence social perceptions and discourses, expand networks of cooperation, establish new principles and duties for states and private entities, and strengthen people's overall political reach.

Moving from an analysis of direct action for climate justice as an arena of convergence, I attempt to identify the tactics that could help us build broad social fronts and bring together diverse actors.

Direct action and climate mobilizations

In recent years, the climate movement has reignited interest in direct action, sparking debates about its scope, forms and goals. In order to halt projects, shut down facilities, draw attention to or exert pressure for policy change, climate activists have blockaded or occupied extraction sites, mines, oil terminals and oil rigs, ports, plastic and fertilizer factories, city centres, highways, railways, construction sites, government buildings, corporate offices, museums, malls, and more.

Activist coalitions have formed in Europe to specifically target fossil fuel extraction and infrastructure. *Ende Gelände* ("Here and no further"), a German coalition blocking coal mines and fossil fuel facilities since 2014, is one prominent example. *Folk Mot Fossilgas* (People against fossil gas) in Sweden successfully blocked the expansion of the Gothenburg gas terminal in 2019, after a three-year campaign culminating in a camp and a blockade. Since 2018, Extinction Rebellion's (XR) meteoric rise, mostly in Global North cities, has had the merit of involving larger constituencies in what they define as nonviolent direct action to effect changes in climate narratives and policies. They have done so through mass gatherings that block city centres, avoiding confrontation and instead accepting, even promoting, arrests and charges. More recently, there has been a proliferation of Extinction Rebellion's offshoot groups, such as *Ultima Generazione* in Italy and Just Stop Oil in UK, who raise the bar of nonviolent direct action by continuously repeating blockades of busy highways and fossil facilities for days on end, and by multiplying sites of attack to ask for bolder climate action. Tactics of mild sabotage are also spreading, with the proliferation of Tyre Extinguishers groups who deflate SUV cars in cities, and even Extinction Rebellion activists turning to the breaking of windows of banks, financial institutions and corporations.

Building on traditions of resistance stretching back centuries (Estes 2019), Indigenous movements around the world have also deployed direct action to contest fossil fuel projects on their territories, through occupations and more confrontational tactics. In North America, the Standing Rock camp built to fight against the Dakota Access Pipeline[1] provided a platform for the coming together of Indigenous Nations, environmentalists, anarchists and residents. The activists utilized the language of climate justice and Indigenous self-determination to animate an explicitly anticapitalist and anticolonial project of transformation and decolonization for all (The Red Nation 2021).

These direct action movements share some objectives but also diverge on theories of change, ultimate goals and how to achieve them. They have provided, in different ways, platforms of convergence and at the same time made enemies and deepened divisions. Now the question is how to nurture confluence among them and other social groups, and how to avoid fragmentation and repression. Issues that an explicit politics of convergence on the frontlines may address include: the lack of broader social legitimacy; the costs to individuals and to the movements posed by arrests, militarization and counter-insurgency techniques; and the need to join the task of achieving broad socio-economic and political transformations with the building of autonomous structures that prefigure alternative modes of life. In the next sections, I will address these issues by focusing on how a politics of convergence can be pursued through the following tactics: connection, escalation, prefiguration, just transition, preparation and litigation.

Converging on the frontlines

Connection

Direct action coalitions have pursued convergence by expanding the frontlines in space, linking the focus point of an action to globally interconnected sites of destruction that create sacrifice zones in some places while wealth is drained elsewhere (De Rosa 2022). This tactic of connection in practices and narratives evades charges of particularism and sustains the internationalist solidarity at the core of climate justice politics (Derman 2020).

In Sweden, *Folk mot Fossilgas* framed their opposition to the Gothenburg gas terminal as an action with global ramifications: the gas shipped to Sweden comes from Indigenous territories ravaged by extraction; therefore, fighting a specific facility is a way for activists in the Global North to affect larger geographies and (infra)structures of oppression. Activists from North America, Ireland and Argentina were invited to the camp in solidarity, together drawing the map of collaborations against distributed networks of extraction. Similar solidarities have been brought forward by networks of Caribbean activists establishing connections along the "death route" of coal: from Colombia (where coal is mined), to Puerto Rico (where it is burned), to the Dominican Republic (where toxic ashes are buried) (Lloréns and Santiago 2018). A last example, at the global scale, is the youth climate movement of Fridays for Future, which has put political emphasis on the "Most Affected People and Areas" hit by climate disasters front and centre, emphasizing climate debt and reparations in school strikes and demonstrations. Internationalist solidarity thus remains a crucial tool of composition within and between movements in the Global North and South.

Escalation

Beyond blockades and demonstrations that weave global solidarities, a debate is ongoing about the possibility to escalate direct action tactics for climate justice. Activists are questioning what violence under climate breakdown is, and what role militant disruption has, considering the long tradition of sabotage of private property, which characterized important emancipatory struggles of the past (Sovacool 2022; Sovacool and Dunlap 2022). Some have criticized the dogmatic nonviolence exemplified by XR, pointing to the shortcomings of direct action conceived solely as an instrument to make visible demands rather than concretely stopping facilities (Malm 2021). Even among more combative European climate justice coalitions, nonviolence as a principle is agreed upon in the action consensus framing the actions. But is it reasonable to continue this path in the absence of material gains (i.e., carbon emitters shutting down and emissions falling to zero)?

Instead, a variety of tactics, including forms of sabotage that focus on property but safeguard lives, could become part of the repertoire of climate movements within a strategy aimed at breaking the current stalemate. Small groups devoted to sabotage and property destruction may finally provide "the risk of investment" that could hurt corporate gains while at the same time creating a space of negotiation between governments and the moderate flanks of the movements. Convergence would be dependent on the division of labour among activists. To be effective, sabotage should not be a vanguardist task disconnected from the larger movement. Instead, the latter should complement sabotage by offering a way out to the establishment through negotiations. Some evidence confirms that "the use of radical tactics, such as property destruction or violence, ... by one flank led the more moderate faction to appear less radical" (Simpson et al. 2022).

Critics of such an agenda highlight the costs for those who engage in sabotage in the absence of dedicated structures of support and of widespread social acceptance. The radical environmental movements of Earth First! and the Earth Liberation Front, active in the 1980s and '90s, had to contend with harsh repression for their monkey-wrenching actions during the so-called "Green Scare." As a result, they developed a "security culture" to evade surveillance and forge strong bonds of mutual care to support prisoners (ffitch 2022). The development of such structures in the face of repression, during the prosecution of activists in court, and by creating narratives that justify sabotage, provide fertile ground for convergence.

Earth First! logo: a monkey wrench and a stone tomahawk (1980). Source: Wikipedia.

However, cutting across both nonviolent and more militant forms of direct action is the issue of the choice of targets. Tactics that disrupt the life of ordinary citizens are increasingly met by retaliation and misunderstanding by the people impacted, risking an increase in social polarization rather than attracting support. Instead, a reorientation towards disruption of sites of capital accumulation more clearly connected to the ongoing ecological destruction might be more fruitful.

Prefiguration

According to Bue Rübner Hansen, however, the exclusive emphasis on will and action that often underpins sabotage risks to be self-defeating (Rübner Hansen 2021). A strategy that *only* targets fossil fuels, capital accumulation or people's mobility through direct action, *without* doing the political work to recompose broad societal interests around a climate justice agenda, is doomed to provoke backlash from potential allies and prevent broad convergence. Other, non-combative forms of direct action reminiscent of organized labour societies and of customary practices in Indigenous communities, rooted in mutual help networks, autonomous forms of service provisions and social reproduction support, are also required for building popular counter-power and attending to the work of class formation. The main issue is how to disentangle the reproduction of life from fossil capital and capitalism in general, which still shape both the expectations and the livelihoods of many (Rübner Hansen 2021). Therefore, combative direct action climate politics must be accompanied by the nurturing of "popular autonomy that transforms social desires." Occupations and blockades can be made acceptable and even desirable for the majority only by turning the post-carbon world into an achievable and attractive reality announced by concrete practices of sustenance, involvement and engagement.

Strategies of regeneration and flourishing of communities and ecosystems — such as social cooperatives, shared urban gardens, collective purchase groups, swapping and repair shops, and other forms of mutual help and solidarity economies — provide a necessary bedrock to strategies of disruption, insofar as they nurture new desires and break toxic attachments (Fletcher 2018). A potential convergence around self-organized forms of social reproduction could then be sought through associations, coalitions and new political parties. Moreover, this approach is in line with decolonial practices and Indigenous calls to reweave networks of interdependence between social and ecological processes, away from capitalist metabolisms and towards infrastructures of care (LaDuke and Cowen 2020) and cultures of reciprocity (Kimmerer 2013).

Contextually, to avoid acting in a vacuum and to connect with alternative world-making practices that struggle to exist, it becomes critical to build relations with and between the frontlines of localized battles and the sparsely populated rural areas, where local communities and permanent activist occupations engage in land defence and water protection against various forms of authoritarian "development," be it fossil, military or low-carbon. There is already a direct relationship between the climate movement and long-standing occupations against destruction like the *Zone à défendre* (zone to defend, ZAD) of Notre-Dames-des-Landes (born out of a struggle against an airport), the *No Tav* in the Italian Val Susa (a decades-long opposition to a high-speed railway cutting through the Alps), and the occupations of the Hambach Forest and of Lützerath in Germany (to prevent the expansion of coal extraction). One such conflict is ongoing in Atlanta, US, led by the Defend the Atlanta Forest coalition, aiming to stop the construction of "Cop City," a police training compound. It has shown how the protection of a forest can become a point of convergence between residents, environmentalists, climate activists, abolitionists, anti-militarists and antiracists.[2] Through a decentralized and autonomous approach, grounded in what Hugh Farrell calls a "strategy of composition" (Farrell 2023) to weld together heterogeneous sectors, battles and movements, the coalition has not only resisted eviction but also attracted substantial national and global support. Many such conflicts are scattered across the map, where local struggles already have clear climate connections, but which are not always articulated or receive the support they need.

Some of these links are being made explicit in the "camp," a tactical companion to direct action and a space of convergence in its own right. Temporary climate camps were one of the first iterations of the reorganization of grassroots environmental movements around climatic concerns. They now accompany direct actions and bring activists and sympathizers together for days of self-formation and coalition building. Yet, another crucial component is its pedagogical dimension (McGregor 2015), particularly the training and formation of a new cadre of activists from younger generations.

In addition, a climate justice camp is a powerful device of prefiguration: realizing here and now the kind of world for which we are fighting. Being based on autonomy and self-organization, it favours practices of mutualism and cooperation over the pursuit of self-interest and competition. The experience of participation can be transformative for individuals insofar as it renders tangible in practice alternative social and ecological relations and, besides providing concrete tools of resistance, makes room for forms of interaction and values that disrupt dominant knowledge and value systems.

Just transition

Climate activists' relations with workers and unions remains a complex issue that would require more space to explore. Next to the risk of entire sectors and workplaces disappearing, the many impacts of top-down "ecological" transition designs on production are forcing workers to take positions in relation to the climate crisis. Some workers' movements are seizing the moment and exploring possibilities for convergence with climate movements. Primarily, this could be seen as an effort to avoid becoming sacrificial victims of a purported green agenda and therefore to resist imposed restructuring, but also influence what and how to produce. Both these issues — the need to safeguard wages and income, and the ambition of workers to exert influence on the production process — should become central concerns for a climate justice politics that is not trapped in a reductionist reading of the climate and ecological crises.

Convergence in practice from the frontlines of workers struggles going on the counterattack shows that it is possible to join the imperatives of the ecological transition with the radical registers of climate justice movements. A hint of potential paths towards this goal comes from the workers of the GKN Driveline, a car-parts factory in Florence, Italy. After receiving mass layoff letters from the plant's owner, the investment fund Melrose, the workers occupied the factory and started a political process in and out of the factory walls. They found support

Leaflet to support GKN workers' crowdfunding, in collaboration with Fridays for Future, Arci and BancaEtica (2023). Source: GKN

in independent research groups, local community struggles, jurists, intellectuals and climate movements. Together they drafted a plan of industrial reconversion to address social and environmental problems and to guarantee employment, sustainability and rights. In essence, the plan proposes to focus production on mechanical components for ecological public transport rather than for luxury combustion cars, integrating venues for training, research and development. It is currently the only concrete plan available for reconversion of the GKN (Collettivo GKN et al. 2023).

Emerging arenas: Disaster preparation and litigation in court

Preparation

An emerging role for direct action in an increasingly uncertain climate includes self-organized disaster preparation and response for the most vulnerable and disenfranchised in areas hit by extreme weather events. This further connects solidarity work and mutual aid for post-disaster recovery with demands for climate justice and just transitions.

Grassroots solidarity brigades intervening where states fail to protect or recover citizens have been already witnessed in post-earthquake settings (Forino 2015; Hajek 2013), during the worst days of the pandemic (Pleyers 2020), and in post-hurricane settings. In the US, remarkable instances of social movements turning into post-disaster support structures for the poorest and most marginalized include the Occupy movement in New York City after Hurricane Sandy (Dawson 2017), which coordinated more than 60.000 volunteers at the height of its organizing; or the coming together of anarchists and leftists in New Orleans after Hurricane Katrina in the Common Ground collective, which under the slogan "solidarity not charity" provided fundamental support to stranded victims (crow 2014). Similarly, in Puerto Rico, organizations like the Climate Justice Alliance (CJA) and the anarchist Mutual Aid Disaster Relief network[3] were crucial to connecting struggles for a just recovery,[4] carried out through international solidarity brigades, with demands for climate justice and with resistance to disaster capitalism.

Such a proactive grassroots climate agenda addresses the very fabric of society. It does not imply a dismissal of activism for mitigation, but demands a welding of mitigation concerns with the urgent, so-far overlooked (even by climate activists) issues of adaptation, preparedness, prevention of losses and damages, disaster response and just recovery. Vulnerability to climate extremes is directly correlated to structural determinants that are social, historical and political in origin — concerning class, racism, patriarchy and exclusion. Therefore, if climate justice movements want to deal with demands for adaptation and disaster-response they must engage more seriously with social justice movements and campaigns across scales.

At the global level, campaigns to cancel the debt and to address unjust trade imbalances of developing countries have a direct relationship with the provision of resources to respond to disasters, besides nurturing an international platform rooted in anti-imperialism and climate justice.[5] In urban contexts, the knowledge of social ills and vulnerabilities by local activists could be increasingly harnessed by fast-growing climate movements to drive upward political demands linked to a social justice agenda (De Rosa et al. 2022).

Moreover, when disasters strike, the logistical and relational capacity of social centres, networks of mutual help, agroecological movements, refugee support groups and other grassroots coalitions rooted in place, provides essential contributions to save lives and to support just recovery in the absence, delay or discrimination of institutional responses. However, this only happens through a prior political work of convergence: a conscious and willful construction of platforms of collaboration between climate-focused movements and other groups on the frontlines of social justice struggles. These collaborations constitute the building blocks of social infrastructures of adaptation — not with the aim of substituting the political work of driving demands for fair adaptation at the heart of decision-making, but rather by complementing advocacy and pressure for policy changes with direct action, training and self-organization. Such a program also expands the reach of climate justice claims by turning them into principles and rights that are immediately relevant to the everyday life of scattered social constituencies, thereby advancing a process of common articulation.

Litigation

Repression of direct action for climate justice is on the rise, with most governments around the world increasingly criminalizing activism. In this light, the needed convergence may benefit from widespread shifts in common sense, namely that fossil fuel companies, their investors and the governments that back them are indeed the real criminals, directly responsible for the suffering and death of millions, now and in the future. Achieving such societal awareness would also help turn those who sabotage infrastructure from felons to protectors in public perception. And, further, in the courts, once their role in utilizing radical means to avoid harm for the many is recognized as such also by judges and by new developments in the relations between activism, law and science. In this sense, the correlation between the inside and outside of courts during litigation processes related to climate and activism already constitute an arena of convergence.

Climate litigation as a tactic of legal mobilization complements and extends grassroots political organizing to effect social change. It is also increasingly a tool in the broader repertoire of action of social movements and civil society to exert influence in the climate politics arena, considered "strategic" when its overall aim goes beyond the case at hand, attempting to affect broader policy and societal changes. Legal climate action may challenge government policies and corporate activities that are inconsistent with climate targets or human-rights obligations. A landmark case in May 2021 in the Netherlands held the energy company Royal Dutch Shell legally responsible for greenhouse gas emissions from its entire value chain, ordering to reduce its worldwide CO_2 emissions (Milieudefensie 2021). This decision marks the first time any court in the world has imposed a duty on a company to do its share to prevent dangerous climate change.

Climate lawsuits also rely on developments in attribution science to make causal arguments. So far, cases seeking compensation for climate change impacts have been unsuccessful. A major challenge is to prove a causal link between emitters' contributions to global climate change and the plaintiffs' losses. Greater use of climate attribution evidence that can support legal findings for causality might improve the prospects of causal claims in court (Stuart-Smith et al. 2021). Conversely, when the causality between specific emitters and extreme events is evidenced by science, certified by courts and amplified by activists, this could shift the public standing of fossil fuel companies and open to compensation for climate damages by affected parties. It could also make the issues of reparations and climate debt politically salient (Otto et al. 2022). It would be a blow to narratives of climate impacts as "future" problems; the debate on climate politics would be affected; and a signal would be sent to other jurisdictions, governments and major emitters.

Challenging widely held assumptions on accountability, property and human rights violations through the courts implies synergies between activists, lawyers and scientists. Potential strategies to develop from such collaboration include: joining litigation with campaigns and awareness-raising to create political pressure; turning legal climate cases into collective issues and a basis for mobilization; circulating and disseminating stories of plaintiffs at the forefront of the climate crisis; pointing at gaps in laws and influence legislation, such as on ecocide and rights of nature; and finally triggering mobilization within the legal and scientific professions.

Conclusions

Conscious political work towards a convergence of movements, sectors and civil society is unavoidable at this point in time to deflect catastrophic trajectories and to reclaim the possibility to live otherwise. Climate justice approaches to political organizing provide a framework to link social and ecological issues with historical and geographical awareness of various forms of injustice, exploitation and destruction, drawing paths toward radical emancipation. Direct action tactics of climate justice movements constitute valuable arenas of convergence for repertoires of action and contention from different movements, traditions and settings, to harness social forces around shared agendas of system-wide transformation.

In my contribution, I discussed existing tactics and experiments of direct action on the ground to articulate how this can be done. First, the tactic of connection between dispersed frontlines of resistance to fossil capitalism is crucial to nurture internationalist solidarity and to foster recomposition within and between movements in Global North and South. Second, a potential escalation of direct action towards sabotage, to be effective, needs to complement movements for climate and social justice through a division of labour strategically oriented. Moreover, to avoid social polarization and to prevent repression, disruptive tactics need to be coupled with structures of support to prisoners and with narratives that justify sabotage, also by shifting actions towards sites of capital accumulation. Third, this can be aided by linking resistance with prefiguration of alternative societal organizations. Enlisting mutual help networks, autonomous forms of service provision and social reproduction support is an essential task for a movement that attempts to break attachment to the world as it is and to nurture desires for radical transformations. Joining local conflicts and multiplying sites of lived experience of alternatives, such as the camp, provide further venues for convergence. Fourth, workers' struggles should become central to a climate justice politics that aims to influence a just transition and to build broad social fronts. Existing examples already point to feasible paths of collaboration between workers and climate activists. Fifth, a more recent arena of convergence is emerging in contexts of adaptation needs and post-disaster recovery. Here previous political work provides the basis for collaborations between climate-focused movements and groups on the frontlines of social justice struggles. Such social infrastructures of adaptation and disaster response, based on solidarity and mutual help, should not substitute but complement advocacy and pressure for policy changes. Sixth, climate litigations to influence climate governance already articulate advocacy and mobilizations in and outside of the courtroom. They could become tools to clarify who the real criminals are and a stage where climate activism can gain legitimacy, especially by pursuing synergies between activists, lawyers and scientists.

These ways of articulating direct action tactics to foster convergence are already being tested in a variety of contexts. By drawing them together, this chapter has aimed to offer insights and tools to advance their combination. Movements for climate and social justice need to grow together to build the needed counter-power. Rather than vanguardism and isolation, we need collaboration and mutual strengthening more than ever. The future will be achieved collectively, or there won't be a future at all.

Notes

1. The Dakota Access Pipeline (DAPL), owned by Energy Transfer, is a 1,886 kilometre-long underground pipeline in the United States to transport crude oil from North Dakota to Illinois. Even if currently operating, its fate is tied to an environmental review mandated by the US Supreme Court in February 2022.
2. defendtheatlantaforest.org/
3. mutualaiddisasterrelief.org/
4. climatejusticealliance.org/our-power-puerto-rico-report/
5. debtforclimate.org/

References

Collettivo GKN, Stefano Laszlo Capitani, Armanda Cetrulo et al. 2023. *Un piano per il futuro della fabbrica di Firenze. Dall'ex GKN alla Fabbrica socialmente integrata*. Milano: Fondazione Feltrinelli. At <fondazionefeltrinelli.it/app/uploads/2023/01/Finale_Futuro-per-la-fabbrica-di-Firenze.pdf>.

crow, scott. 2014. *Black Flags and Windmills: Hope, Anarchy, and the Common Ground Collective*. Oakland, CA: PM Press.

Dawson, Ashley. 2017. *Extreme Cities: The Peril and Promise of Urban Life in the Age of Climate Change*. London: Verso.

De Rosa, Salvatore P. 2022. "Breaking Consensus, Transforming Metabolisms: Notes on Direct Action against Fossil Fuels through Urban Political Ecology." *Social Text* 40, 1: 135–155.

De Rosa, Salvatore P., Joost de Moor, and Marwa Dabaieh. 2022. "Vulnerability and activism in urban climate politics: An actor-centered approach to transformational adaptation in Malmö (Sweden)." *Cities* 130, article 103848.

Derman, Brandon B. 2020. *Struggles for Climate Justice: Uneven Geographies and the Politics of Connection*. Cham, Switzerland: Springer Nature.

Estes, Nick. 2019. *Our History Is the Future: Standing Rock versus the Dakota Access Pipeline, and the Long Tradition of Indigenous Resistance*. London: Verso.

Farrell, Hugh. 2023. *The Strategy of Composition*. Ill Will Editions.

ffitch, Madeline. 2022. "A Frontline Response to Andreas Malm." In J. Kindig (ed.), *Property Will Cost Us the Earth. Direct Action and the Future of the Global Climate Movement*. London: Verso.

Fletcher, Robert. 2018. "Beyond the End of the World: Breaking Attachment to a Dying Planet." In I. Kapoor (ed.), *Psychoanalysis and the Global*: 48–69. Lincoln, NB: Univeristy of Nebraska Press.

Forino, Giuseppe. 2015. "Disaster Recovery: Narrating the Resilience Process in the Reconstruction of L'Aquila (Italy)." *Geografisk Tidsskrift-Danish Journal of Geography* 115, 1: 1–13.

Graeber, David. 2009. *Direct Action: An Ethnography*. Chico, CA: AK Press.
Hajek, Andrea. 2013. "Learning from L'Aquila: Grassroots Mobilization in Post-Earthquake Emilia-Romagna." *Journal of Modern Italian Studies* 18, 5: 627–643.
Kimmerer, Robin W. 2013. *Braiding Sweetgrass: Indigenous Wisdom, Scientific Knowledge and the Teachings of Plants*. Minneapolis: Milkweed Editions.
LaDuke, Winona, and Deborah Cowen. 2020. "Beyond wiindigo infrastructure." *South Atlantic Quarterly* 119, 2: 243–268.
Lloréns, Hilda, and Ruth Santiago. 2018. "Traveling on Coal's Death Route: From Puerto Rico's Jobos Bay to La Guajira, Colombia." *Latino Rebels*, August 14. At <latinorebels.com/2018/08/14/coaldeathroute/>.
Malm, Andreas. 2021. *How to Blow up a Pipeline*. London: Verso.
McGregor, Callum. 2015. "Direct Climate Action as Public Pedagogy: The Cultural Politics of the Camp for Climate Action." *Environmental Politics* 24, 3: 343–362.
Milieudefensie/Friends of the Earth Netherlands. 2021. "How we defeated Shell." At <milieudefensie.nl/actueel/md_how_we_defeated_shell_en_final.pdf>.
Otto, Friederike E.L., Petra Minnerop, Emmanuel Raju et al. 2022. "Causality and the fate of climate litigation: The role of the social superstructure narrative." *Global Policy* 5: 736–750.
Pleyers, Geoffrey. 2020. "The Pandemic is a battlefield. Social movements in the COVID-19 lockdown." *Journal of Civil Society* 16, 4: 295–312.
The Red Nation. 2021. *The Red Deal. Indigenous Action to Save our Earth*. New York: Common Notions.
Rübner Hansen, Bue. 2021. "The Kaleidoscope of Catastrophe: On the Clarities and Blind Spots of Andreas Malm." *Viewpoint Magazine*, April 14. At <viewpoint-mag.com/2021/04/14/the-kaleidoscope-of-catastrophe-on-the-clarities-and-blind-spots-of-andreas-malm/>.
Simpson, Brent, Robb Willer, and Matthew Feinberg. 2022. "Radical flanks of social movements can increase support for moderate factions." *PNAS Nexus* 1, 3.
Sovacool, Benjamin K. 2022. "Beyond Science and Policy: Typologizing and Harnessing Social Movements for Transformational Social Change." *Energy Research & Social Science* 94, article 102857.
Sovacool, Benjamin K., and Alexander Dunlap. 2022. "Anarchy, War, or Revolt? Radical Perspectives for Climate Protection, Insurgency and Civil Disobedience in a Low-Carbon Era." *Energy Research & Social Science* 86, article 102416.
Stuart-Smith, Rupert F., Friederike E.L. Otto, Aisha I. Saad et al. 2021. "Filling the evidentiary gap in climate litigation." *Nature Climate Change* 11: 651–655.
Tilly, Charles, and Sidney Tarrow. 2007. *Contentious Politics*. Boulder and London: Paradigm Publishers.

IMAGINING JUST TRANSITIONS

Julie Sze, in conversation with Gopal Dayaneni

Climate justice and Just Transition are activist concepts and terms that are gaining wide-scale acceptance in multiple policy and academic contexts. However, like "sustainability" and "nature," the popularization of climate justice and Just Transition presents opportunities and dangers insofar as they lose core shared values, politics or theories. Climate justice activists and movements within the US use the term fenceline/frontline to foreground issues of race, class, indigeneity, citizenship and gender to highlight the disparities of who is most impacted and most responsible. Fenceline/frontline climate justice activists use a radical framework to distinguish its position against mainstream, technologically driven conversations around climate policy. Within the US, climate justice approaches to climate change and Just Transitions are informed by and aligned with a number of diverse social movements. Decolonial and anticapitalist critique emerging from within the Global South are one such foundational influence. Another important influence is transformative justice, emerging out of activism on prison abolition and criminal justice policy and practice. Transformative justice seeks to "respond to violence without creating more violence and/or engaging in harm reduction to lessen the violence and … [is] a way of 'making things right,' getting in 'right relation,' or creating justice together" (Mingus 2019). Queer Liberation, Black Liberation and Reparations, Indigenous Sovereignty, Food Sovereignty and many other radical movements are core to the identity and politics of the fenceline/frontline Climate Justice Movement (see Mingus 2019).

This chapter draws on ongoing interviews and conversations with Gopal Dayaneni, one of the founding members of Movement Generation: Justice and Ecology Project,[1] and Movement Generation documents (Mascarenhas-Swan 2017; Movement Generation 2009; 2016; 2020).[2] Movement Generation was formed in 2002 as a study and strategy space for organizers co-convened by Movement Strategy Center and the School of Unity and Liberation. In 2006, the effort evolved into Movement Generation: Justice and Ecology Project, a collective of organizers who came out of union organizing, environmental justice, ecology, economic justice, workers' rights, racial justice, Global Justice, anti-war organizing and Indigenous sovereignty movements. At the same time, the increasing visibility of the climate crisis and the acute impact of Hurricane Katrina motivated the founding members to focus on the relationship between social injustice and ecological erosion (Mascarenhas and Llewellyn 2020). Movement Generation is a key architect of the Just Transition framework (2016).[3] Just Transition has its origins in the labour movement and the Environmental Justice movement, and the Just Transition framework builds on that foundation as an articulation of shared vision and strategy. Movement Generation is motivated, in part, by radical activist Grace Lee Boggs, who asks us "What time is it on the clock of the world?" (Boggs 2008 [1974]). To answer this question, Dayaneni argues that "What is demanded of us right now by the material, cultural and ecological conditions is a *new way of thinking about ... or really an old way remembered about ... organizing*. We need to remember/re-imagine organizing and to realign our movement strategy with the healing powers of the living world."

The Movement Generation Just Transition framework was conceptualized specifically to address the dangerous disintegration of issues, strategies, constituencies and movements into silos. "From the foundation of Movement Generation, some of us were antagonistic even to 'climate' as a frame because it focuses the gaze on atmospheric concentrations of CO_2 in the sky, rather than on the erosion of seed, soil and story and the exploitation of land, labour and living systems," says Dayaneni. The Just Transition framework is a powerful visualization of critique and creation. On the one side are the problems of the Extractive Economy, and on the other is the need to move toward a Living Economy. The Extractive Economy is not limited to mining or fossil fuels alone but involves five dimensions: an Extractive Worldview (consumerism and colonial mind-set), Purpose (enclosure of wealth and power), Governance (militarism) and Resources (extraction: dig/burn/dump) and foundationally, the exploitation of human labour. To move beyond critique of the problem and into action, the framework posits a shift of values, resources and action towards Living Economies based on a different set of pillars: Worldviews (caring and sacredness), Purpose (ecological and social well-being), Governance (deep democracy), Resources (regeneration) and Labour organized through consent and cooperation. The problems are not just mining oil, coal and gas, but systems of extractivism, or, as Dayaneni put it, the "uncommoning and enclosure of the wealth of the living world."

According to Michelle Mascarenhas-Swan (2017), a Movement Generation collective founding member, "The question is, how is that [carbon] transition going to go? Is it going to be one that continues on a path of inequity, violence, scarcity and the hoarding of resources by some while others go without? Or is it going to be a Just Transition?" To answer these questions, Movement Generation posits the Just Transition framework as a radical imagining of history, politics, economy, and futures that understands the problem of carbon and oil as intimately tied to exploitations of land and labour. This articulation directly opposed a dominant techno-scientific problem of engineering and policy-tinkering that keep capitalism and colonialism intact. Thus, framework builds complex articulations between different political struggles to help bring just transitions of all stripes forward. In 2009, Movement Generation co-led a delegation of US grassroots groups to the UN Climate Change Conference in Copenhagen, in opposition to mainstream environmental organizations and their failure to address the "root causes of the climate crisis." These groups organized what would later become the Climate Justice Alliance that comprises over seventy urban, rural and Indigenous frontline organizations and supporting networks that are "locally, tribally, and regionally-based racial and economic justice organizations of Indigenous Peoples, African American, Latinx, Asian Pacific Islander, and poor white communities who share legacies of racial and economic oppression and social justice organizing."[4] The Just Transition framework emerges out of political struggle and through its practice, bends and grows a radical climate politics drawing from environmental, antiracist, feminist, Indigenous, unions and worker rights.

This chapter highlights how the Just Transition framework *imagines* a radical climate politics to nurture and create convergence in climate justice fenceline/frontline worldviews, strategies and actions. It articulates the implications of the Just Transition framework, organized into the following sections: *articulations* of climate justice and just transition; *elaborations* of extraction and enclosure; *intersecting* struggles and some examples of how the theoretical framework (including engaging contradictions and conflicts) has been used in practice.

The framework rejects a "carbon fundamentalism" that masks all kinds of injustice. As Dayaneni says,

> The world could reduce carbon and be equally unjust in ways that will continue to erode the life support systems of the planet. If you take your money out of fossil fuels and you put it in Walmart or prisons or the banks that finance the fossil fuel industry you are reproducing extractivism. We can "decarbonize" the economy, but if we still exploit the labour of the living world, we will perpetuate the crisis. The climate crisis is not the problem ... it's the emergent *consequence* of the actual problem which is exploiting communities and ecosystems everywhere at once.

It is the fundamental structure of economies that are at the root of climate crisis, economies that extract, exploit and degrade demands endless new frontiers of extractivism on the planetary scale that have a long temporal scale, as in the book *The History of the World in Seven Cheap Things* (Patel and Moore 2017).

In other words, Movement Generation believes that transitions are inevitable, but justice is not. Without justice, Dayaneni warns, "the transition will be just epic scales of suffering that will be inequitably distributed." To shift the transitions to a more just outcome, the framework draws upon abolitionist imaginaries that bends climate activism and policy development in radical directions, towards anticapitalist, decolonial and demilitarized visions. He says simply and powerfully that:

> You cannot convert the Labour of the living world into stuff faster than its capacity to regenerate and get away with it. It does not matter who supposedly controls the means of production, but also the nature of production itself. It isn't just about the gross accumulation of the wealth of the living world it is also about being out of balance with the living systems, upon which we depend. Indeed, who actually controls the means of production on planet earth? The photosynthesizing organisms. The plants, and forests and algae. That is who controls the means of production. They are the only ones who can

directly take the energy of the sun, convert it into power to do work. We are all just living off their labour.

To do so, is, simply to argue for revolution. He writes:

> The basis of revolution is not the struggle for power. The basis of revolution is *rights*. When peoples and communities are organized enough to assert rights, they are able to contest the legitimacy of existing authority. And the only way to assert rights is to exercise them. So we must organize ourselves to exercise our rights in such a way that contests the legitimacy of existing authority. The rights we are interested in asserting are Rights of Mother Earth and the rights and responsibilities to create an economy that advances, defends and is constrained by those rights.

Thus, climate justice is a revolutionary politics.

What is Climate Justice? What is the Just Transition?

To address — and reframe — these questions, the Just Transition framework establishes a way of talking about capitalist and corporate economies that allows us to contrast the organization of extractive structures and regenerative economies as a way of explaining the problem, broadcasting a vision of liberatory futures based on social and ecological well-being and articulating a strategy. Economy, in a broad historical sense, is explained as having five key elements: resources from the living world combined with human work towards some purpose(s) with worldview/cosmology that justifies it and a form of governance to facilitate activity towards the purpose. In an Extractive Economy, these elements are: Extractive Worldview (consumerism and colonial mind-set), Purpose (enclosure of wealth and power), Governance (militarism), Resources (extraction: dig/burn/dump) and Work (exploitation).

Although the climate crisis is dominantly framed as caused *by* fossil fuels and their attendant institutions (oil, coal and gas), the Just Transition framework's conceptualization of the climate crisis goes far beyond fossil fuels or atmospheric concentration of CO_2. Politically, the questions of climate disruption, water security, land security, erosion of biological and cultural diversity, and food security are inextricably linked

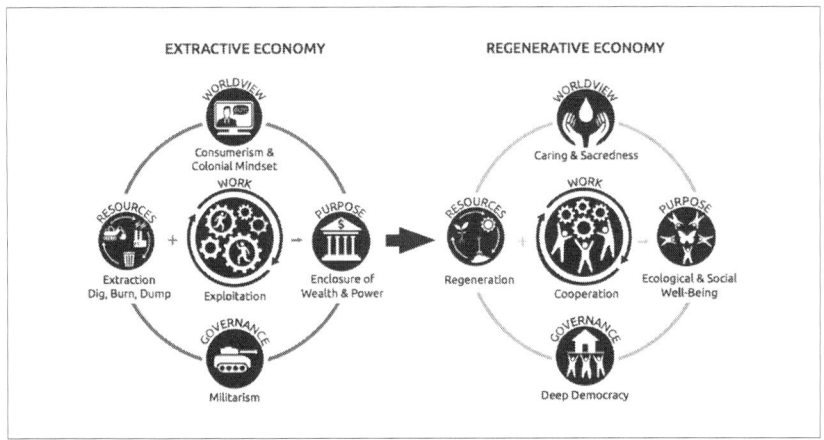

The Just Transition framework identifies a strategy for moving from an Extractive Economy to a living or regenerative one, through a combination of actions to disinvest from and stop the bad (opposition), and invest in and build the new (vision). Source: Movement Generation (2016) and Climate Justice Alliance.

to race, indigeneity, poverty and global economic development.[5] Rather, the task is to "look down" at the organization of the economy, not to "look up" at the atmosphere and count carbon to track success or failure for climate movements, or in climate policy. For Movement Generation, economy means in the broadest sense, "stewardship, management or care of *home*" from its Greek roots of (*oikonomia*). Dayaneni says,

> The Economy is all these elements interacting. All economies have an ecological basis. Economies are nested in ecosystems. And economies mediate all of our relationships to each other and the rest of the living world. So while you might think of the crisis as an ecological crisis, the landscape of struggle — and the strategic points of intervention — are all about the economy. Thinking of climate crisis as about economies means understanding economies as a central landscape of responses to climate crisis and the just transition. Instead of thinking we need to intervene at the planetary scale (like geoengineering) we can see opportunities for transforming economy and governance everywhere all around us. Local and community-based organizing can be decentralized and distributed and democratized in ways that allow us to act everywhere at once.

Using this analysis, the problems and solutions are not based on "business as usual" (i.e., unjust economic and political systems based on solar or renewables) or an engineering or policy fix. Rather, he writes,

> We are able to get to scale not by creating massive silver-bullet solutions but by aggregating to scale through trans-local organizing. This principle of Translocal Organizing is important to the Just Transition Framework and the Climate Justice movements. Movement Generation defines "Trans-local Organizing" as autonomous place-based organizing to address real conditions in a community, with unifying visions, shared strategies, common frames and connective tissue across communities aligned in common cause.

Extraction and enclosure

One of the pillars of the Extractive Economy is enclosure of wealth and power — essentially, property. Dayaneni says:

> Ultimately all enclosures must be enforced through violence. It doesn't matter if it's fence around my house and the police that patrol it or the border around the nation state and the army that secures it — all enclosures are ultimately enforced through violence. That's why we have militarism and systemic violence as the defining feature of governance; because ultimately, that is what it takes to maintain an economy based on ever expanding enclosures and endless extractivism.

Violence is required to both enforce and expand enclosures.

Movement Generation's theory of change posits "two distinct possible futures: Economic Transition or Ecological Collapse. If we stay the current course of a globalized industrial model, collapse is inevitable. We must, instead, create an intentional pathway — a Just Transition — towards local, living, loving economies." Divesting from the Extractive Economy and its enclosures, requires re-investing (or investing back into) a *cooperative* economy based on commons and consent. Movement Generation warns against falling into the trap of thinking that divesting from fossil fuels is enough. Dayaneni writes, "Payday lending is extractive. Walmart is extractive. Apple Computers and Tesla are extractive. The very process of making money off the movement/ownership of money is extractive, and, according to the vast majority of the world's cultures, a sin." He continues that "*demands for* energy democracy, food sovereignty, worker ownership, transformative justice all become the *answers* to the climate crisis." What is missing is the *mechanisms* to absorb the divestment resources and put them in to communities in a way that: "creates the opportunity for community ownership of wealth: commons of capital, commons of land, commons of energy, commons of food and water."

Enclosures, extractivism, exploitation all rely on an expectation that the way things are result from some natural and unchangeable state of (capitalist and colonial) being. In *Ugly Freedoms*, US political scientist Elisabeth Anker (2021) examines the various appeals to freedoms in contemporary political thought and how ideologies and practices of American freedom legitimate other forms of oppressions. She writes: "Stories about freedom, about people's imbrication in something called nature, and about agency are important for climate politics ... any large-scale effort to halt global warming will depend upon reworking the stories underpinning destructive relationships to the planet and, I would add, reworking stories about freedom." In other words, she reminds us that "How we tell stories of freedom matters." In *A Planet to Win: Why We Need a Green New Deal,* Naomi Klein's (2019) preface similarly chides the environmental movement for its "imaginative asphyxiation."

In sharp contrast to a denuded generic "climate justice" language that valourizes renewables at the expense of a broader political critique or historical understanding, fenceline/frontline climate justice movements posit fundamentally different worldviews and stories of freedom than those that currently exist in political, economic and cultural systems. Anker (2021) posits, and fenceline/frontline climate justice confirms that,

> If the freedom to participate in and help compose a world alongside others is premised on a subject that is not a masculinized heroic individual who self-wills his action, but a collaborative amalgamation of acts from many nonhuman and human creatures that form an agentic ecosystem, then different stories of freedom will emerge from that vision.

Frontline/fenceline environmental justice offers a utopian vision of freedoms for climate justice, one grounded in freedom from fear, freedom from toil, freedom to move and freedom to live.

These ideas of freedom are capacious, far beyond the dominant notions of freedom as individualist, property based and a negative freedom "from" (environmental laws, or masks in the case of COVID). Dayaneni expands on these capacious and generative definitions of freedoms:

> We confront the existing structures that do not meet our needs and, in fact, infringe upon our rights and freedoms and well-being. We demonstrate that our capacity to self-govern is better than the supposed mandate of corporations and the state to govern. The more we meet our needs by building an economy of care, cooperation and consent, the more we are asserting our rights that are violated by the existing dominant economy. Along with this economic power we must build real political power in our communities. Our inability to self-govern routinely butts up against the mandate of the state and corporations to govern and no matter how badly they do it, no matter how poorly it meets our needs, no matter how many communities are disposed of in the process — until we demonstrate that their mandate is not legitimate and that we have the capacity to actually meet these problems ourselves, we will end up always defaulting to calling the cops to deal with harm and hurting and relying on the state to supposedly solve our problems or trust Amazon to sell us what we need.

Rather than relying on the state as an agent of violence and protecting enclosures and extractions, fenceline/frontline climate justice activists claim their leadership into the Just Transition. This leadership is based on histories that demanded the theft of their land and labour to bring the current world into being. In addition to these histories, the ongoing legacies of such reverberate into different visions for the future. Dayaneni continues that:

> If we believe we can live in a world without policing and prisons, then we have to actually figure out how we are going to self-govern our way through harm and hurting. And if we don't know how to do that, we have no business suggesting that we can live in a world without policing. The existence of policing and prisons makes it hard to practice self-governing

"Just Transition within a Green New Deal" logo. The logo shows the importance of vision and narrative ("changing the story"), through the voices of frontline/fenceline communities, as part of the Just Transition strategy. Source: Climate Justice Alliance.

our way through harm and hurting, of course. In the same way that you know you have to weed the garden to grow the food you can't just say, "I'm going to grow food and I'm going to leave the weeds" … Either you have to reimagine your relationship to the weeds or you have to remove them to create space for what you want to grow. And in the same way it is true that policing and prisons is choking out the space for us to live a different way. It is also the case that living a different way, is the only way to demonstrate our capacity to self-govern. We have to be both confronting the illegitimacy of policing and prisons *by demonstrating* that transformative justice works. And we have to erode policing and prisons to expand the fertile ground for transformative justice.

Dayaneni suggests how different political struggles are linked and how these visions for the regenerative future are imagined, and crucially, practiced through struggle and in community across space, species and temporal scales.

Interweaving struggles

Politically and ideologically, Movement Generation and the Just Transition framework were inspired and shaped by the wisdom of many radical movements, including the Chipko movement in India, the Zapatistas, the Latin American left (the MST), the Black Panthers, and Occupy the Farm, an experiment in land reform in which Movement Generation participated. The Chipkos were the first tree huggers. For the Chipko movement, their slogan in the 1970s was "ecology is permanent economy." To understand the economy in that way means, according to Dayaneni, to shift from (political) borders to (ecological) boundaries:

> If your economy is situated within its ecological boundaries, it will be permanent … when your economy exceeds ecological balance, there are problems … Borders are arbitrary, inflexible, rigid and literally imposed upon living systems and human communities by colonialism and the nation state (or more accurately, *nation-statism*). In contrast, ecological boundaries that are permeable flexible culturally and ecologically defined that the shape of governance is different for what it is you're trying to govern like watersheds are governed very, very differently than energy sheds or food sheds or trade sheds.

He reminds us that "expressions and examples of the Regenerative Economy — or Local, living, loving economies — are everywhere all around us." Struggles for food sovereignty, energy democracy, Indigenous sovereignty, worker and community cooperative ownership, transformative justice or the work generally create "commons of capital" to finance cooperatives without subordinating them to debt. They are concrete examples, and "living manifestations of Just Transition, whether they identify as that or not," says Dayaneni. What all these movements have in common is the commons — they are expressions of commoning, predicated on cooperation, care and consent rather than a politics of hierarchy, extraction and enclosure.

Regarding the integration of theory and praxis and the challenge of working through ideological differences, at Movement Generation, Dayaneni says, "We don't have a political line, we have a political line of inquiry." They didn't come from a place of position, but of shared learning and exploration. Within the US, the Just Transition framework emerged in large part out of student fossil fuel divestment campaigns and the environmental justice movement. Students fighting for fossil fuel divestment at Swarthmore College had alliances and relationships with communities and organizers in Appalachia, fighting mountaintop removal and the devastation of those lands. Swarthmore students studied efforts such as the anti-apartheid movement and built a divestment campaign to target fossil fuels and the university in solidarity with frontline communities. It was only after these campaigns that the larger environmental movement, including groups like 350.org, joined the fossil fuel divestment movement. The Just Transition Alliance (JTA) articulated a labour notion of Just Transition: What does it mean to transition workers from polluting, dirty industries to clean industries and clean jobs? Just Transition initially focused on point source pollution, and Alinsky models of community-organizing that focused on individual and community harm. What the climate justice movement focused on from these roots was translocal organizing. What the divestment movement did was adapt and transform, so that the goal was not a *bigger* scale of organizing, but a *balanced* scale. The focus was on building and supporting autonomous grassroots movements, drawn together through an alliance of values, and what became named Resilience-Based Organizing (RBO).

The goal of many different and smaller networks, and the focus on translocal organizing, is a concrete result of past lessons and political analysis. The focus of the Just Transition framework on local communities aligned through their values and RBO, rejects, rather than assumes a top-down hierarchical system based on domination. That impacts the structure and leadership away from a single organization or figure. The movement thus practices deep democracy in action, which does not negate or deny political conflict or contentiousness to assume a politics of uniformity. Dayaneni explains that there are many challenges to enacting these articulations in practice. The framework is "just that, it is not intended to be prescriptive. It doesn't tell us *what* to do — it offers a way of thinking *about* strategy. The two biggest challenges that emerge are navigating contradictions and co-optation."

Transition is always, thus in part, the *process* of navigating change and emergent contradictions. He continues:

> It isn't as simple as having a vision; or even a theory of revolution — but it requires us to make difficult decisions every step

of the way as we move from the world we are in, to the world we know we need and deserve. To navigate contradictions well takes two things: 1) a finely tuned and regularly maintained moral compass. and (2) a community of practice (which helps maintain the compass and engages in the struggle). To this end, it is always and only ever about *relationships*. We don't always have perfect answers, but we are constantly trying to navigate the contradictions with an eye towards social and ecological well-being.

Thus, the framework forms a connective tissue of expressions of social movements to be in right relation with one another. These examples, according to Dayaneni,

> [navigate] ... the inherent contradictions of transitioning from the dominant extractive economy to deeply democratic regenerative economies. In fact, sometimes it isn't even a transition — it is a defence of what was already the right answer before the imposition of extractivism. These movements, such as the Food Sovereignty and land reform movements; the movement for Energy Democracy; the development of cooperative economics and what we call "a commons of capital," to disrupt dominant finance; Indigenous Sovereignty and so much more. These are all expressions of defending, remembering, restoring or rebuilding the kinds of pre-existing conditions of freedom and commoning that are threatened, eroded, infringed upon through exploitation, extractivism and enclosure. Many of these movements don't even identify with Just Transition, and that is totally okay. We seek to create a framework that can uplift all of the amazing interventions that are adding up to a powerful tapestry of transformative movements. We were never interested in having everything be Just Transition or have everyone have to use just one framework. We instead were seeking to share some strategies and insights we see reflected in diverse movements.

There are many concrete examples of how the framework has been used to build climate justice. The framework acts, Dayaneni writes, "as a resource to help us consider new approaches and strategies and to help us articulate a shared vision of what we are for — in as much radical diversity as possible. The possibilities are endless, from organizers in Portland, Oregon who used the framework to advance the Portland Clean Energy Fund — an incredibly inspiring strategy to finance clean energy with environmental justice principles through taxing mega-retailers." Other adaptations and evolutions of the JT framework come from Native Movement in Alaska, PUSH Buffalo in New York, the Our Power Coalition in Richmond, California, and many more. Indigenous nations, such as Native Movement, are working to "rematriate land," or "land-back" strategies for returning land to Indigenous care and commons-based governance. Indigenous land trusts, such as Sogorea Te' Land Trust in Ohlone territories, are a concrete example where there are contradictions, in that "to liberate land from enclosure you have to have access or control of the land and currently, the most expeditious way to protect land is to buy it for the last time. These are real contradictions, but through communities of practice and constant reflection on values and purpose, organizations are finding ways to navigate the politics and contradictions." These examples are wildly different in their content, region and response and yet, they share common values and vision but are deeply place-based and responsive to local communities.

It is equally important to recognize the gaps in the Just Transition framework as living vs. static. Movement Generation, in parallel conversation with diverse radical movements, has been evolving and adapting the framework to respond to gaps and emergent wisdom from the Disability Justice movements, the Queer Liberation movements, internationalist critiques of how we can be more responsive to the needs of Global South social movements.

Conclusion

The power of the Just Transition framework is in its simultaneous simplicity and complexity. On the one hand, its "value" is simply in enlarging the frames of what needs transition to go beyond carbon. The JT framework has become very popular, but it is often thought of as "build the good, stop the bad" (which it is). But it is much more than that. As Movement Generation argues, and Dayaneni articulates, the framework is "fundamentally about building strategy towards the assertion of rights as the basis of revolution. I notice this is often lost or ignored. For us, isn't about just pre-figurative alternatives — it is about self-governance as the strategy to contest for power and the legitimacy of existing authority."

This project of tying everything back together and with the biggest question of insurgency, and articulations for radical/deep transformation is not unique to the JT framework. Others like Marco Armiero, along with Italian feminist Silvia Federici and many others, are sharing histories and vocabularies of regenerative thinking and practice. As Armiero writes in his recent book on the idea of what he calls the *Wasteocene,* a process of extraction that produces wasted peoples and places: "exploitation and oppression are always embedded within the bodies of humans and nonhumans. It tells us that for a radical emancipatory project taking control of the means of production is not enough unless we do not change the socioecological relationships from wasting to commoning" (Armiero 2021: 59).

I have seen the power of the Just Transition framework in transforming my students' worldviews and political analyses. While the dominant discourse on climate is alienating in some respects (as a technical issue of dense policy and climate science), the framework moves those who are not particularly radical in massive ways. When Dayaneni says that "We as a society cannot extract from a finite system faster than its capacity to regenerate without consequences," my students who have been raised at the teat of common-sense capitalism remember the deep lessons that they knew as children and which attendant institutions, including educational and political structures, have beaten out of them. The framework rejects endless growth and corporate capitalism, the ongoing legacies of colonialisms, and supremacy and domination writ large of whiteness, gender and heteronormativity, and of human over nonhuman natures. Its "value" is in its radical vision and politics and what communities do with it in their local contexts to grow commoning and to remake the common-sense to a deeply remembered sense of connection and community.

Notes

1 See <movementgeneration.org/about/>.
2 See also <movementgeneration.org/resources/>.
3 For more on this history, practice and for more on the framework, see also <climatejusticealliance.org>.
4 At <climatejusticealliance.org/about/>.
5 At <movementgeneration.org/about/our-theory-of-change/>.

References

Anker, Elisabeth R. 2021. *Ugly Freedoms*. Durham: Duke University Press.

Armiero, Marco. 2021. *Wasteocene: Stories from the Global Dump*. Cambridge, UK: Cambridge University Press.

Boggs, James, and Grace Lee Boggs. 2008. *Revolution and Evolution in the Twentieth Century*. New York: Monthly Review Press.

Klein, Naomi. 2019. "Foreword." In Kate Aronoff, Alyssa Battistoni, Daniel A. Cohen, and Thea Riofrancos, *A Planet to Win: Why We Need a Green New Deal*. London: Verso Books.

Mascarenhas-Swan, Michelle. 2017. "The Case for a Just Transition." In D. Fairchild and A. Weinrub (eds.), *Energy Democracy: Advancing Equity in Clean Energy Solutions*. Washington: Island Press.

Mascarenhas, Michelle, and Tom Llewellyn. 2020. "Just Transition and Permanently Organized Communities with Michelle Mascarenhas." From podcast series *The People's Covid-19 Response* from Shareable. April 30. At <shareable.net/podcasts/just-transition-and-permanently-organized-communities-with-michelle-mascarenhas-swan/>.

Mingus, Mia. 2019. "Transformative Justice: A Brief Description." *TransformHarm*. At <transformharm.org/transformative-justice-a-brief-description/>.

Movement Generation. 2009. "Ecological Justice: A Call for Action." At <movementgeneration.org/wp-content/uploads/2014/08/MG.CurriculumManual.pdf>.

———. 2016. "From Banks and Tanks to Cooperation and Caring: A Strategic Framework for a Just Transition." At <movementgeneration.org/wp-content/uploads/2016/11/JT_booklet_English_SPREADs_web.pdf>.

———. 2020. "Propagate, Pollinate, Practice: Curriculum Tools for a Just Transition." At <movementgeneration.org/wp-content/uploads/2018/12/Propagate-Pollinate-Practice-Final.pdf>.

Patel, Raj, and Jason Moore. 2017. *The History of the World in Seven Cheap Things*. Berkeley: University of California Press.

COUNTERHEGEMONIC FLOWS

Expanding Renewable Energy Struggles in Turkey

Ethemcan Turhan and Cem İskender Aydın

Despite some setbacks from major players, global energy transformation is well underway, driven by geopolitical realignments and by the global decarbonization imperative. This transformation is already having significant socioecological, spatial and political impacts on communities across the Global South. On the one hand, the promise of transition to renewables is to provide less dependence on centralized energy generation and distribution. On the other hand, these very renewables provide new avenues for accumulation by dispossession, while sacrificing communities and landscapes. The key issue at stake for the communities at the frontlines of this transformation, therefore, is the democratic ownership, planning and control of renewable energy sources.

Turkey, as an upper middle-income country that has undergone significant social, political and economic changes in the past two decades, is no exception. The energy sector in Turkey became one of the fastest growing in the world in this period, ranking second to China in the increase in electricity and natural gas demand globally (Ministry of Foreign Affairs n.d.). The International Energy Agency's (IEA) Renewables 2020 report suggests that Turkey will lead both hydropower growth in Europe and global geothermal expansion (together with Indonesia, Kenya and the Philippines) in the coming decade. This massive growth of Turkey's energy sector hinges on an intricate relation between the state and the market as further elaborated in recent debates on state capitalism, crony capitalism and authoritarian neoliberalism in the Turkish context (Güven 2022; Altinörs and Akçay 2022). In an attempt to scratch the surface of environmentalist opposition to Erdoğan's hegemonic bloc, this chapter will focus on the continuities and ruptures in environmental struggles in the past decade in Turkey. In doing so, it will explore the grassroots opposition to run-of-river hydropower and geothermal energy as counterhegemonic flows of environmentalism in Turkey's energyscapes.

The high cost of Turkey's energy expansion

Once hailed as the "model country" for the Middle East, Turkey today undergoes a significant economic crunch, in part due to crony capitalism, the consolidation of executive and judicial powers in a single hand, and a complete overhaul of state institutions under two decades of Erdoğan's rule. During this time, both the state elites and international counterparts played their cards to favour higher energy consumption as a precondition for economic development, with electricity generation playing a key role in the process. This, in turn, resulted in an aggressive and authoritarian neoliberal push towards an "all-of-the-above" energy policy: a rush to hydropower, domestic lignite, geothermal, nuclear, wind and solar power all at once (Özkaynak et al. 2020; Bayülgen 2022).

By increasing electricity generation using both domestic and imported fossil fuels, as well as non-fossil resources, Erdoğan's ambition to expand energy generation by all means sought to meet the increasing (yet almost always overestimated) energy demand during the country's period of debt-fueled rapid economic growth. This was made possible thanks to the availability of cheap credits and a favourable geopolitical position in the aftermath of the 2008/09 global financial meltdown, which enabled access to energy imports — with clear consequences that today manifest in a looming balance of payments crisis. The same period witnessed the regime's unparalleled push to provide energy for domestic consumption, leading to a more than threefold increase in installed capacity of electricity generation between 2000 and 2021 from 27.2 GW to 99.8 GW. It also shaped the ambitions of state elites to turn the country in to a *regional energy hub*, transporting both primary energy (i.e., natural gas) and transmitting electricity to high demand regions in Europe. The recently released National Energy Strategy claims to target an additional 96.9 GW until 2035, thereby doubling the existing installed capacity (Ministry of Energy and Natural Resources 2022).

This particular growth strategy involves urgent land expropriations, arbitrary top-down decision mechanisms, and a lack of transparency and genuine public participation. The period in which rapid liberalization of the country's electricity sector took off — by bringing down the share of public ownership from 59 percent to 21 percent between 2006 and 2021 — also gave rise to numerous environmental conflicts around energy infrastructures, large and small, fossil and renewable (Erensü 2018; Aydın 2019). The recent ratification of the Paris Agreement and the related net zero emission target by 2053 complicates the clean energy transition even further. Such a target requires a phasing out of the coal and gas power plants and a large-scale deployment of renewable capacity (including wind, solar, hydro and geothermal). While there is a steep increase in renewables during the last decade, these investments do not seem to substitute fossil fuels nor reduce the carbon intensity of the economy (Gümüş, 2024). Moreover, such an expansion has consequences for land-use as well as control and ownership of resources already well-documented by the literature on renewables-driven land transformations (Knuth et al. 2022).

In what follows, we narrate the changing and transforming faces of grassroots struggles against the expansion of renewable energy in Turkey in two distinct but overlapping periods. In doing so, we trace anti-hydropower and anti-geothermal power struggles, which surfaced roughly ten years apart. The juxtaposition of anti-hydropower and anti-geothermal struggles in the country reveals that such grassroots movements can only achieve enduring success insofar as they up the ante by politicizing their socioecological woes. As the history of environmentalism in the country has shown, earlier environmental resistances were often successful (or at least, raised their local concerns to the national stage), owing to a convergence between mass popular mobilization, confrontational legal struggles and parliamentary support (Turhan et al. 2019). However, the increasing deterioration of the rule of law, a gradual loss of effectiveness of formal politics and the rapid criminalization of street mobilization has decidedly limited the options available to environmental opposition. This remains a major political battlefield in Turkey, where the state capture by Erdoğan's authoritarian regime is almost complete despite facing a significant pushback from opposition coalitions. We argue that Turkey proves to be a good example where the burning need to transition to renewables takes its toll on the livelihoods of local communities and the very same communities fight back with counterhegemonic arguments.

Against the flows of power:
The rise and fall of anti-hydropower struggles

Tapping hydroelectricity is in fact not a novelty for Turkey. The country has relied on it heavily since the 1950s, when the public infrastructure agency, State Hydraulic Works, began building relatively large dams with large reservoirs with the intention of fostering the nation's technical and economic development. The novelty of Erdoğan's regime, however, was its ability to tap further into the hydropower potential by aggregating the smaller capacities of rivers and creeks. By encouraging private investors to pursue forty-nine-year transfers of water-use rights, which provided lucrative returns through electricity purchase guarantee programs and exemptions from environmental regulations (Harris and Islar 2014; Islar 2012), a massive increase in small-scale hydropower plants was observed since the second half of the 2000s. This rush for small hydropower in a country with a long history of hydro-developmentalism was perhaps not surprising, but the scale of societal resistance catapulted the topic to both activist and scholarly relevance (Aksu et al. 2016; Yaka 2018).

One of the reasons, which triggered a significant backlash from local communities, is the Turkish government's preferred method of acquisition of water and land resources with "urgent expropriation" (*acele kamulaştırma* in Turkish) decisions. Originally designed as a post-World War II-era measure in 1956 and used for the first time in 1978, urgent expropriation decisions were used at an accelerating pace after 2010, the great majority of these being legitimized by energy investments. This land appropriation tool involved a ministerial cabinet (and now a presidential) decree to expropriate private land that is required for the building of plants, transportation routes and transmission lines. Additionally, legal reforms were put in place to make it easier to transfer the user rights of publicly held land and property to private companies engaged in the production or distribution of energy (Islar 2012). For instance, numerous environmental and social obstacles to hydropower development were removed thanks to changes made to laws like the Renewable Energy Law and the Law on Expropriation (Kutlu 2022). Such expropriations frequently resulted in the loss of livelihoods for rural communities reliant on privately owned or rented land from the government, or on common lands like pastures, ponds or creeks. They also often resulted in the destruction of forests and prairies rich in terms of biodiversity, to make way for transmission lines and transportation roads.

Run-of-river hydropower plants, which are considered to be more environmentally benign than reservoir-type hydropower plants for having little to no water storage requirement, are often branded as clean renewable energy sources. Yet, despite the efforts of national and international investors to brand these projects as clean, the geographic concentration and local implications of these projects led to long-standing socioecological conflicts in Turkey. An example of the impact these run-off river type plants have is the obstruction of fish migration routes from downstream to upstream due to the use of pipes to divert the water from the riverbed into the electricity generation plants (Şekercioğlu et al. 2011). Additionally, diverting water into pipes creates a specific form of water grabbing (Islar 2012) grounded in the neoliberal logic of efficiency (Eren 2018). This practice denies the water flows available to the animals and people around the sources despite the political and legal battles sought to ensure lifeline water (*can suyu,* the minimum ecological flow required to maintain the riverbed; see also Erensü 2013a).

One of the first examples of local anti-hydropower resistance was against a series of planned run-of-river hydropower plants in the Fırtına Valley in the Eastern Black Sea Region in the late 1990s. After the mid-2000s, local protests against hydropower plants spread across the country (Aksu et al. 2016). Some emblematic resistances such as Yuvarlakçay (Western Anatolia), Munzur (Eastern Anatolia), and Hasankeyf (Southeastern Anatolia) precipitated in the contemporary form of the ecologist movement in Turkey and led to the formation of nationwide coalitions such as the Fraternity of the Rivers Platform.[1] As Erensü (2013b) also points out, the Gezi Park protests, which took place across the country in 2013, despite their resemblance to the Occupy! or Arab Spring movements, were actually the culmination of a decade of socio-environmental unrest about the plunder of urban-rural ecosystems (Özkaynak et al. 2015). Hence, the anti-hydropower movement became a model for grassroots environmental opposition and an inspiration for other local resistances, thereby significantly shaping contemporary environmentalism in Turkey.

After the first half of the 2010s, the rate of new investments in hydropower plants slowed down due to the saturation of the market. This led the crony capital to seek other avenues of accumulation such as solar, wind and geothermal. Numerous small creeks and streams were already heavily choked with hydropower plants and new investments became less profitable due to the government's preferential treatment of solar and geothermal investments, which received considerably higher feed-in-tariffs. This decline, in part, was also achieved due to the visibility of popular opposition and the social unrest around hydropower plants — many of which were in rural areas with a significant voter base of Erdoğan's party, AKP.

The rise and fall of anti-hydropower movements shaped the ecologist agenda in Turkey in a way that propelled environmental issues to their rightful position in opposition politics. Akbulut et al. (2018: 105) argue that this is mainly due to the failure of the privately owned and operated hydropower plants, catered to crony capital by the Turkish state's judicial and executive powers, to "mobilise reciprocity and mutuality … through which the ideal of modernisation/developmentalism could be articulated as a collective interest." Hence, with the pretext of development as collective emancipation long gone in ruins under the authoritarian whims of neoliberal developmentalism, the anti-hydropower struggles of the 2010s brought back environmentalism in Turkey to its lost ideological home since the early 1990s: questioning of an economic model in delivering collective well-being and a higher common good while socio-natures are sacrificed ruthlessly.

Transforming flows from ground up: Struggles against geothermal power

As Turkey's hydropower capacity reached maturity towards the mid-2010s, the private sector looked for new profit-making opportunities in other renewables. At the same time, international climate finance became available for other renewable sources with lesser public contestation. That is when geothermal energy came into the picture as a new outlet for capital accumulation. It also meant that people in places like Germencik, Aydın in western Turkey had to learn the hard way that, contrary to what the signboard at the entrance of their town said — "Germencik, the home of figs and geothermal" — figs and geothermal power plants could not co-exist. Large numbers of fig trees were cut down and huge pipes transporting geothermal fluids appeared in the village to pave the way for the establishment of geothermal power plants. As such, geothermal power development emerged as a key field of socioecological contestation in the late 2010s and led to the emergence of a new line of environmental opposition, which framed its message with the bold slogan "geothermal is the stepbrother of the atomic bomb" (Evrensel 2021).

In principle, geothermal energy is a highly efficient renewable energy source that taps into the heat stored in underground aquifers, which is essentially dissipated heat from earthquake fault lines and volcanic terrain (Spijkerboer et al. 2022). Multiple uses of geothermal exist due to differences in enthalpy (i.e., useful heat as the sum of internal energy) in different reservoirs: low enthalpy fields (providing heat around 20-70°C) are used for heating purposes in spas, swimming pools and fishponds, whereas high enthalpy fields (providing heat more than 150°C) are profitable for electricity generation. While dwarfed by massive growth in solar and wind energy and limited by its geographic availability, geothermal energy continues to be a highly attractive energy source due to its baseload capabilities. It can produce 24/7 for 365 days a year; hence it does not have the intermittency problems of solar and wind when the sun doesn't shine or wind doesn't blow.

However, the Turkish geothermal sector, by and large, remained dormant until the liberalization of the energy sector in the early 2000s. The enactment of a law on Geothermal Resources and Natural Mineralized Waters in 2007 immediately led to the privatization of existing geothermal sites and the wholesale of licenses to drill (Kutlu 2020). Consequently, the installed capacity of electricity generation from geothermal power plants skyrocketed from 15 MW to 1,686 MW between 2005 and 2022 (with an average annual increase of 40 percent), placing Turkey in the fourth position globally. This massive growth, however, was not distributed equally across the country. It remained geographically concentrated in two regions — Gediz and Büyük Menderes — both of which have been home to some of the most agriculturally productive lands of western Anatolia for millennia. With underground temperatures reaching up to 295°C, these regions were targeted by two thirds of all geothermal power plant investments between 2011 and 2021.

This "gold rush" to geothermal power generation was enabled by the government's feed-in-tariff mechanism (YEKDEM), which provided windfall profits for geothermal investors and was backed up with cheap credit lines and risk-sharing mechanisms offered by international financial institutions such as the World Bank and the European Bank for Reconstruction and Development (EBRD). Despite the talk about local benefits of direct-use applications (such as greenhouse heating, district heating, etc.), it is quite telling that the bulk of the investment materialized in electricity generation due to lucrative deals for geothermal companies.

This situation led to rapid, albeit unplanned, growth of geothermal power generation where multiple overlapping licenses were often handed out over two-dimensional parcels with no attention to the integrity of three-dimensional reservoirs and subterranean structures (Chamber of Mechanical Engineers 2022). Adding insult to injury were the reports showing that geothermal power plants in Gediz and Büyük Menderes regions were by no means zero-carbon investments and, due to specific geological conditions, were in fact emitting CO_2 almost on par with coal-fired power plants (Hirtenstein 2016).[2] This finding led the EBRD and the Ministry of Environment and Urbanization to conduct a Cumulative Impact Assessment study in 2020, whose findings indicated a serious lack of social and environmental checks and balances. However, due to the lack of comprehensive monitoring of geothermal emissions, attempts to legally challenge geothermal investments for their environmental impacts often fail.

As the reported cases of socioecological impacts[3] increased, opposition to geothermal power plants also became increasingly visible at the national level in the late 2010s. The geographic concentration of geothermal power plants and drilling operations in one of the most fertile agricultural-export zones of Turkey led the grassroots opposition to use a multitude of tactics and strategies, handed over from earlier environmental movements in the region and beyond. First of all, the proliferation of anti-geothermal struggles in Gediz and Büyük Menderes regions led to a consolidation of opposition groups in well-connected activist platforms such as Aydın Environmental Platform (AYÇEP), Germencik Environmental Platform, and Aydın Ecology Platform. Particularly AYÇEP's activism — which merged legal action, confrontational tactics against company representatives (in one case leading to the detention of a drilling operations manager by local village women only to be saved by gendarmerie later on) and political lobbying — yielded a significant success in delaying or cancelling a number of geothermal projects.

Yet these tactics to counter the geothermal offensive faced an increasingly uneven playing field where market and state actors co-operate. One clear instance of this was the case of the deputy governor of Aydın, when his pictures on a luxury boat with geothermal power plant owners surfaced (Akdemir 2020). Earlier, following an attack by gendarmerie under his command against villagers protesting geothermal drilling operations, he was recorded on camera suggesting "it's only pepper spray, you are exaggerating it." On the one hand, confrontational direct action through the establishment of impromptu guard-posts at the village entrance often leads to arrests of many villagers. On the other hand, costly legal actions against the state and companies often face defeat in the courtrooms, or at best provide manoeuvring space to companies to amend their projects on the basis of incomplete environmental impact assessments.

Last but not least, by mobilizing political action through lobbying, these movements managed to get the biggest opposition party in the parliament (CHP) to prepare a special report on the environmental impacts of geothermal power plants — the first of its kind — in which a mainstream political party actively calls for a moratorium on new geothermal licenses in the Gediz and Büyük Menderes regions. By referring to the "ecological devastation" wreaked by geothermal power plants, which is not experienced as a "clean energy" model in the region, this report calls for compulsory cumulative impact assessments, the removal of exceptions and privileges granted to power plants in operation, the enforcement of basin-wise strategic planning and the strengthening of energy cooperatives to take ownership of local geothermal resources.

Women protesting geothermal power plant in Mezeköy, Aydın in front of the military police barricade. Photo credit: Deniz Mine Öztürk.

Counter-hegemonic struggles for energy democracy

Arguably, what matters most for the communities at the frontlines of energy transformation is the democratic ownership, planning and control of renewable energy sources. Whether it is to reap the power of water running down mountains, as in the case of hydropower, or to harness the heat under our feet, as in the case of geothermal power, the state's preferential treatment of private interests over the common good in Turkey has created and continues to create local struggles. Overcoming this conundrum will require not only ensuring social acceptance from communities, but also their active involvement in navigating the energy transformation so that it fulfils their needs, demands and aspirations. Even under increasingly autocratic circumstances, uncanny coalitions of coercive state power and the capital's push to reap profits by creating consent with "green talk" can no longer yield social acceptance in Turkey. The limits of authoritarian energy governance are now being drawn by ecologist movements politicizing their actions through a triad of popular mobilization, courtroom battles and political lobbying (Şorman and Turhan 2022).

Although the anti-hydropower and anti-geothermal movements took root in different periods and in different spatial contexts, it is clear that there are a lot of commonalities in their discourses to confront the hegemonic energy offensive of Erdoğan's government. While these movements share repertoires of contention in their actions on the street, in the courtroom and in the halls of political power, they have also shaped the trajectory of grassroots environmentalism in Turkey — a dynamic we refer to as counterhegemonic flows.

For instance, what emerged as local discontent against urgent expropriations, in both cases often rapidly evolved into discourses questioning the real need for energy in the country. In a similar fashion, the historical continuities between the anti-hydropower and anti-geothermal movements can be traced back to similar languages of valuation[4] against the destruction of rural livelihoods (as exemplified by the importance assigned to nonhuman nature in both cases, merging the defence of land with the defence of water, fish, figs and olives). It will not be an overstatement to suggest that participants of these movements had their trust in the state injured and started questioning the real role of the state, after facing the rural police defending private interests with batons and pepper spray and, to their surprise, witnessing the state siding with energy companies. In many instances, local communities opposing hydroelectric plants or geothermal power plants expressed that their feelings had been betrayed and let down by the state — a common rupture point leading to the questioning of the sovereign rule, which shaped these movements' discourses and actions.

Thus, the continuities and ruptures we observe between these spatially and temporally distinct moments of opposition are due to the ongoing transformation of environmental activism in the country. The proliferation of the anti-hydropower movement partly paved the way for the Gezi Park protests in 2013. And as a result of the Gezi protest episode (another big rupture point), discourses and actions of local opposition movements became widely heard at the national level, leading to the formation of the Ecology Union (*Ekoloji Birliği*), a national platform of grassroots ecologist movements. Such platforms enable mutual learning between activists in their fights against coal-fired power plants, extractivism, urban transformation or green grabbing by renewable energy projects. This mutual learning also helped produce counterhegemonic knowledge by grassroots groups through their interaction with other activists, networks of likeminded scholars (mostly political ecologists), lawyers, politicians and different social movement participants (see, for instance, the work of Center for Spatial Justice 2019).

Finally, it can be said that the flows of capital and coercive power in the capillaries of the Turkish state do not go uncontested, even if this comes at a price for the local communities involved. The material flows of water, be it from rivers or from underground reservoirs, only make meaning insofar as there is a community to take the control and channel these flows to the improvement of their living conditions. However, the state-sanctioned transformation of material flows of resources into commodities aiming at the fastest return on investment happens at the expense of material and immaterial values of anti-hydropower and anti-geothermal activists in Turkey. This calls us political ecologists to shed further light on the histories and politics of socio-natures as well as the visions of energy democracy, as propagated by communities from the ground up. We consider it essential to explore how materialities of energy flows can be read side by side with the ebbs and flows of environmental justice movements, paying attention to counterhegemony as flows of ideas, actions and people.

This is also a call to go beyond the defensive. We argue that ecological activism needs to think actively towards a convergence of mass popular mobilization, transformative legal action, and radical politics positioning local communities at the helm of power in energy transition. In the absence of this triad, the emergent possibilities of a socioecological transformation may easily swing towards right-wing rural populism (Karataşlı and Kumral 2023). Assembling an emancipatory energy system that doesn't trespass ecological limits will require not only attention to alternative visions of the future but also to a re-definition of collective material well-being. Until then, as the impacts of hydropower on the lifeline support of rural communities continue to grow or the aggressive build-up of geothermal boreholes crisscrossing rural landscapes expand, so will the repertoires of contention of grassroots movements to counter these claims of "clean energy."

Notes

1. Original in Turkish is "Derelerin Kardeşliği Platformu" (DEKAP) and is also translated in some texts as the "Sisterhood" or "Brotherhood" of Streams/Rivers.
2. This is mainly due to the calcareous geology of these regions with high geothermal potential. Subterranean limestone emits significant carbon dioxide when it comes in contact with high-temperature steam. Recent modelling studies suggest that these emissions gradually decline as geothermal operations continue.
3. Reported impacts include: dispossession due to urgent expropriation decisions; decline in yield/quality in agricultural products; environmental damages due to misconduct in geothermal operations (e.g., discharge of geothermal fluids to water bodies running through villages); odor problems due to excessive H_2S emissions; and impacts on public health due to heavy metal accumulation in ground and surface waters.
4. One can associate values to nature beyond monetary measures and different languages of valuation may exist regarding the sacredness of nature, environmental justice, livelihoods, rights of nature and so on (Zografos 2023).

References

Akbulut, Bengi, Fikret Adaman, and Murat Arsel. 2018. "Troubled Waters of Hegemony: Consent and Contestation in Turkey's Hydropower Landscapes." In F. Menga and E. Swyngedouw (eds.), *Water, Technology and the Nation-State*. Abingdon: Routledge.

Akdemir, Özer. 2020. "Aydın Vali Yardımcısının JES'çilerle yat keyfi tartışma yarattı." *Evrensel*, May 16, 2020. At <evrensel.net/haber/404906/aydin-vali-yardimcisi-nin-jescilerle-yat-keyfi-tartisma-yaratti>.

Aksu, Cemil, Sinan Erensü, and Erdem Evren (eds.). 2016. *Sudan Sebepler: Türkiye'de Neoliberal Su-Enerji Politikaları ve Direnişleri*. Istanbul: İletişim.

Altınörs, Görkem, and Ümit Akçay. 2022. "Authoritarian Neoliberalism, Crisis, and Consolidation: The Political Economy of Regime Change in Turkey." *Globalizations* 19, 7.

Aydın, Cem İskender. 2019. "Identifying Ecological Distribution Conflicts around the Inter-regional Flow of Energy in Turkey: A Mapping Exercise." *Frontiers in Energy Research* 7, 33.

Bayülgen, Oksan. 2022. *Twisting in the Wind: The Politics of Tepid Transitions to Renewable Energy*. Ann Arbor: University of Michigan Press.

Center for Spatial Justice. 2019. "Melet: Bütunleşik Havza Yıkımı (Melet: Integrated Basin Destruction)." March 2019. At <mekandaadalet.org/wp-content/uploads/2020/09/MELET-BUTUNLESIK-HAVZA-YIKIMI.pdf>.

Chamber of Mechanical Engineers. 2022. "Türkiye'nin Enerji Görünümü 2022." At <mmo.org.tr/kitaplar/turkiyenin-enerji-gorunumu-2022>.

Eren, Ayşen. 2018. "Transformation of the Water-Energy Nexus in Turkey: Reimagining Hydroelectricity Infrastructure." *Energy Research & Social Science* 41.

Erensü, Sinan. 2013a. "Abundance and Scarcity Amidst the Crisis of 'Modern Water': The Changing Water-Energy Nexus in Turkey." In L.M. Harris, J.A. Goldin, and C. Sneddon (eds.), *Contemporary Water Governance in the Global South: Scarcity, Marketization and Participation*. Abingdon: Routledge.

_____. 2013b. "Gezi Parkı Direnişinin İlhamını Yerelde Aramak." *Bianet*, June 10, 2013. At <bianet.org/bianet/siyaset/147400-gezi-parki-direnisinin-ilhamini-yerelde-aramak>.

_____. 2018. "The Contradictions of Turkey's Rush to Energy." *Middle East Report* 288.

Evrensel. 2021. "Danıştay, Uzundere'ye JES projesinin iptal kararını onadı." July 18, 2021. At <evrensel.net/haber/442991/danistay-uzundereye-jes-projesinin-iptal-kararini-onadi>.

Gümüş, B. 2024. "Türkiye Electricity Review 2024." At <ember-climate.org/app/uploads/2024/03/Turkiye-Electricity-Review-2024.pdf>.

Güven, Ali Burak. 2022. "Towards a New Political Economy of Turkish Capitalism: Three Worlds." *Turkish Studies* 24, 1.

Harris, Leila M., and Mine Islar. 2014. "Neoliberalism, Nature, and Changing Modalities of Environmental Governance in Contemporary Turkey." In Y. Atasoy (ed.), *Global Economic Crisis and the Politics of Diversity*. London: Palgrave MacMillan.

Hirtenstein, Anna. 2016. "These Clean Energy Projects Pollute More than Coal Power Plants." *Bloomberg*, July 21, 2016. At <bloomberg.com/news/articles/2016-07-21/these-clean-energy-projects-pollute-more-than-coal-power-plants?leadSource=uverify%20wall>.

Islar, Mine. 2012. "Privatised Hydropower Development in Turkey: A Case of Water Grabbing?" *Water Alternatives* 5, 2.

Karataşlı, Şahan Savaş, and Şefika Kumral. 2023. "Crisis of Capitalism and Cycles of Right-wing Populism in Contemporary Turkey: The Making and Unmaking of Erdoğanist Hegemony." *Journal of Agrarian Change* 23, 1.

Knuth, Sarah, Ingrid Behrsin, Anthony Levenda, and James McCarthy. 2022. "New Political Ecologies of Renewable Energy." *Environment and Planning E: Nature and Space* 5, 3.

Kutlu, Kutay. 2020. "'Yeşil devlet' kavramı ve Türkiye'deki yenilenebilir enerji politikası. / The concept of 'green state' and renewable energy policy in Turkey." PhD Thesis, Marmara University Department of Political Science and International Relations. At <tez.yok.gov.tr/UlusalTezMerkezi/tezSorguSonucYeni.jsp>.

Kutlu, Kutay. 2022. "The Need to Look Beyond the Right to Property: An Assessment of the Constitutional Court of Turkey's Judgments on Urgent Expropriations for Hydropower Plants." In I. Borsuk, P. Dinç, S. Kavak and P. Sayan (eds.), *Authoritarian Neoliberalism and Resistance in Turkey: Construction, Consolidation and Contestation*. Singapore: Palgrave Macmillan.

Ministry of Energy and Natural Resources. 2022. "Türkiye Ulusal Enerji Planı (Turkey's National Energy Plan)." At <enerji.gov.tr//Media/Dizin/EIGM/tr/Raporlar/TUEP/T%C3%BCrkiye_Ulusal_Enerji_Plan%C4%B1.pdf>.

Minitry of Foreign Affairs. n.d. "Turkey's International Energy Strategy." At <mfa.gov.tr/turkeys-energy-strategy.en.mfa>.

Özkaynak, Begüm, Cem İskender Aydın, Pınar Ertör-Akyazı, and Irmak Ertör. 2015. "The Gezi Park Resistance from an Environmental Justice and Social Metabolism Perspective." *Capitalism Nature Socialism* 26, 1.

Özkaynak, Begüm, Ethemcan Turhan, and Cem İskender Aydın. 2020. "The Politics of Energy in Turkey: Running Engines on Geopolitical, Discursive, and Coercive Power." In G.M. Tezcür (ed.), *The Oxford Handbook of Turkish Politics*. Oxford: Oxford University Press.

Şekercioğlu, Çağan H., Sean Anderson, Erol Akçay et al. 2011. "Turkey's Globally Important Biodiversity in Crisis." *Biological Conservation* 144, 12.

Şorman, Alevgül H., and Ethemcan Turhan. 2022. "The Limits of Authoritarian Energy Governance: Energy, Democracy and Public Contestation in Turkey." In M. Nadesan, M. Pasqualetti and J. Keahey (eds.), *Energy Democracies for Sustainable Futures*. Amsterdam: Elsevier.

Spijkerboer, Rozanne C., Ethemcan Turhan, Andreas Roos et al. 2022. "Out of Steam? A Social Science and Humanities Research Agenda for Geothermal Energy." *Energy Research & Social Science* 92.

Turhan, Ethemcan, Begüm Özkaynak, and Cem İskender Aydın. 2019. "Coal, Ash, and Other Tales: The Making and Remaking of the Anti-Coal Movement in Aliağa, Turkey." In O. İnal and E. Turhan (eds.), *Transforming Socio-Natures in Turkey: Landscapes, State and Environmental Movements*. Abingdon: Routledge.

Yaka, Özge. 2018. "Rethinking Justice: Struggles for Environmental Commons and the Notion of Socio-Ecological Justice." *Antipode* 51, 1.

Zografos, Christos. 2023. "Languages of Valuation." In S. Villamayor-Tomas and R. Muradian (eds.), *The Barcelona School of Ecological Economics and Political Ecology: A Companion in Honour of Joan Martinez-Alier*. Cham: Springer

PART FOUR

FEMINISMS

INTRODUCTION TO PART FOUR

Panagiota Kotsila, Ilenia Iengo and Irene Leonardelli

How do socioenvironmental movements construct alliances and coevolve with feminist movements' theories, activism and praxis, against the current backdrop of the climate crisis? For more than forty years, we have seen the emergence and collision of debates and struggles binding together different forms of feminism and environmentalism. Irreducible to one-dimensional genealogies, the contributions of feminist thinking to environmental questions have been and continue to be manifold. Feminist issues, like gender-based violence and inequalities, care work, knowledge/power dynamics in society, the making of subjectivity, are brought together to critically interrogate environmental conflicts, the social construction of nature, and imaginaries of better socioecological futures. At the same time, in a climate-altered world where connections between local and global scales, and between human and more-than-human life and well-being, are becoming more visible and powerful than ever, environmental and climate justice issues open up different and deeper questions about how extractivism and environmental degradation relate to gender-based injustices, the devaluing of the work of socioecological reproduction, and the increasingly contested nexus between health and environment.

Gender-based struggles around access to environmental resources, and sociopolitical processes related to their management and use, have been historically at the centre of confronting patriarchal systems of power in society. The interests and practices around specific ecological processes and resource management have been heavily gendered. The role of women, for example, in creating and protecting land and food commons, and the impacts they experienced as a result of land dispossessions, informed women's struggles to resist the commercialization of agriculture (Federici 2012). Ecofeminism, as a composite field of activism and thought, has drawn the links between the parallel domination of women (and other subordinated groups and identities) and of nature, via patriarchy and extractive capitalism, and has inspired environmental movements across the world. Similar struggles can be traced to a result of unequal and gendered impacts of environmental pollution on women's health, but questions of environmental justice and politics have moved beyond a mono-dimensional consideration of gender and towards an intersectional analysis of such exposures, vulnerabilities and impacts. Intersectionality, a concept rooted in Black feminism, highlights how gender, race, class, sexuality and ability, among other aspects of social differentiation, are co-constituted (Crenshaw 1991). In relation to socio-environmental movements, an intersectional lens recognizes the plurality of experiences related to environmental and climate impacts depending on how people are situated along different intersecting axes of oppression and privilege (Ranganathan 2017).

Feminisms have further contributed to a deeper epistemological questioning of concepts and "grand narratives" stemming from Western knowledge traditions and tied to the interpretation and control of nature. In fact, the very dualism of nature versus society is part of the logic serving to sustain other dualisms such as reason/matter, male/female, mind/body, master/slave, subject/object, or culture/nature. Such normalized categories and dichotomies build on knowledge/power dynamics reveal how no knowledge produced is "neutral" or free of bias, but contingent to power relations. Feminisms bring about an understanding of science as an embodied and situated process of knowledge production, where subjugated perspectives can provide partial and critical accounts of the world (Haraway 1988). From the inclusion of gender questions in development of the 1950s to the ecofeminism of the 1970s, and landing to current feminist and decolonial political ecologies (Harcourt et al. 2023) elaborations, feminisms have provided extensive critiques of mainstream discourses around progress and development that normalized environmental injustice and promoted modernization and growth at all costs, while reproducing and sustaining colonial dynamics and discourses that erased different cosmovisions while marginalizing and erasing whole communities.

Bringing feminism into environmentalism also involved engagement with and inspiration from queer theories. This meant to queer our ideas of "nature" and "natural," including aspects of gender and health, and to understand how sexual relations "organize and influence both the material world of nature and our perceptions, experiences, and constitutions of that world" (Mortimer-Sandilands and Erickson 2010). In their chapter, Kusiani and Kotsila bring together insights from queer ecologies, queer environmentalism and urban political ecology, to contesting heteronormative urban environments and the way they are mobilized by neoliberal growth-oriented institutions in order to reorganize and control previously "unruly" socionatures, such as those inhabited by and coevolving with sexual dissidents, non-binary and queer communities in a green area of Tbilisi, Georgia. They show how these unruly natures served to provide a place of refuge, of personal expression and of work, for which becoming imperceptible was a crucial tactic of survival, but also of subversion and resistance.

Foregrounding the importance of gender equality for implementing socially just and ecologically sustainable food systems, Desmarais and Calvário's chapter presents the case of La Vía Campesina, a global movement bringing together 182 organizations of peasants, small-scale farmers, rural women, Indigenous peoples and farmworkers. They reflect on how a feminist perspective came to be central to the movement only after years of women's commitment and work to gain more space. In particular, they point to how feminist activism was fundamental in shaping food sovereignty as a political project within the movement, and to propose it as an alternative and radical critique to neoliberal rural development and food politics. This project importantly entails addressing all violence against discriminated and marginalized groups in its multiple forms and spaces, including homes, fields and organizations, as well as ensuring that actions are grounded in local realities.

Starting from the lived experiences of Indigenous, peasant and rural women fighting against multiple forms of violence and dispossession in Abya Yala, Cruz Hernández's chapter presents the body-territory-land conceptualization. The mobilization of this concept is at the centre of different *territorial community feminisms* building collective strategies and southern alliances against the interweaving of neocolonialism, capitalism and patriarchy. The juxtaposition of body, territory and land is not just a linear, symbolic continuity but is rooted in the understanding of the body, especially of rural, Indigenous, Black and impoverished women and gender-non-conforming people as the first territory that is subject to being conquered, violated and contaminated, while, at the same time, it is the material site of resistance and liberation from oppression and violence, both within the local community and at the state and international corporate level. Cruz Hernández clarifies that territorial community feminism should not be inscribed within a specific feminist wave. Rather, these struggles embodied by Indigenous, peasant and rural women constitute a crack in colonial temporalities, breaking linear Eurocentric understandings and instead propose an ontology of interdependence rooted in alliances and resistances of bodies-territories-land (Colectivo de Miradas Críticas del Territorio desde el Feminismo 2019).

References

Colectivo Miradas Críticas del Territorio desde el Feminismo. 2019. "(Re) Patriarcalización de los territorios. La lucha de las mujeres y los megaproyectos extractivos." In T.D. Cruz Hernández and M. Bayón Jiménez (eds.), *Cuerpos, territorios y feminismos: Compilación latinoamericana de teorías, metodologías y prácticas políticas*. Quito: Ediciones Abya-Yala.

Crenshaw, Kimberlé. 1991. "Mapping the Margins: Intersectionality, Identity Politics, and Violence against Women of Color." *Stanford Law Review* 43.

Federici, Silvia. 2012. *Revolution at Point Zero: Housework, Reproduction, and Feminist Struggle*. Oakland, CA: PM Press.

Haraway, Donna. 1988. "Situated Knowledges: The Science Question in Feminism and the Privilege of Partial Perspective." *Feminist Studies* 14, 3.

Harcourt, Wendy, Ana Agostino, Rebecca Elmhirst, Marlen Gomez, and Panagiota Kotsila (eds.). 2023. *Contours of Feminist Political Ecology*. Cham: Palgrave Macmillan.

Mortimer-Sandilands, Catriona, and Bruce Erickson. 2010. *Queer Ecologies: Sex, Nature, Politics, Desire*. Bloomington: Indiana University Press.

Ranganathan, Malini. 2017. "The Environment as Freedom: A Decolonial Reimagining." Social Science Research Council. *Items*, June 13. At <items.ssrc.org/just-environments/the-environment-as-freedom-a-decolonial-reimagining/>.

QUEER CRUISERS AND SEX WORKERS RESISTING AND REDEFINING URBAN SOCIONATURES IN TBILISI, GEORGIA

Tornike Kusiani and Panagiota Kotsila

The activism of queer sex workers and cruisers as they resist urban "green" redevelopment in Tbilisi, Georgia, contributes a queer environmental justice lens to urban politics and movements that focuses on how sexuality and sexual relations organize and influence both the material world of cities and our perceptions, experiences, and constitutions of them (Mortimer-Sandilands and Erickson 2010). This chapter focuses on one such "unruly green space" of resistance — the Heroes Square in the centre of the city. The term "queer" refers to non-heterosexuality, and in general to a critique of gender binaries and normativity. As such, it also allows questioning and queering other socially constructed dichotomies, such as that of nature versus culture. The queer lens helps us to capture the hetero-ecological dynamics of urban green space developments and suggests ways to dismantle hetero/homo binaries embodied in them, while also situating sexuality within complex systems of power in urban developments (Heynen 2018).

In this chapter we look at how queer communities are affected by and may transcend processes of neoliberal urbanism — understood as the privatization and/or redevelopment of public space for the benefit of private investors, the tourist or real estate industry, or economic growth in general — as often happens through big urban greening or regeneration interventions. We address this question by looking at the everyday practices and collective actions of queer communities at Heroes Square. We draw on queer and intersectional urban political ecology approaches that question how urban space and nature are imagined and (re)produced through power, and often concern the conflict between heteronormative urban planning versus queer (urban) ecologies (Mortimer-Sandilands

2016). A queer ecological lens can facilitate understandings of how different forms of eco-queer activism can shape urbanism, including by building solidarities and new coalitions between green and queer actors in civil society.

Urban redevelopment in Heroes Square, Tbilisi, Georgia, during the years 2009–2019 transformed local ecologies and infrastructures but also pushed towards the exclusion of queer communities who used this space both for socializing, cruising, and sex work. By urban greening we understand the kinds of changes made in the material infrastructure of urban green and non-green environments (buildings, abandoned facilities, etc.) to create ecological amenities such as gardens, green buildings (walls, roofs, yards), renovated plantations, green streets, etc. (Anguelovski et al. 2020). We revisit ongoing and past struggles, paying attention to connections among sites, scales and subjectivities, and critiquing urban redevelopment strategies through which silencing and violence takes place in heteronormative, sexist, and racist societies.

We base our study on the textual discourse analysis of media materials, as well as on eight qualitative interviews with members of the queer community as part of participatory ethnography, and activist research conducted during the summer of 2019 by Tornike Kusiani, with the theoretical and analytical contribution of Panagiota Kotsila. During the research, our ontological stance is not "strong objectivism," but "partial objectivism," as Haraway (1991) suggests. Tornike is a queer, non-binary person, who has lived in Tbilisi and has to some degree shared the struggles with people involved in this research, having professional and leisure connections with Heroes Square, and having been the victim of police brutality in public spaces because of his queer identity. Holding this insider-outsider status (Dwyer and Buckle 2009) allowed Tornike to build connections with participants, while being conscious of the fact that our informants stand on very different positions and were highly vulnerable to violence due to their gender identity and work.

These stories shed light on how queer communities are persevering defendants of public and inclusive urban natures, despite their persistent marginalization and continuous targeting often camouflaged behind urban redevelopment plans from the City Hall and backed up by police violence, while also facing discrimination from passersby. Through their everyday struggles and resistances, queer communities contribute to questioning processes of heteronormative urban planning, speaking to intersectional socioenvironmental justice in terms of distribution, recognition, and participation in relation to greening (Anguelovski et al. 2020). The practices of queer communities bring into light ways in which: relationships between communities and urban space/nature are nourished; place attachment, place dependence and place-based identities are created (Steil and Delgado 2019); transgressive and disobedient socioecological existences are carved out.

Discrimination and violence against LGBTQIA+ in Georgia

In Georgia, LGBTQIA+ people are among the most discriminated groups, and their rights of assembly and expression are limited. LGBTQIA+ visibility is manipulated and distorted in the discourses and propaganda of homosexuality by ultranationalists or religious groups[1] to further exclude them from public spaces and turn public opinion against them. The self-proclaiming centre-left governing party — Georgian dream (ქართული ოცნება) — has been using such precedents of violence since 2012 to cause fear and intimidate LGBTQIA+ activists in terms of the safety of any upcoming demonstrations. In essence, the queer community struggles to obtain guarantees for protection and safety during such events from the government. Some have reported that the government is working with ultranationalists to cause fear and force the queer community to pull back from demonstrating. By doing so, they satisfy the homophobic sentiments of their electorate, while not appearing to officially ban such demonstrations and thus avoiding international pressure and criticism.[2]

As an example, on the International Day Against Homophobia, Transphobia and Biphobia (IDAHOT) — which was first celebrated in the country in 2012 — the Orthodox Church repeatedly mobilizes haters against the LGBTQIA+ community, claiming that its visibility is a "propaganda of homosexuality." In 2013, thirty thousand men, including priests, attacked queer activists while the government did nearly nothing to protect protesters. Every year since, every attempt for visibility, whether a Pride march or an IDAHOT demonstration, has been the target of violent attacks. Such attacks reflect geopolitical tensions, too (see endnote 2). In 2018 the LGBTQIA+ community refused to hold an IDAHOT demonstration in order to avoid the risk of being violently attacked, but also as a rejection of continuing to be instruments of mainstream political actors in their campaign against the country's entry in the European Union. This gave more ground to existing discourses from parts of the left that LGBTQIA+ issues are not relevant or are overshadowing more important axes of struggle like class and labour politics, with some actors from the left even linking identity politics to Western imperialism and capitalism. It is noteworthy that since 2018, LGBTQIA+ activists were often excluded from Georgia's left-wing spaces and attempts to build coalitions between queer movements and mainstream leftists have ended in calls to: "lower the flag." They have been told "now is not the time," and "do not stand here."

At the same time, the queer communities have been experiencing a long history of policing and violence in Tbilisi. Our interviewees recalled different instances and forms of oppression, with police, for example, occasionally detaining sex workers to gather information, refusing to let clients pull over, or telling them that having a transgender person in the car is illegal. Police have also assisted perpetrators in preparing charges against transgender women to gather proof of sex work. As one interviewee said, "If we protested these behaviours or aggressive males hitting us, the police would utilize these methods to punish us." The excessive presence and violence of the police around places where queers and sex workers use to socialize or work has been normalized to the public opinion under a discourse of public safety.

Even though the binary and heteronormative views on gender and sexuality shrink the public space for LGBTQIA+ people — so that they often limit themselves to exclusively private spaces — they have also employed a constellation of counter-practices to challenge dominant discourse around public space usage. One such place is the centrally located Heroes Square, occupying approximately 0.56 km² in the centre of the city. This space has been, since the early 2000s, the largest central location for cruising[3] and sex work in Tbilisi. The woodland area features a vast network of paths leading to the Circus building, which is positioned at the centre and serves as the forest's distinguishing feature. This land is now encircled by walls, with two entrances and several secret entrances through the woods. The queer community calls it *"pleshka,"* which is a name of cruising space from the Soviet Union times.

The entire woodland is a mix of public and private land, whose ownership and management (public/private) are not clearly apparent to the public. This makes the park correspond to Gandy's description of "unruly spaces": without a "clearly defined role, or which are characterized by ill-defined use or ownership, or that have been appropriated for uses other than those for which they were originally intended" (Gandy 2006: 734). Such spaces, engaged by the queer community, expose the characteristics of queer-green space illuminating material and cultural constellations in connection to nature. These "queer natures" forge a reconceptualization and reappropriation of urban ecological marginal territory. These connections subvert the active production of "straight" (hetero)sexualized spaces (Binnie 1997: 223) and remind us of how efforts to control, manage and design nature emanate from imaginaries of "wild natures" connected to deviant sexualities (Mortimer-Sandilands and Erickson 2010). In short, queer communities in Heroes Square have been actively questioning and embodying the denial of socionatural spaces as reflecting particular sexual subjectivities, as they fight against discourses of heteronormativity embedded in mainstream urban nature management practices and conceptualizations.

Queering resistance through marginal urban nature

Urban nature as a place of identity formation and survival for queer communities

Queer communities have always engaged with urban nature, reclaiming their place in urban space. In Tbilisi there were at least ten urban areas where queer communities were largely present, embodying the "unruliness" of ill-defined use/ownership of those spaces — ranging from abandoned buildings with some green cover, to railways, to very centrally located squares. Such spaces offered possibility of cruising, considering the need to keep visibility low. Nevertheless, urban growth has taken over most of these spaces, except for Heroes Square. This space provides a natural shelter and safety for the expression of non-heteronormative forms of gender and sexuality. While trans sex workers need to be cis-passing for safety reasons in public, the shadows of trees and the secret passages allow transgender women to change their clothes, having to go there with the clothing that reflects the gender they were assigned at birth. Often, when young transgender women are kicked out of their homes, these spaces become their only shelter; newcomers or homeless queers often sleep in the woods before they earn enough to rent an apartment. Such spaces bring them economic income, as the unruliness of the space also attracts men who are seeking sex with men or trans sex workers. Sex workers can follow their clients or use the woodlands, which is safer than a private room, as they can ask for help if the client attacks them or refuses to pay. Sofia, a transgender sex worker, says, "we are a community, we stand together, and we fight together; we often have to protect each other from group attacks or police raids."

In the winter, such urban nature also provides protection from the cold. Trans sex workers often clear it from branches and burn them to get warm. They carve out new passageways, find new entrances and clean up the natural waste of the woodland. Such practices constantly change urban nature biophysically but also in terms of meanings and provisions. The queers of Heroes Square have a relationship with its urban ecologies that is not based on idealizing or monumentalizing urban nature but surviving from and through it. Moreover, such practices promote place attachment and contribute to formation of place-based identity. While they survive through the space utilizing its ecological amenities or earning money, they also call each other different adjectives directly connected to space, such as *"tsirkis bozo"* (circus slut) or *"pleshkis bozo"* (pleshka slut) and many others, proudly embracing such terms.

The heteronormative discourse of urban redevelopment and its impact on the queer community

Heroes Square suffered its first urban change already in 1935, as the newly constructed King Tamar Avenue divided the woodland into a northern and eastern part, cutting the rocky hill northeast of the square. Among other developments, King Tamar Bridge was constructed between 1932 and 1937, along with an eleven-storey tower house on the square in 1939, followed by the Circus complex on the hillside in 1940. As a result, what used to be a significant green public area became an aggressively car-oriented infrastructure.

The most recent redevelopment of Heroes Square started with the City Hall paying 40 million euros to private companies to design and construct a 252-metre reinforced concrete monolithic highway that overpasses Heroes Square between 2009 and 2013. During the same period, the road connecting to Heroes Square in Vere River valley was constructed. Street action by local neighbours followed the announcement of this project, and locals collected nearly two thousand signatures against its construction, contesting the destruction of existing natural landscapes and the increase of car traffic.

It is worth noting that public space had been shrinking since a new bureaucratic unit was instituted in the Tbilisi City Government in 2009 — the "Zonal Council" has jurisdiction to decide how and what to develop. In nine years, more than 25,000 applications were submitted and approved to build taller and broader than officially permitted, and to change the land status to allow for construction. The Tbilisi City Hall issued these paid permits as one-time exceptions, while the city government — the main investors — has paid more than 18 million euros towards such permits. In this way, private developers have shown their power in changing the very fabric of the city, as a clear expression of neoliberal urbanism unfolding in Tbilisi. This has created and exploited sociospatial disparities, while benefiting investors, constructors, and political elites.

In 2010, the mountain rock demolition in Heroes Square started. Since then, plenty of work has been done on Heroes Square. Specifically, dismantling the existing fountain, cutting the trees, excavating, and covering the Heroes Square tunnel, laying asphalt pavement, installing streetlights, a protective wall, overpass metal railings, multicoloured lighting, and the beam from a war memorial. Such work has been done where trans and gay sex workers used to work. While gay sex workers left the space, trans sex workers relocated to one part of the park ("Tsirki raise") and cruising was pushed further into the woods. In short, the redevelopment was not only pushing sex workers and queers out of the park, but it also impacted the ecology of the Vere River valley, damaging its perennial plants, and affected the wider public, turning Heroes Square from a green amenity to an aggressively car-dominated traffic hub.

These changes were accompanied by significant economic investments and public funds circulation from the City Council to private companies. City Hall conducted two calls for tenders for construction and allowed private companies to operate against the city development plan. For cutting down the trees, which could be treated instead, and placing potted variegated ivy plants all over the overpasses, the city hired the tender-winning company Greenservice, which belonged to a former politician. The official service cost was 38,350.84 euros, with this being only part of a tenders Greenservice had won from 2010 to 2012 that was worth a total of 4 million euros. However, Tbilisi remains one of the least green cities in the country and in Europe. Critiques point to how the motive behind the decisions related to greening is to circulate city funding to friendly businesses. A former employee of Greenservice realized the company planned to cut down the trees and sued the company in the prosecutor's office but was unsuccessful. In response, she started the biggest guerilla gardening protest in 2013, planting catalpa trees on the overpasses in Heroes Square, and was joined by trans women sex workers, symbolically marking the start of queer-environmental activism coalitions.

In 2015, a significant flood occurred in the Vere River valley in Tbilisi, resulting in at least twenty human deaths and impacting the Tbilisi Zoo, leaving half of its animal inhabitants either dead or on the loose. In Heroes Square, the tunnel and the underground were flooded too. While the highway was soon reopened, the underground was rehabilitated and opened again in 2017, with new painting works and surveillance cameras to rebrand the place as "clean" and free of "danger" and "crime," as the mayor proudly claimed. As part of the works, City Hall installed green grass cover, new paths, and a lighting system, as well as various new low growing plants, while at the same time, in 2018 again cutting down more pine trees in the woodland. The motivation of these changes was clear. The old underground, and the shade of the trees

The entrance of Heroes Square's underground before the repainting. Republished with permission from <facebook.com/gabo.ge>.

around the whole square, were places used by the queer community. On the walls of the underground, before the renovation, there existed paintings which displayed writings by cruisers and one massive rainbow illustration with the Georgian poet Kote Kubaneishvili's phrase on the wall: "whence it is dark inside, calmly inwards do slide." By erasing these paintings, the queer community itself was targeted for erasure. While City Hall was operating under a discourse of neutrality regarding urban nature and urban infrastructure, urban planning and redevelopment held an essential function in sociospatial governance, preserving a "government-sanctioned limitation of what actions in public places are considered suitable" (Catungal and McCann 2010: 85). Recognizing the value of urban green space but repeatedly removing trees was a ruse to eradicate queer bodies and practices and enforce heteronormativity in the neighbourhood. Coupled with the use of new lights and surveillance cameras, the redevelopment contributed to establishing a regime that acted as a behaviour filter.

The removal of tall trees and fences around the woodland exposed the space and restricted access to the woods for refuge or sex, and for transgender people to change their clothes. As well, the Circus administration started to frequently paint the benches where trans women sat to discourage their use. As a result, the risk of abuse during work increased for sex workers, as they had to start following their clients somewhere else. Instead of perceiving the new infrastructures of Heroes Square as apolitical and idle, we see these changes as intentional exposure and thus "as an active participant in the constitution and manipulation of urban society" (Gabriel 2014: 41). But these practices were not left unchallenged by the queer community itself.

Queer resistance and diversified strategies

Direct actions of resistance involved transgender sex workers planting new trees as part of guerrilla gardening activism and breaking new lights that were being installed in the woodland. Moreover, they deployed their deep knowledge of the space and carved out new passageways to continue using it. By trying to re-appropriate the natural conditions and restoring the characteristic shade produced by the woodland, they were challenging the very neoliberal nature of the revitalization process that aimed to take such conditions away from them. In 2017, an organization established by trans women — Transgender Women's Center

— requested that City Council name a small area "Transgender Square" in memory of transgender women who were victims of violence and oppression.

Although enforcing rules is a fundamental instrument of power, resistance manifests in people's yearning to find a place within uneven geographies, where space is denied, limited, and entirely governed (Keith and Pile 2013). Queer communities' resistance through their occupation and defence of "unruly spaces" represents a broader struggle for sociospatial and urban environmental justice. Comprehending the resistance of Heroes Square requires analyzing the ideas that refute the widely held belief that resistance is only about valiant struggles or grand gestures of opposition. Instead, resistance can frequently entail fights for empowerment and day-to-day survival. Typical forms of such resistance aim to occupy new areas, forge new geographies, and claim their place on the map (Scott 1986). In the case of the queer communities of Heroes Square, we see both day-to-day survival struggles during their work and in their interactions with the police or violent passersby, as well as more organized struggle for gaining visibility and bringing their problems and needs in the public political sphere. The media coverage they generated throughout their resistance is widespread, and the forms they utilized are provokingly self-sacrificial. For example, after being attacked, one transgender woman cut her stomach in Heroes Square to force protection from the police. Another one tried to burn herself on Labour Day (also known as International Workers' Day), on May 1, 2020, to draw attention to the livelihood challenges she was facing. Due to the COVID-19 pandemic and resulting quarantine, she could not work or use Heroes Square and thus could not pay for rent. "I am a transgender woman, and because the Georgian government does not care about me, I will kill myself," she said. In this context, a group of activists prepared a video about jobless transgender people to spread word about their struggles.

Despite transgender women involved in sex work experiencing one of the most criminalized, underpaid, and dangerous jobs, their working conditions were never a part of labour rights discussions in left-wing movements. Their oppression is often considered "cultural" and thus rendered insignificant or secondary. Often, during LGBTQIA+ demonstrations like IDAHOT day or the Pride parade, leftist environmental platforms like the Greens[4] in Georgia, often led by heterosexual men, would accuse queers of overshadowing economic oppression with identity politics. But queer activists have called for integrating their identity politics into the left movement. As mentioned, a suicide attempt by a transgender woman on May 1st was met with a disturbing indifference in left-wing circles, including by the Greens, as if trans-based oppression did not have an economic (and specifically, working class) dimension.

As a result, however, the queer members of the Greens did start to criticize a much-internalized homophobia of the party and asked the leadership to resign. In the following general assembly of the Greens, the leadership indeed resigned. Their new politics recognized that the oppression due to gender identity is inextricably linked to economic status, and a new leadership was elected consisting of queer, non-binary persons and women only. At the same time, new initiatives and approaches emerged. This includes some community gatherings/discussions promoted by the Greens and Pride to promote equality and support trans women.

Notes

1. Georgian National Unity, Alt Info, The Union of Orthodox Parents, to name a few.
2. Georgia has entered negotiations with European leaders to become part of the European Union, for which freedom of LGBTQIA+ assembly is a mandatory requirement. In public this feeds a tension: between becoming a European country with shared European values in freedom of expression and assembly and a post-soviet past rooted in sexism and homophobia, which is being celebrated with the support of Russian-led anti-LGBT and anti-European propaganda. The latter is often expressed through radical far-right groups and through targeted fake news in the mainstream media and social networks.
3. The practice of finding sex between men, usually anonymously and often in public or semi-public indoor and outdoor spaces, allowing bodily expression to function free from ideas about heteronormativity.
4. Greens are a queer-feminist movement that has existed for over fourteen years, with the ambition to create an intersectional political party.

References

Anguelovski, Isabelle, Anna Livia Brand, James JT Connolly et al. 2020. "Expanding the Boundaries of Justice in Urban Greening Scholarship: Toward an Emancipatory, Antisubordination, Intersectional, and Relational Approach." *Annals of the American Association of Geographers* 110, 6.

Binnie, Jon. 1997. "Coming out of Geography: Towards a Queer Epistemology?" *Environment and Planning D: Society and Space* 15, 2.

Catungal, John Paul, and Eugene J. McCann. 2010. "Governing Sexuality and Park Space: Acts of Regulation in Vancouver, BC." *Social & Cultural Geography* 11, 1.

Dwyer, Sonya Corbin, and Jennifer L. Buckle. 2009. "The Space Between: On Being an Insider-Outsider in Qualitative Research." *International Journal of Qualitative Methods* 8, 1: 54–63.

Gabriel, Nate. 2014. "Urban Political Ecology: Environmental Imaginary, Governance, and the Non-Human." *Geography Compass* 8, 1: 38–48.

Gandy, Matthew. 2006. "Urban Nature and the Ecological Imaginary." In N. Heynen, M. Kaika and E. Swyngedouw (eds.), *In the Nature of Cities: Urban Political Ecology and the Politics of Urban Metabolism,*. New York: Routledge.

Haraway, Donna, 1991. "Situated Knowledges: The Science Question in Feminism and the Privilege of Partial Perspective." In *Simians, Cyborgs and Women: The Reinvention of Nature*. London: Free Association Books.

Heynen, Nik. 2018. "Urban Political Ecology III: The Feminist and Queer Century." *Progress in Human Geography* 42, 3: 446–452.

Keith, Michael, and Steven Pile (eds.). 2013. *Geographies of Resistance*. London: Routledge.

Mortimer-Sandilands, Catriona, and Bruce Erickson. 2010. "Introduction: A Genealogy of Queer Ecologies." In *Queer Ecologies: Sex, Nature, Politics, Desire*. Bloomington: Indiana University Press.

Mortimer-Sandilands, Catriona. 2016. "Queer Ecology." In J. Adamson, W.A. Gleason, D.N. Pellow (eds.), *Keywords for Environmental Studies*. New York: New York University Press. 169–171.

Scott, James. 1986. "Everyday Forms of Peasant Resistance." *The Journal of Peasant Studies* 13, 2: 5–35.

Steil, Justin P., and Laura Humm Delgado. 2019. "Limits of Diversity: Jane Jacobs, the Just City, and Anti-Subordination." *Cities* 91: 39–48.

RADICALIZING FOOD SOVEREIGNTY

The Power of La Vía Campesina's Feminist Politics

Annette Aurélie Desmarais and Rita Calvário

> The feminism that we propose recognizes our cultural diversity and the very different conditions that we face in each region, country and place. We are building it from the daily struggles which women across the planet fight. Struggles for our autonomy, social transformation, the defence and protection of peasant agriculture, and food sovereignty. From this, new men and women will emerge with new gender relationships based on equality, respect, cooperation and mutual recognition. This feminism is transformative, rebellious and autonomous. (La Vía Campesina 2017a)

At the World Food Summit held in October 1996, the transnational agrarian movement, La Vía Campesina, introduced a peasant notion of food sovereignty as a radical critique and alternative to neoliberal approaches to rural development and food politics. Initially conceived as "we have the right to produce our own food in our own territory" (La Vía Campesina 1996), food sovereignty effectively politicized food systems by focusing on key questions: *What* food is being produced and harvested? *Who* produces and harvests food? *Where, why* and *how* is it produced and gathered, and at *what scale?* (La Vía Campesina 2000a). Answering these questions meant analyzing who is making decisions and who has the power to decide. Thus, right from the start, La Vía Campesina's notion of food sovereignty centred on power relations and sought to place decision-making concerning agriculture and food into the hands of local communities.

Twenty-five years later, on October 13, 2021, La Vía Campesina released its "Manifesto for the Future of the Planet," a document that declares how crucial feminism is to both La Vía Campesina and food sovereignty. Beginning with "Food sovereignty is a philosophy of life," the manifesto asserts that,

> Social peace, *gender justice* and solidarity economies are essential pre-conditions for realizing food sovereignty … It [food sovereignty] calls for a society that *rejects discrimination in all forms — caste, class, racial and gender —* and urges people to fight *patriarchy* and parochialism. … *Peasant women and other oppressed gender minorities* must find equal space in the leadership of our movement at all levels. We must sow the seeds of solidarity in our communities and address all forms of discrimination that keep rural societies divided. … Food sovereignty offers a manifesto for the future, a *feminist vision* that embraces diversity. It is an idea that unites humanity and puts us at the service of Mother Earth that feeds and nourishes us. (authors' emphasis, La Vía Campesina 2021)

How did gender equality and feminism come to be so central to the movement's political project of food sovereignty? And what has been the role of women's struggles within the movement in this process? This chapter draws on a careful examination and analysis of several of the movement's main documents, such as the declarations of its International Conferences, Women's Assemblies and Youth Assemblies. Since these gatherings are spaces of deliberation and debate, as well as being the highest decision-making and representative political spaces within the movement, the declarations and accompanying documents provide important insights into the movement's analysis, dynamics, vision, actions and paths forward.

La Vía Campesina formally emerged in 1993, and today it brings together 182 organizations of peasants, small-scale farmers, rural women, Indigenous peoples, and farmworkers from eighty-one countries located throughout the Americas, Europe, Africa, Asia and the MENA (Middle East and North Africa) region. Many scholar-activists consider it to be the world's most politically significant rural transnational movement at the forefront of global resistance to ongoing dispossession, displacement and human rights violations in rural areas unleashed by the further expansion of the corporate-led and state-supported neoliberal food system.

Women are currently a visible and active force within La Vía Campesina, as is evident when observing movement mobilizations, actions and gatherings. A quick scan of the La Vía Campesina website also provides many insights into the extent of women's activism within the movement. But this was not always the case. The fact that gender issues as they relate to women and feminism are now so central to La Vía Campesina and its conceptualization of food sovereignty is the result of a thirty-year-long struggle of women within the movement involving, as Doreen Massey (2009) would put it, a whole lot of "invention and hard work." In this chapter, we focus on two specific dimensions of women's feminist work within the movement: the creation of women's autonomous spaces and the priority to end all forms of violence against women. In doing so, we discuss how this feminist work has been key to radicalize the movement politics and vision of food sovereignty. We conclude by reflecting on how feminism adds to La Vía Campesina's and food sovereignty counterhegemonic potential.

Carving out women's spaces to elevate women's presence, voices and demands

The founding International Conference of La Vía Campesina held in 1993 and its Framework of Action did recognize men and women's rights to land, and particularly women's important roles in peasant organizations and the need to "guarantee their full participation" (La Vía Campesina 1993). Yet, although women represented 20 percent of the delegates, the Mons Declaration resulting from the conference mentions women producers (as "s/he") only once. Further, only men were elected as regional leaders and no mechanisms were established to ensure participation of women in future meetings (Desmarais 2007). It was not until the Second and Third International Conferences of La Vía Campesina, held in 1996 and 2000 respectively, that La Vía Campesina took important steps in relation to women's rights and equality.

At the Second International Conference held in Tlaxcala, Mexico, women delegates (again representing only 20 percent of the delegates) pushed for actions aimed at addressing gender inequalities (between men and women) within the movement. They argued that the important first step was to form a special women's committee — consisting of one appointed representative from each of the Vía Campesina regions, which subsequently became known as the Vía Campesina Women's Commission

Poster of La Vía Campesina for the celebrations of the International Women's Day on March 8, 2022. Source: <viacampesina.org/>.

— whose work was to "develop strategies, mechanisms and a plan of action to ensure women's equal participation and representation at all levels of Vía Campesina, and establish coordination and communication among women" (in Desmarais 2007: 163). Women delegates did not consider this first women's autonomous space as an end in itself — thus rejecting the idea of ghettoizing women's struggles and of turning gender issues into a sideline to the main struggle of the peasant movement. Instead, they envisioned the newly formed Women's Commission as being a driving force of "freer" spaces untainted by sexist culture in which women from different regions of the world could come together to discuss among themselves their shared and specific concerns, needs and interests, engage in collective analysis, and strategize on how to challenge the male-dominated organizational models in rural organizations. Women aimed at making these organizations more effective in addressing women's specific interests and priorities, including the growing transnational agrarian movement itself (Desmarais 2003 and 2007).

In pushing this vision forward, the Women's Commission created various women's autonomous spaces. This involved organizing women's meetings immediately prior to major international events where La Vía Campesina delegations gathered at the time, such as the World Food Summit in 1996 and the World Trade Organization protests in Seattle three years later. In its first four years, the Women's Commission worked hand in hand with the women leaders of peasant organizations in Central and South America and the Caribbean to hold a series of women's workshops and exchanges themed "Peasant women on the Frontiers of Food Sovereignty."[1] These, together with other women's gatherings organized by the regional peasant movements, were instrumental in creating the kind of freer spaces mentioned above where peasant women from diverse rural organizations members of La Vía Campesina could learn more about each other's experiences, share stories of success and defeat, laugh and sing, voice their views and proposals, debate among peers, and become more wholeheartedly engaged in La Vía Campesina and its politics. It is here that women gained more confidence to participate in political spaces and speak in public, reinforced their analytical tools for understanding the world surrounding them, and acquired more experience in debating politics and engaging in activism, while also collectively imagining a more equal world. With similar processes and results, on the other side of the world, in August 1999, women organized the Asian Peasant Women's Workshop, bringing together peasant women from Thailand, Vietnam, Laos, Malaysia, Indonesia, Philippines, Korea and Japan. There is no doubt that these experiences enabled the Women's Commission to successfully convene La Vía Campesina's First International Women's Assembly held just prior to the movement's Third International Conference held in 2000, in Bangalore, India.

In many ways, this Conference was a turning point for La Vía Campesina as it enacted significant advances to guaranteeing women's political equality within the movement by introducing parity in leadership positions and engaging in debates about how best to embed a gender analysis as a foundational part of the movement's way of understanding and changing the world and social relations. Following considerable debate amongst women in the First Women's Assembly, the Conference approved, unanimously, a significant change to its international structure. Thereafter, La Vía Campesina's International Coordinating Committee (ICC) was expanded from one to two elected coordinators per region, one woman and one man. Additionally, the female Regional Coordinators would now constitute the International Women's Commission (subsequently renamed the International Women's Articulation) and meet prior to each ICC meeting (Desmarais 2003 and 2007).

Importantly, the Bangalore Conference also discussed a Gender Position document that included a detailed action plan with ambitious measures to achieve gender equality in political representation and participation. These included: ensuring gender parity at all policy-making events within member organizations and at all levels; having 50 percent women delegates in all La Vía Campesina committees and conferences; and ensuring that women take positions of leadership within member organizations (La Vía Campesina 2000b). The action plan also pushed La Vía Campesina to integrate a gender perspective as transversal in the everyday political life of the movement, signalling attention to multiple oppressions: "All members in all participating Vía Campesina organizations must accept the importance of developing a gender, class and ethnicity perspective and integrate this into their frameworks" (La Vía Campesina 2000b).

Fifth La Vía Campesina Women's Assembly, July 18–19, 2017, where women decided on their action plan for the next four years and inputs for the VII La Vía Campesina Conference, July 19–22, 2017, in Derio, the Basque Country (Spain). Source: <viacampesina.org/>.

Since this precedent-setting Women's First Assembly, a Women's Assembly is held prior to each of the movement's much larger International Conferences that take place every four years. It is difficult to put into words the potential and power that these assemblies hold. The diversity of women, the exuberance, the energy, the commitment to solidarity, the exchange of experiences and the strategic decision-making on the path forward — all are certainly inspiring accomplishments. And between the international conferences, women have held organizational exchanges within and among regions, regional conferences and participated in international campaigns, all of which provide much-needed time to collectively reflect, analyze, dream and strategize for how best to work together in building new futures based on food sovereignty. The creation of multiple women's autonomous spaces has been and continues to be instrumental to women's greater participation, representation, visibility, voice and power within the movement and in their efforts to transform La Vía Campesina itself and radicalize its politics and conceptualizations of food sovereignty with a feminist perspective.

Radicalizing food sovereignty with a feminist perspective: Ending *all forms* of violence against women

One of the key struggles that La Vía Campesina women shared and pushed forward within the movement focused on ending *all forms* of violence against women. This struggle is a clear example of how women's specific interests and priorities as experienced in their daily lives are worked on by women in constructing a feminist perspective, which is then translated into the movement's conceptualization and praxis of food sovereignty. Through this labouring of a "feminism from below," food sovereignty becomes much more than just about food and agriculture; it embraces toppling social inequity and uneven power relations of all kinds.

The Gender Position paper discussed at the First Women's Assembly in 2000 clearly recognizes the "sexual as well as physical abuse of women and girls" in processes of intimidation, displacement and militarization in the countryside, calling for an end to these human rights violations (La Vía Campesina 2000b). This document also emphasizes respecting the "right of women to be free from domestic violence" considering that "the confidence, self-esteem and human potential of women is cruelly undermined by the subjugation and abuse many experience within their own homes" (La Vía Campesina 2000b). Four years later, the Second Women's Assembly held in São Paulo, in 2004, calls for "the immediate application of measures to eradicate all forms of physical, sexual, verbal and psychological violence" (La Vía Campesina 2004a).

It is at La Vía Campesina's Fourth International Conference in 2004 that women's demands to stop violence against women became a call for the movement as a whole. La Vía Campesina's São Paulo Declaration expands the movement's understanding of violence against women by considering it not only "criminal violence" but that it is also structural and includes the marginalization effects of "the privatization of basic services, the concentration of land ownership, and the destruction of local markets" (La Vía Campesina 2004b). Moreover, the São Paulo Declaration points to the links between, and rejection of, the violence of patriarchy and aggressions of capitalism: "We are equally committed to the struggle against the patriarchal system that only accentuates the aberrations of capitalism" (La Vía Campesina 2004b). In this perspective, gender inequalities are understood as structural, systemic, and a result of the intricacies between patriarchy and capitalism.

By 2008, the La Vía Campesina takes a more public and proactive stance in the struggle to end violence against women. Whereas the previous declarations identified the problem and its multiple dimensions, the Maputo Declaration presents an analysis of the origins, causes, and implications of violence against women for the peasant movement. It also signals a path forward:

> One issue was very clear in this V conference, that all the forms of violence that women face in our societies — among them physical, economic, social, cultural and macho violence, and violence based on differences of power — are also present in rural communities, and as a result, in our organizations. This, in addition to being a principal source of injustice, also limits the success of our struggles. We recognize the intimate relationships between capitalism, patriarchy, machismo and neoliberalism, in detriment to women peasants and farmers of the world. All of us together, women and men of La Vía Campesina, make a responsible commitment to build new and better human relationships among us, as a necessary part

of the construction of the new societies to which we aspire. For this reason during this V Conference we decided to break the silence on these issues, and are launching the World Campaign "For an End to Violence Against Women." (La Vía Campesina 2008b)

There are some critical aspects of this quote that are worth noting: violence against women is seen as being multidimensional, non-geographically specific, and rooted in structural sexism and patriarchy; macho culture and patriarchal relations are understood as being intertwined in capitalism and neoliberalism — thus, struggles for food sovereignty must be anticapitalist and feminist; addressing violence against women is necessary to move food sovereignty forward. Linked to this is the La Vía Campesina's position that ending violence against women is also about building new, changed gender relations in everyday life, including within the movement and its member organizations. As the Maputo Declaration urges: "If we do not eradicate violence towards women within our movement, we will not advance in our struggles, and if we do not create new gender relations, we will not be able to build a new society" (La Vía Campesina 2008b). As such, the campaign's goal goes far beyond just raising awareness as it includes a commitment for each woman and man to take action in their own spaces of living, working, and organizing to effect change in the ways they interact and relate to others of a different sex and gender. This is a campaign that seeks fundamental change in gender relations in households, peasant organizations and rural communities around the world.

La Vía Campesina's commitment to ending gender-based violence continues while expanding its views of what this violence means and encompasses. The Jakarta Declaration in 2013 includes a mentioning of violence against women as a problem occurring in both "rural and urban areas," thus calling for feminist solidarity among all, both rural and urban women (La Vía Campesina 2013b). This Declaration reaffirms a commitment to place the campaign to stop violence against women at the heart of La Vía Campesina struggles, considered to be a key step for advancing the movement's struggle for food sovereignty. This position is no doubt influenced by the Women's Manifesto resulting from its IV International Women's Assembly held in Jakarta that demanded "Initiating immediate actions and measures in order to eradicate violent sexist practices and

Banner for the mobilization week to mark the International Day for the Elimination of Violence against Women, November 25–30, 2019, within La Vía Campesina international campaign to end violence against women. Source: <viacampesina.org/>.

physical, verbal and psychological aggressions in our organizations, in our families and in society" (La Vía Campesina 2013a). The Derio Declaration in 2017 reiterates a commitment to continue to fight against "all forms of violence against women: physical, sexual, psychological, and economic" while also signaling the importance of "increasing our capacities to understand and create positive environments around gender, within our organizations and in our alliances" (La Vía Campesina 2017c). The Derio Declaration also reflects, still timidly, an emergent but powerful debate on gender diversity and LGBTQIA+ rights in the movement, which broadens understandings of gender and violence.

The campaign to stop violence against women set in motion since 2008 is global in scope, while much of the work has concentrated more at the regional and national levels as part of La Vía Campesina local organizations' agendas. An evaluation of this work is still pending. The persistent call to end all forms of violence against women by La Vía Campesina women and its translation into La Vía Campesina's International Declarations — and concretely into the work of local organizations — signals that this is a permanent, ongoing struggle, one that requires everyday attention and priority.

Building a feminist notion of food sovereignty as counterhegemony

The work of women within La Vía Campesina reveals their power in radicalizing food sovereignty and La Vía Campesina politics. Through women's engagement in critical self-reflection and political analysis, collective decision-making, building ties of friendship and solidarity across borders by working together to create and nurture women's autonomous spaces and set a collective agenda, they have consistently voiced their demands both within the movement and beyond — for instance, by establishing alliances with the World March of Women.[2] In the process, La Vía Campesina women became active political subjects in "making their own history" and they have remained united in their efforts to build a different world based on a feminist notion of food sovereignty. As the Derio Women's Assembly declared: "We are building a feminism out of our peasant and popular identity as a tool for our organizations and in the social emancipation process for men and women… [We are] Building the movement to change the world with feminism and food sovereignty" (La Vía Campesina 2017a).

Women's ways of working and their demands within La Vía Campesina have had a powerful impact on the movement as a whole. We have pointed to specific examples of how these have changed the structure of the movement, expanded and deepened the conceptualization of food sovereignty to include self-organization, ending violence against women and building new gender relations. Thus, food sovereignty came to mean much more than just agriculture and food: it is about radical social change writ large. Perhaps more importantly, it has also led the movement to embrace a radical feminism that moves well beyond strands of gender equality or liberal feminism that focus on formal rights and women's increased market participation without changing structures and cultures of violence, hierarchy and inequality. This is also a feminism that comes from peasant and rural women's own analysis and activism embedded in their own lived realities and differences, not from external, declarative ideas of what is or is not "real" or "proper" feminism.

La Vía Campesina women have done a whole lot more work in expanding and infusing radical notions of feminism into food sovereignty — from discussions about patriarchy and capitalism, to the need to understand intersectionality and tackle conjointly all types of oppression and discrimination, to more recent formulations of a "popular peasant feminism" — that we were not able to approach in the limited space of this chapter. Our goal was to shed light on the efforts of La Vía Campesina women's initial steps at building a "feminism from below" and their role of translating a radical feminism into the whole movement and its organizations in ways that radicalize the conceptualizations and struggles for food sovereignty. We did this by focusing on two dimensions of women's work within the movement: creating women's autonomous spaces and their demand to end all forms of violence against women.

For many within La Vía Campesina, the movement's adoption of feminism has been a thirty-year struggle. This is not to suggest that La Vía Campesina has reached some kind of feminist-infused utopia, as numerous obstacles remain both within the women's spaces, the movement as a whole, and many of its local organizations. As is often the case with transnational movements, although women's spaces have been absolutely critical, they are not free of tensions and conflicts, regional dominance, louder voices silencing others, and exclusion (Desmarais 2007).

La Vía Campesina and its member organizations are no stranger to the numerous difficulties involved in continuing to build, consolidate and strengthen a transnational movement with strong regional and local organizations over the long term, and in increasingly adverse political-economic and climate-environmental global conditions. That the movement remains the most politically significant transnational agrarian movement today attests to its capacity to respond to shifting terrains of struggle and to embrace diversity while finding common ground. For La Vía Campesina women, a large part of that common ground is violence against women, in all its forms: from direct to structural violence, in their homes, fields and organizations to elsewhere in society. Importantly, in tackling this head-on, La Vía Campesina women sought both internal and external change. As the Derio Women's Assembly stressed: "The struggle against violence toward women begins in our hearts and consciences. Let us unify our wills to build a rural world without violence, starting with the creation of a new woman and man" (La Vía Campesina 2017a). Importantly, as the Derio Youth Declaration stressed, this perspective includes gender diversity: "[T]here is no food sovereignty or justice without feminism and equality of all people. We must recognize and respect diversity of all forms, including race, gender, sexuality and class. We will root out patriarchy and discrimination wherever it exists" (La Vía Campesina 2017b).

All of this, we argue, adds considerable power to food sovereignty as a counterhegemonic force to dominant powers and elites in the rural world. First, by integrating a view of women's oppression and patriarchy as being constitutive of and reinforced by the ways capitalism and the neoliberal food system is organized and governed. Without specifically addressing and overcoming women's oppressions, "there is no food sovereignty." Second, by expanding conceptualizations of gender and inequalities through an intersectional lens, to include and unite diverse social groupings suffering from multiple forms of oppression, in a perspective of radical social change.

We are convinced that La Vía Campesina's ongoing strength and legitimacy will depend on its proven ability to continue to embrace diversity, build solidarity, engage in open debates, ensure that demands and actions are grounded in local and daily realities, and establish common ground for action, among women and within the movement as a whole.

Notes

1 The main regional organizations were the Coordinadora Latinoamericana de Organizaciones del Campo (CLOC), the Asociación de Organizaciones Campesinas Centroamericanas para la Cooperación y el Desarrollo (ASOCODE), and the Windward Islands Farmers Association (WINFA).
2 The websites of La Vía Campesina (viacampesina.org) and the World March of Women (marchemondiale.org) reveal the various ways in which both movements collaborate and engage in solidarity. Depending on the country/region, these can range from developing joint positions on issues as well as jointly organizing workshops, exchanges and campaigns. As just one example of the solidarity between the two movements, see <viacampesina.org/en/gallery-peasant-struggles-and-food-sovereignty/>.

References

Desmarais, Annette Aurélie. 2003. "The Vía Campesina: Peasant Women at the Frontiers of Food Sovereignty." *Canadian Woman Studies* 23, 1: 140–145.
_____. 2007. *La Vía Campesina: Globalization and the Power of Peasants*. Halifax and London: Fernwood Publishing and Pluto Books.
La Vía Campesina. 1993. "Mons Declaration: The Vía Campesina Follow-up to the Managua Declaration." Mons, Belgium. May 15–16.
_____. 1996. "The Right to Produce and Access to Land." Vía Campesina Position on Food Sovereignty presented at the World Food Summit. Rome, Italy. November 13–17.
_____. 2000a. "Food Sovereignty and International Trade." Position paper approved at the Third International Conference of the Vía Campesina. Bangalore, India. October 3–6,
_____. 2000b. "Gender Position Paper." Discussed at Vía Campesina Third International Conference. Bangalore, India. October 3–6.
_____. 2000c. "Bangalore Declaration of the Vía Campesina." Declaration at the Third International Conference of the Vía Campesina. Bangalore, India. October 3–6.

_____. 2004a. "Declaration of the Second International Assembly of Rural Women." Itaici, São Paulo, Brazil. June 12–13.

_____. 2004b. "Declaration of the Vía Campesina's Fourth International Conference." Itaici, São Paulo, Brazil. June 14–19.

_____. 2008a. "Declaration of the III Assembly of the Women of Vía Campesina." Maputo, Mozambique. October 17–18.

_____. 2008b. "Declaration of Maputo: V International Conference of Vía Campesina." Maputo, Mozambique. October 19–22.

_____. 2013a. "Women of Vía Campesina International Manifesto of the IV Women's Assembly." Jakarta, Indonesia. June 7.

_____. 2013b. "The Jakarta Call of the VI Conference of La Vía Campesina." Jakarta, Indonesia. June 9–13.

_____. 2017a. "V Women's Assembly La Vía Campesina Declaration." Derio, Euskal Herria/Basque Country, Spain. July 18.

_____. 2017b. "Youth IV International Conference Declaration." Derio, Euskal Herria/Basque Country, Spain.

_____. 2017c. "VII International Conference, La Vía Campesina: Euskal Herria Declaration." Derio, Euskal Herria/Basque Country, Spain. July 16–24.

_____. 2021. "Food Sovereignty: A Manifesto for the Future of Our Planet. Official Statement from La Vía Campesina." October 13. At <viacampesina.org/en/food-sovereignty-a-manifesto-for-the-future-of-our-planet-la-via-campesina/>.

Massey, Doreen. 2009. "Invention and Hard Work." In J. Pugh (ed.), *What Is Radical Politics Today?* London: Palgrave Macmillan.

COMMUNITARIAN TERRITORIAL FEMINISMS OF ABYA YALA

Women Organized against Violence and Dispossession and the Experience of Community Networks in Chiapas, Mexico[1]

Delmy Tania Cruz Hernández

Since the end of the last century, the South has been in a geopolitical context where extractivism has increased, shaping environmental scenarios of appropriation and dispossession. In the case of Mexico, the State has built economic policies that generate favourable conditions for the development of extractive industries, welcoming transnational capital in territories with rich natural resources that are regularly inhabited by native peoples. The capitalist siege against Indigenous peoples is not a new record. It is the history of capitalism, which, like a hydra, launches a reactivated offensive that, time and again, is determined to destroy the conditions of stability collectively achieved, based on the efforts of struggle.

It is key to mention that the capitalist siege constantly experienced by peoples must be understood within the framework of what Gutiérrez (2011) calls "community networks" ("*entramados comunitarios*"): "multiple worlds of human life that populate and generate the world under different patterns of respect, collaboration, affection, dignity and reciprocity, not fully subject to the logics of capital accumulation, although attacked and often overwhelmed by them." The activities that sustain community life are mainly carried out by women, who also put their bodies into the struggle. Women who build collectivity in their territories try to crack the wall that surrounds them, bursting onto stage with their voice and presence, questioning the contradictions in their community networks. Undoubtedly, the alliance between patriarchy, colonialism and extractivism oppresses the daily struggles embodied and led by organized women. Focusing on the multiple weaving of bridges that is built from the struggles can give us clues to the possible horizons that have been intertwined and that can crack the logics of capital.

This essay began as a reflection in the 2015 seminar "Pensamiento Crítico Frente a la Hidra Capitalista" ("Critical Thinking against the Capitalist Hydra") organized by the Zapatista support bases at the Universidad de la Tierra (CIDECI) in San Cristóbal de las Casas, Chiapas. This encounter was organized with the questions: How are we? And what follows now?, in what the Zapatistas called a "seedbed" (*semillero*), stating: "let the heart that we are open the word, that it speaks and listens. And from between words we choose the best seed" (Galeano 2015: 7). I participated out of conviction, as I have been part of the Sixth National of the Zapatistas since 2006.[2]

At the time, I was organized as part of the Colectivo Miradas Críticas al Territorio desde el Feminismo (Feminist Critical Perspectives on the Territory Collective),[3] which I co-founded in Quito, and Mujeres Transformando Mundos — MUTRAM (Women Transforming Worlds), which I had just started with my life partner, Noelia.[4] After the seminar, Noelia and I came out with a question that persists to this day: what follows for us to face the scenes of death and devastation that exist in the territories we walk on, the patriarchal oppressions within our feminist organizations, and the low-intensity war in Chiapas? With the power of the encounter and our conversations, we went to the Domínguez Committee with our life allies from the Centro de Educación Integral de Base — CEIBA (Centre for Grassroots Integral Education)[5] to tell them about our experience. We saw it as necessary for our bodies to anchor ourselves in our territories and accompany each other in our organizational endeavours. We spent a day talking, crying, remembering. They listened and resonated with our thought-feelings. After this heartfelt conversation, we decided to start a journey together, which we continue today.

This chapter documents the resonances that we have been carrying out since that time as part of these multiple collectives. They come from a situated feminist research from the South, which means articulating diverse languages, taking part and contributing to opening dialogues in the territories between the diverse people that we are. These "heartings" (*corazonares*) are essential to understand that when I argue, I do so from a collective path that gives me the possibility of going down to earth, to always build in dialogue, from a thought from below and to the left. I do not intend to "box" my comrades (*compañeras*) as feminists, but rather, to try to elucidate what paths we are weaving together in this dialogue, between popular urban worlds and rural, Indigenous peasants. While many of the women with whom we share community construction do not call themselves feminists, they are not antagonistic to the feminist keys on violence, rights, land and defence of territories, and indeed, they deploy community strategies that are clearly a fight against the patriarchy that oppresses them.

Theoretical-political approaches from Abya Yala feminisms

Abya Yala has a long tradition of anticolonial and anticapitalist struggles, where organized women have put up walls to the colonial and modern project of death. Undoubtedly, as Margara Millán Moncayo (2011) refers, feminisms came to destabilize the abstract universal masculine subject proposed by the modern paradigm. But feminisms of the South are the ones that have come to dismantle the colonial blindness that feminisms themselves reproduce (Alvarado et al. 2020). These feminisms, born in different cardinal points of Abya Yala, have no waves; they are embodied in the land and in the feminized bodies resisting in these territories. They attempt to break the ontological barrier drawn by the coloniality of being (Alvarado et al. 2020), of knowledge and gender (Lugones 2008).

The arguments of Mohanty (1984) are once again urgent, in which she warns us of the danger of drawing female subjects without analyzing the particular context in which women struggle against all forms of domination. I understand that as women we occupy different steps in the hierarchies that mark the oppressions, but as a result of the patriarchal connection we live on a historical continuum of oppressions given by the system we inhabit. A fundamental contribution of southern feminisms is that they have brought the renewed struggle against extractivist projects into the theoretical and political debate. Key antecedents in Abya Yala were the 1992 Indigenous uprisings in Ecuador and in 1994 in Chiapas, Mexico, where Indigenous women and men took up the just demand for land and territory. The territory became a place of dispute, and in our colonized south the key opponents are the organized women from different latitudes who propose the re-existence of an interconnected land.

I will briefly review some theoretical-methodological contributions that attempt to explain the relationship between women and territories in Abya Yala. In particular, I will focus on some arguments of the so-called ecofeminisms of the South, feminist political ecology and the proposals put forward by the anti-patriarchal community feminisms. I do not pretend to say which theoretical arguments fit in the reality of Abya Yala; I consider that each organized space of Indigenous, peasant, rural, impoverished, Black women and organized people of sexual-gender dissidence, have their own ways of naming the struggle against the racist, speciesist, adultcentric and classist patriarchy. I carry out this exercise to show a brief archaeology that helps me to present the contributions that I leave and take from each position in order to build what I call territorial community feminisms.

Ecofeminisms and embodied studies of feminist political ecology

Ecological feminism is the name given to the variety of feminist perspectives that study the connections between the domination of women (and the oppressed) and the domination of nature. A common point among the various positions has been the commitment to overcome the rigid and passive conception of nature as conceived by the West. Another commonality is many of the current attempts to break the binary and hierarchical conception between nature and culture. Mies and Shiva (1993) are referent authors who have proposed that ecofeminisms — besides being a key theory to dismantle the patriarchal capitalist pact, which hierarchizes human and nonhuman lives — must also be articulated as a social movement.

Interesting contributions to ecofeminism have emerged in some parts of Abya Yala. For example, Trevilla (2018) articulates arguments from feminist economics to put care economy into the debate. From Uruguay, with a more critical view towards certain ecofeminist positions, Migliaro and Rodríguez express the interest of approaching ecofeminist positions as a political bet to denounce the unsustainability of the patriarchal capitalist system and provide clues on how to crack Anthropocene logics (Migliaro and Rodríguez 2020). However, there is a lack of studies that are embodied in rural, peasant or Indigenous contexts in Abya Yala. Furthermore, what I consider missing from the ecofeminist proposals is a theoretical-political discussion on the meaning of territory, fundamental to understand all the realities of Abya Yala.

Bina Agarwal (2004) dissociates herself from ecofeminism and proposes an alternative framework that she calls feminist environmentalism. The primary challenge that Agarwal posed was the need to think of ecologism in a materialistic key. She was also one of the pioneers in provoking environmentalism to take feminist arguments into account, and for in-vogue feminisms to make environmentalist goals their main objective, a point that was also adopted by feminist political ecology.

For the precursors of feminist political ecology (Bilder 2013; Rocheleau et al. 2004), it has been essential to turn the association between women and nature into a political bond. Following in some ways the line proposed by ecological environmentalism, they intend to place gender as a critical category to analyze access to and control of resources (Rocheleau et al. 2004) and examine resistances in various community networks. Feminist political ecology recognizes contributions from feminist economics, the ethics of care and attachment to life as fundamental ways to build different relationships between humanity and other living beings.

I recognize in feminist political ecology a fertile field for the construction of knowledge, which allows us to understand that the hierarchical relationship and domination between humans and nonhumans will depend on the material and subjective conditions that exist in community networks. In addition, feminist political ecology marks a point of analysis of the capitalist siege that each context experiences. It also retakes territory as a theoretical-political category to understand space, as always in dispute. One of the main premises here is that environmental change is not a neutral process susceptible to management, and that political agency emerges from complex subjectivities (gender, race, class, sexuality), which produce diverse territorial strategies deployed mainly by organized women.

Without waves and with land: Community feminisms

The voices of Indigenous, Black, rural and peasant women have always been present within feminisms. It is true that many times they have not been heard. However, their theoretical and political contributions disrupt hegemonic feminisms and reveal their inconsistencies and contradictions. Community feminisms are in this line. One of the most important contributions in this field is to dismantle the idea that gender is a category constructed and given by the West. Therefore, it should not be understood in the same way in all latitudes. Moreover, decolonizing gender is not only an ideological position but an epistemic political stance.

It has been important to emphasize that time is a cultural construct for community feminisms. They dissociate themselves from arguments that pigeonhole their contributions as part of the fourth wave (Martínez 2019) and posit that community feminisms have been present for a longer time. However, the impossibility of listening to their demands and political proposals comes from the kind of relationships that are constructed in hegemonic feminisms. Furthermore, it is alleged that there is no grammatical framework that allows for the encounter, as the possibility of constructing new ethical paths between us and others, to allow us to let ourselves be with the other without hiding our multiple differences. "We do not have waves" states Guzmán (2019), referring to the fact that we do not come from Eurocentric ancestors. We have our own references of struggle, and they are the ones that mark the history of the political project, in order to recover the memory stolen by colonization. Therefore, many of these references are becoming part of the struggle, against any form of capitalist and patriarchal oppression. Community feminism, as Guzmán (2019: 28) rightly frames it, is a transforming political project; a "horizon of possibilities, as utopia that is built, and that is why its enunciation is from the proposal, communitarian feminism, a single word because the community is not a theory or an ideology, the community simply or complexly 'is.'"

Community is being in practice. Community feminisms, like the struggles of organized Indigenous peoples, come to put on the table that the Indigenous is not an essentialist identity, nor the community a pristine space. Rather, both are projects in the process of becoming, in possible horizons, which are built from the everyday life in the territories. From our political project, one of the strong contributions that has helped us to think about the different dispossessions we have experienced in our territories and to create strategies is the concept of the "body-territory-land" (*cuerpo-territorio-tierra*). The body-territory-land concept was proposed by Indigenous Mayan thinkers in Guatemala and Bolivia. The contribution these thinkers make is to understand that bodies are territories and territories are social bodies, and both have an indissoluble link (Cruz 2020).

The conception of the body has been in dispute. The body is not something given, but a constructed category that has never been absent, since it served to understand the other:

> Women, primitives, Jews, Africans, the poor, all those who were labelled "different" in different historical epochs, have been considered bodily, dominated then by instinct and affection, reason being beyond themselves. They are the other and the other is a body. (Oyěwùmí 1997: 3)

Oyěwùmí (1997), reminds us of how central the body has been in the construction of difference in the dominant Western culture. From the latitudes of Abya Yala, community feminisms make it possible to understand the body itself and as mediation. That is to say, the body is the vehicle through which we mediate our commitments with others, with the territory and with the other; simply put, it exists insofar as it is a relationship (Cruz 2020). These arguments open the possibility to begin a dialogue on the decoloniality of the body, not as an individual place, nor as a passive agent, but as a diversity of embodied experiences that bring memory and exist in relation to other diverse spatialities. Therefore, the body-territory-land is a mediation, an ontology and an epistemic crack, because it generates a displacement towards a new bodily dissonance, which renames the ontology of interdependence from Abya Yala feminisms.

Territorial community feminisms

Thanks to the collective commitment that we promote as Mujeres Transformando Mundos — MUTRAM (Women Transforming Worlds), and the Centro de Educación Integral de Base — CEIBA (Centre for Grassroots Integral Education) rooted in Chiapas, we have built a house of collectives, where we meet and accompany each other to weave strategies for the defence of the territories. We coincide with the Florecillas (Indigenous women of Chuj roots) of the Trinitaria municipality, the Colibrí rural collective from the municipality of Comitán, the Indigenous and urban women collective Fases de la Luna from the municipality of Margaritas, and the *G-men*, a collective of Indigenous, urban men who reflect on patriarchy and hegemonic masculinity. Together and organized we have sought to build livable, dignified and desirable territories for all the species that inhabit the territories.

The conversations I describe are essential to understand that when I write from a collective journey, that gives me the possibility to go down to earth (*bajar a la tierra*), to build always in dialogue, a thinking from below and to the left. Twice a month, we get together to dialogue, learn and meet. Our ailments, experiences, resistance, work, challenges and joys are the echoes that lead us to build collective territorial strategies to weave a good life for our territories and for ourselves as women. From 2017 to 2018, we had ten conversations to make our counter-cartography. With it we were tracing individual and collective territorial strategies and at the same time it was a space for feminist political self-training. Session after session each one of us talked about the pieces of our territories. Where did we feel happiness, fear or violence? The route that we were tracing of the spaces created a counter-cartography that reflects the places where certain practices of women are shown in a certain spatial way. This collective exercise showed the political, social and cultural factors that allow or prohibit women's political mobility; that is, our counter-mapping narrated the mechanisms of power that are embodied in women's bodies and territories according to the various processes of dispossession. Here are some excerpts from those conversations:

> It seems unbelievable, but you are calm when you are ignorant and do not know. But when you learn more about it, it makes you more uneasy. I have thought a lot about what we have learned in the workshops, the meetings, and I commented to Margarita how worried I am about my daughters. Before I didn't know about the femicides, but now that I have been learning about them, I am always thinking about my daughters and what could happen to them and that makes me anxious, although I know I am not alone.
>
> When we went to that meeting with the Zapatista women, you see we were all in workshops and I went into one where there was a woman who had a sign on her chest, she had a canvas on her chest with a picture of a girl and I wanted to know who that girl was and I found out that it was her daughter and that she had been asking for justice, because she disappeared.

And the authorities do nothing, she said that once they called her to say that they had found her bones, but then they were not hers. Imagine not knowing what happened …

The lady finished telling the story and all of us who were there cried, and I even clutched my chest because it hurt me to hear that, and I imagined myself in her shoes and I understood what we talked about, what violence against women is; in the workshops, what femicide was entered my head and heart … I think of my daughters, as they go out and are on the streets in the city, in public transport, it makes me angry to see so much military.

Counter-cartography done by one of the participants in the sessions. Photo credit: Delmy Tania Cruz Hernández.

In one of our many rehearsals, we began to think about what part of our territory caused us fear, why and what did we feel in our bodies? Zeni shared the story about the city. Gloria echoed her: "I don't know how to read well, and that in the city is important, sometimes I get lost, I feel strange, as if I were nothing." Marcela and Margarita shared the ailment about the loss of their river. Zara talked about the river where she washes and that, although it is far away, she likes to go there to tell her sadness. Malena and Lupi talked about the church square, where they sell their products that they make with plants from the forest, the medicine that has helped them to heal their body and heart. This piece of their territory makes them happy.

During our conversations, we weaved a narrative that

allowed us to understand that the territory is everything that is in it physically, but not as a container, because it is valid insofar as the river, the land, the plants, the church, and the small square have a dialectical and intersubjective relationship with the people who live there. The incarnated territories become symbolic territories; they are a social construct that is rooted in the corporealities. The territory exists when the intersubjectivity in it occurs, not only among human beings but with everything that inhabits it. We have learned this epistemic dissonance to understand the relationship between the body and the territory and the land as a central element that gives us life. Thus, Marcela, when she chose the place where she washes as a place of refuge, the river element took on body-territorial relevance. She goes there to tell the river her sorrows and joys and it takes them away and keeps them; the river acts as an agent of transformation in her life. The river is also an important representative in Margarita's cartography, because it is there where grandmothers, mothers and she used to socialize, where they used to wash and meet, before the river was polluted. Their perception of the river changed from being a space of sociability and safety to an insecure one.

Counter-cartography done by another of the participants in the sessions. Photo credit: Delmy Tania Cruz Hernández.

> Now you can't go through, it stinks … they threw us out of the city, they throw everything around here. We were treated with contempt. The truth is that, some time ago a girl was robbed, since nobody passes by here anymore.

In other words, the capitalist siege marks our lives. In this example we see how it stripped them of a benign spatiality and disrupted their perception of their body-territory-land.

In the narratives presented, the city is a territory that embodies significant experiences and marks women in their condition of gender, but also of race, class, sexuality and age. When Gloria and Zenaida, both Indigenous women, narrate their experiences in the city, they both name fear as the main feeling attached to the urban space because of their condition as women. They recognize that their feminized bodies and those of their daughters are the central target of colonial femicidal violence, which haunts the cities like a ghost. In their stories, there is also a component of racial discrimination. Gloria alludes to feeling bad in the city as she does not understand well certain places because they are Spanish-speaking and mostly literate trenches. Gloria does not read Spanish. In addition, both consider that when they ask for work and the kaxlans (white-mestizo people) see them they think that "we are only good for washing, cleaning or scrubbing toilets."

The reflections I present are to expose that thinking in, with and from the body — the territory we embody — is one of the main components to which territorial community feminisms alludes. These are not strategies or forms of struggle; they are understandings of the territory and the space that corporeality occupies in it. Therefore, the body that we reclaim composes histories and becomes relevant in its relationality with the territory, being anchored to the land.

The violence we face

"To live well we need to live without violence," says Ema (2018), a member of Las Fases de La Luna collective in Margaritas, alongside other women defenders in the northern highlands of Puebla.

> They want to shut us up and we scare them because we don't let them, they know we are organizing and the other time they put up a sign outside the place where we meet that said "you should ALL leave" (TODAS *se van de aquí*). I got scared and we went to report it to the parish. The priest said that this was wrong, but they want us to keep quiet, that we don't get together because they know that things change when women get organized. What doesn't get in their heads is that things also change for men. (Ema, organized woman from Margaritas from the collective Las Fases de la Luna, personal communication July 2018)

From different latitudes of Abya Yala, organized women have denounced the violence they experience within their communities. Nancy, an Amazonian leader, said in a forum organized by FLACSO in 2016: "As women we experience violence in our communities. When we speak within it, they say that we are already feminists, they use that word to label us and accuse us of wanting to divide the community." Making violence visible is essential to address the good life of women in their territories. The active participation that women have had in the territorial struggle has given them the possibility of naming the machismo that exists in their communities. Sometimes, the political organization that they build manages to reduce situations in which acts of violence against women occur, but it is not enough. When women organize themselves, they attack the patriarchal power of the community that is imbricated in the territory.

> I used to dedicate myself to see how I supported women, I have been a victim of my own laws — referring to the community laws — when I started to go out to defend the land and to raise my voice they punished me ... That was because I defended a girl who was being abused by her father and I left the territory and brought her to my house.... I felt sorry for the girl and that's why I did it, but it cost me a lot. (Julia, organized woman from Comitán, personal communication March 2020)

Women and their bodies, in general, are the declared target in the war where territories are defending themselves against the siege of patriarchal capital. Organized women suffer a double danger as they are also a threat because they become subjects that generate knowledge, in dialogue with and listened by more and more women in the communities, and they also interact with the mestizo worlds — to reveal that within the community there is also violence (Cruz 2020).

When talking about violence in community networks, one of the questions that arises within feminisms is: how do women manage to resist the dominant male order, subverting the hegemonic meanings of cultural practices and reusing them for their own purposes and interests? On the one hand, when women become conscious, there is a direct attack on the power structure itself and not only on the consciousness of an autonomous individual, where "the act of resistance is the paradigmatic example of social agency" (Butler 1999: 16-18). Although Butler clarifies that not all resistance is opposed to power, she argues that resistance is always crucial for social transformation. On the other hand, Mahmood (2008: 184–188) suggests that:

> Social agency cannot have only one measuring stick — transformation. Rather, each change must be viewed with its networks, forms and cultures. This turn raises a more flexible category of resistance that not only manifests itself in order to modify a use, custom or power relation; but to remain in it from a different place.

This way of understanding resistance contributes in a fairer way to the interpretation of the reproduction strategies used by organized women in different latitudes of Abya Yala to zig-zag and confront the diverse forms of violence they experience daily. The territorial community feminisms that we are weaving on the border of Chiapas are on the margins, in our own battlefield. The focus is on how we do politics among diverse women and with our communities. We are building community networks that take into account the voices, words and knowledges of women. We are questioning how organized women embody the negotiations to crack the very systems of life and forms of cultural reproduction. The pathways of practices within territorial community feminisms show us that resisting is not always the same as breaking from the territories or communities, sometimes it implies only breaking women's own chains and cracking the daily life in their community networks.

Participants in one of our sessions. Photo credit: Delmy Tania Cruz Hernández.

This already allows them to move to a place where they can reinvent their ways of being Indigenous, peasant, rural and urban-marginalized women. Collectivity is the starting point of the movement.

Why add the "territorial" to community feminism? I want to clarify that it is not an annex, it is one more window into the communitarian perspective. I believe that the contributions of territorial community feminism should be read within the framework of the struggles for the defence of the territories. It is important to remember the prolonged dispossession of Indigenous territories and that those who have faced the racist extractive violence are the organized peoples, where women have played a vital role.

Undoubtedly, the contributions that we have discovered in our collective journey can be intertwined with what I call territorial community feminisms, since they open up new ways to understand the territorial contributions of women who weave organization. As diverse women who come together, when we think of defence, we do not do it only from a position of "holding on or resisting" but from one of insurgency, which builds, proposes, dreams and concretizes. We think about the defence of our lives and that of the territories that we embody in the long term, in the continuous dialogues where we fight asking ourselves: if I don't do it, what are we going to leave to our sons and daughters?

Organized women who build territories in the framework of dispossession have put at the centre of the agenda that the reproduction of life, and the multiple activities contained in such reproduction, are central to defend and build livable spaces (Cruz 2020). In addition, women organized in the framework of the territorial struggle inject the movement with the notion that the emotional is political: "I want to live free in my territory," "I love my land," "I suffer for my community and what happens to it," "my heart hurts because there is no justice in my territory." Being affected becomes affectivity and political action.

Territorial community feminisms are shaped by our collective practices, in community networks that confront the long-standing dispossession of the body-territory. They have positioned the body as a construct that is not merely individual but inseparable from the territory-land. Likewise, the community is conceived as a social relationship in which women play an essential role. When we face territorial violence, we stealthily organize ourselves to crack these patriarchal and colonial counter-attacks, often embodied in the cultures of our territories.

Women who deploy territorial strategies in community networks do not usually break with our communities, because we are part of them and being there is usually a political challenge, as long as the community is questioned and transformed. Our non-breaking does not mean standing still, but it is through our territorial strategies that we build spatialities where we feel safe and networked, to continue cracking the invisible wall that surrounds us. Within the spaces we inhabit, we are trying to build a utopia — non-patriarchal, non-separatist, anticolonial and of course anti-systemic organizations.

The itineraries that we have been walking together for more than six years reveal to us that territorial community feminisms are a proposal and a perspective incarnated in our latitudes — through dialogue, debate and development — which we build in daily action and that arises from our theoretical-political practice of transformation.

Notes

1   A longer version of this essay was originally published in Spanish in 2020 in *Revista Estudios Psicosociales Latinoamericanos* 3, 1: 88–107.
2   The Sixth Declaration of the Lacandon Jungle is a political-organizational proposal that was issued by the EZLN in June 2005. One of the central arguments is organizing, being collective, and rethinking — that is the only solution to building possible worlds. I'm from the Sixth because I adhere to the Sixth Declaration, because I support the Zapatista movement, and I believe in its organizational ethical-political ideas. I learned from my oppressions as a woman and as an Indigenous person through my struggles, and I organize myself together with others, because I also affirm that this is the only possible way to build a world where many can fit.
3   A space for militant and feminist research-action, created in Quito, Ecuador in 2012. We are diverse partners with political activists that believe in villages, collectives and communities from Ecuador, Mexico, Peru, Uruguay, Brazil and Colombia. We share desires to build dissident and communal knowledge. See <territorioyfeminismos.org>.
4   MUTRAM was born in 2010 and was legally established in 2014. The dream was started by two women (me and Noelia). We were joined by six women committed to social change, but not with the same political perspective. This situation led to a major breakup in 2017 and resulted in the departure of four colleagues. In 2019, like phoenixes we reviewed ourselves, thought-felt ourselves again and rebuilt. Currently, we are five women who make up the organization. One of MUTRAM's greatest strengths is believing in the possibility of building new ways of doing politics among women, and from there accompanying the fabric of possible worlds together with other women, young girls and their peoples. Since the beginning of our formation, we have been allies of the CEIBA, who are key civil society actors within the border region of

Chiapas. Little by little and together with them, we have been making way for our political unity.
5   CEIBA is a popular education team that promotes the construction of subjective conditions for social change. They seek to develop capabilities for transformative action by supporting collective processes and responding to the educational needs of each process. Since the beginning of our formation, we have been allies of the CEIBA, who are key civil society actors within the border region of Chiapas. Little by little, and together with them, we have been making way for our political unity. See <ceibacomitan.wixsite.com/ceibacomitan>.

References

Alvarado, Mariana, Delmy Tania Cruz Hernández, and Lisset Coba Mejía. 2020. "Feminismos en Movimientos en América Latina y el Caribe. Intersecciones Entre Pensamiento y Acción Política." *Millcayac – Revista Digital De Ciencias Sociales* 7, 12.

Agarwal, Bina. 2004. "The Gender and Environment Debate: Lessons from India." In V. Vázquez and M. Velásquez (eds.), *Miradas al Futuro. Hacia la Construcción de Sociedades Sustentables con Equidad de Género*. Ciudad de México: Universidad Autónoma de México.

Bilder, Marisa. 2013. "Las mujeres como sujetos políticos en las luchas contra la megaminería en Argentina." *X Jornadas De Sociología*. Faculty of Social Sciences, University of Buenos Aires, Buenos Aires. At <cdsa.aacademica.org/000-038/346.pdf>.

Butler, Judith. 1999. *Gender Trouble. Feminism and the Subversion of Identity*. New York: Routledge.

Cruz Hernández, Delmy T. 2020. "Nosotras como mujeres que somos: Entre la desposesión, la insubordinación y la defensa de los cuerpos-territorios." Doctoral dissertation, Ciesas-Sureste, Chiapas. At <ciesas.repositorioinstitucional.mx/jspui/handle/1015/1035>.

Galeano, Subcomandante. 2015. "De Cómo Llegamos a la Cofa del Vigía y Lo Que Desde Ahí Miramos." In *El Pensamiento Crítico Frente a la Hidra Capitalista*, Vol. 1.

Gutiérrez, Raquel. 2011. "Entramados comunitarios y formas de lo político." In *Palabras para tejernos, resistir y transformar en la época que estamos viviendo*. Oaxaca: Pez en el Árbol.

Guzmán, Adriana. 2019. *Decolonizar la Memoria, Descolonizar los Feminismos*. La Paz: Redición Llojeta.

Lugones, Maria. 2008. "Colonialidad Y Género: Hacia Un Feminismo Descolonial." In W. Mignolo (ed.), *Género Y Descolonialidad*. Buenos Aires: Signo.

Mahmood, Saba. 2008. "Teoría feminista y el agente social dócil: Algunas reflexiones sobre el Renacimiento Islámico en Egipto." In L. Suárez Nava and R.A. Hernández Castillo (eds.), *Descolonizando el Feminismo: Teorías y Prácticas desde los Márgenes*. Catedra: University of Valencia.

Martínez A., Luis. 2019. *Feminismos a la contra. Entre-vistas al Sur Global*. Santader: Editorial Lavoragine.

Mies, Maria, and Vandana Shiva. 1993. *Ecofeminism*. London: Zed Books.

Migliaro González, Alicia Isabel, and Lorena Rodríguez Lezica. 2020. "Ecofeminismos al Sur. Claves para pensar la vida en el centro en el Uruguay." *Bajo el volcán* 1, 2: 143–174.

Millán Moncayo, Márgara. 2011. "Feminismos, Postcolonialidad, Descolonización: Del Centro a Los Márgenes." *Andamios. Revista de Investigación Social* 17.

Mohanty, Chandra Talpade. 1984. "Under Western Eyes: Feminist Scholarship and Colonial Discourses." *boundary 2*, 12–13.

Oyěwùmí, Oyèrónkẹ́. 1997. *La invención de las mujeres. Una perspectiva africana sobre los discursos occidentales del g*énero. Bogotá: En La Frontera.

Rocheleau, Dianne, Barbara Thomas-Slayter, and Esther Wangari. 2004. "Genero y ambiente: una perspectiva de la ecología política feminista." In V. Vázquez, and M. Velásquez (eds.), *Miradas al futuro. Hacia la construcción de sociedades sustentables con equidad de g*énero. Ciudad de México: Universidad Autónoma De México.

Trevilla Espinal, Diana Lilia. 2018. "Ecofeminismos y agroecología en diálogo para la defensa de la vida." *Biodiversidad la Revista*. At <biodiversidadla.org/Documentos/Ecofeminismos_y_agroecologia_en_dialogo_para_la_defensa_de_la_vida>.

PART FIVE

LABOUR

INTRODUCTION TO PART FIVE

Giorgos Velegrakis, Diego Andreucci and Gustavo García-López

Political ecology scholars have so far offered important theoretical thinking on the ways in which nature and labour are intrinsically linked (Räthzel and Uzzell 2013); on how worker and environmental alliances are critical to advancing economic and environmental transformation (Russell 2018); and rethinking ecological politics in class terms today (Barca 2019). All these attempts aim at bridging a double historical gap. First, academically, between the environmental studies (that have taken little account of labour) and labour studies (that have largely ignored the environment). Second, in terms of political strategy, between the environmental and labour movements (that have seen each other as opponents in several cases).

We propose understanding the expropriation of natural resources and the exploitation of labour as two sides of the same coin. The central questions of this book — "What is to be done, by whom, and how?" — are at the core of this section. Additionally, the section follows Barca's (2017) proposition to build a political strategy for socioecological transformation upon a more solid analysis of the social forces involved, their mutual relations and common interests. In such a strategy, the labour movement, including trade unions and other working-class organizations, have a dual role. On one hand, they are vital as the political subjects of any radical transformative strategy. On the other, they are crucial for engaging (both theoretically and politically) in environmental justice activism. To this end, it is important for working-class struggle to broaden its focus beyond income and occupation, to incorporate other subaltern interests and positionalities.

The chapters in this section address the questions posed above, while discussing and possibly reconceptualizing labour environmentalism as forms of environmental activism that aim to effect radical transformations, based on principles of mutual interdependence between production, reproduction and ecology (Barca and Leonardi 2018). Each chapter tells a story of a historical or ongoing socioecological struggle from a different part of the world. The authors describe how communities, activists, trade unions and other organized workers build, out of their interrelated practices, counterhegemonic articulations against intersecting forms of exploitation, oppression and dispossession. In several cases, they successfully create new transformative collective projects through practices of alliance and solidarity. Finally, they put forward questions of new political subjects and organizations beyond traditional trade-unionism or environmentalism.

By doing so, all case studies share several commonalities, including: a) a political ecology approach that highlights the multidimensional links between labour (or class, more broadly) and the environment; b) the study of the crucial role of power relations in structuring unequal socioecological relations; c) the analysis of the way diverse subaltern groups are equally threatened by globalizing capital; and d) the need for understanding (as well as reconceptualizing) working-class ecology and labour environmentalism. These contributions offer important insights for thinking of new and alternative paths towards a "Just Transition."

From an ecosocialist perspective (that all chapters share), a Just Transition refers to the process of transitioning from a capitalist, fossil fuel-based economy to a more sustainable and equitable system that seeks to reduce dependency on fossil fuels while prioritizing social and environmental needs of workers and communities. Ecosocialists argue that a Just Transition must be centred on the principles of social and environmental justice (e.g., Foster 2020; Löwy 2015; Kovel 2013). This also means that those who are most impacted by the transition must have a say in the decisions that affect their lives. Moreover, in ecosocialist terms, a Just Transition involves redefining the concept of work and value, departing from the hegemony of growth and capital accumulation. Within the current climate crisis, all chapters argue, a socioecological and socioeconomic transformation involves a fundamental deconstruction of the currently dominant economic and social system — racial-patriarchal capitalism — toward a more sustainable and equitable one.

In these terms, all chapters historicize and contextualize environmental problems and their interrelation within the socioeconomic sphere, while seeking to develop possible alternatives. Jacklyn Cock argues that a new politics of convergence between labour and environmental justice movements is emerging globally. By focusing on the case of South Africa, she provides evidence of this convergence, as trade unions and environmental civil society organizations are fighting together against extractive activities across the country. According to the author, this common project created new spaces of thinking and organizing for a Just Transition toward a common ecosocialist future, despite the different interests and preoccupations.

In a similar way, Tatiana Roa Avendaño reflects on the efforts of Colombian workers in the energy and mining sectors to converge with environmentalists, Indigenous and peasant communities and other organizations to confront extractivism. It seeks to understand the motives that led the workers to advance these multi-sectorial articulations against extractivism, even when this may affect their source of income; and how worker organizations included in their visions and narratives issues such as the defence of the environment, and the respect for harmonious relations between society and nature.

Giorgos Velegrakis and Danai Liodaki discuss a major socioecological conflict taking place over the last several years in Skouries, Greece. Drawing on interviews and informal conversations with diverse local actors, for and against the mining project, the authors analyze how conflicts around mining shape everyday life in the area. They research if and how confrontation is the only way of belonging in areas and communities with such socioenvironmental conflicts that cut across the social, economic, political and everyday life and affect both local activists and miners.

The chapters in this section do not exhaustively cover the multiple relations between labour and the environment. Yet, they open important questions — such as the role of trade unions; the relations between environmental issues in the Global North and the Global South; practices of the labour movement for environmentally and socially just alternatives to the present modes and relations of production — issues that are at the core of any transformative politics.

References

Barca, Stefania. 2017. "The Labor(s) of Degrowth." *Capitalism Nature Socialism* 30, 2.
_____. 2019. "Labour and the Ecological Crisis: The Eco-Modernist Dilemma in Western Marxism(s) (1970s–2000s)." *Geoforum* 98.
Barca, Stefania, and Emanuele Leonardi. 2018. "Working-Class Ecology and Union Politics: A Conceptual Topology." *Globalizations* 15, 4.
Foster, John Bellamy. 2020. *The Return of Nature: Socialism and Ecology*. New York: Monthly Review Press.
Kovel, Joel. 2013. *The Enemy of Nature: The End of Capitalism or the End of the World?* London: Zed Books.
Löwy, Michael. 2015. *Ecosocialism: A Radical Alternative to Capitalist Catastrophe*. Chicago, Illinois: Haymarket Books.
Räthzel, Nora, and Uzzell, David. 2013. "Mending the breach between labour and nature: A case for environmental labour studies." In N. Räthzel, and D. Uzzell (eds.), *Trade unions in the green economy*. London: Routledge, 1–12.
Russell, E.D. 2018. "Resisting Divide and Conquer: Worker/Environmental Alliances and the Problem of Economic Growth." *Capitalism Nature Socialism* 29, 4.

A TRANSFORMATIVE JUST TRANSITION AS THE DRIVER TO AN ECOSOCIALIST FUTURE IN SOUTH AFRICA

Jacklyn Cock

This chapter suggests that new spaces of thinking and organizing for an ecosocialist future are emerging in South Africa and much of the Global South. Its foundations are connections between radical elements in the labour movement and new organizational and ideological forms from civil society fighting for justice and against extractivism, a mode of accumulation involving the exploitation of labour and natural resources as part of the system of global capitalism. Until now resistance to extractivism has been scattered and episodic. But we are beginning to see a new politics of convergence between the labour and the environmental justice movements globally (Uzzell and Räthzel 2012; Velicu and Barca 2020). The concept of a "Just Transition" is prominent in debates on this convergence but cannot serve as a unifying narrative because it lacks coherence in terms of both modalities and goal. Furthermore, the convergence of interests between the labour and environmental movements is not straightforward. The environmental movement is largely focused on the climate crisis and adamant about the immediate closure of coal mines and some sixteen coal-fired power plants. The labour movement is largely preoccupied with the unemployment crisis, the highest in the world, and the displacement of coal workers. The chapter suggests that a common project would involve a coherent and focused notion of a just transition to mean dismantling capitalism and building an ecofeminist socialist society.

Ecosocialism has been defined as "the convergence of resistance and anticapitalist movements from below, and their practices and critiques that together articulate opposition to relations of exploitation and dispossession, and the defence, establishment, and elaboration of praxes of an alternative political economy and way of being rooted in social and ecological justice" (Brownhill 2022: 3). Gender justice is also relevant and claimed to be "the third foundational line of ecosocialism" (Kovel 2021: 34). The current practices of ecofeminists are recognized in the notion of "ecofeminist socialism." The key principles are justice and sustainability.

The concept of a just transition

The origins of the concept of a just transition lie with the International Trade Union Confederation. The Paris Agreement of 2015 accepted the International Labour Organization's guidelines that the transition from fossil fuels to renewables must promote the creation of more decent jobs, anticipate the impact on employment, provide adequate social protection for job losses and displacement, and promote skills development and social dialogue. Overall, the concept was extremely narrow and reformist. Today there is no consensus on its meaning with competing approaches representing different class interests. These range from a vague conception of "system change" to a minimalist approach involving a low-carbon, resource-efficient economy including the social protection of vulnerable workers with "green jobs" and "green growth." A "green economy" or "green capitalism" relies on expanding market and new technology, leaving existing capitalist relations largely intact (Cock 2014; Swilling 2020).

In the last ten years in South Africa the concept has been stripped of any visionary content, appropriated by powerful elites and narrowed to simply mean a shift to a new (largely privatized) energy regime. For many working-class people, it is an empty concept that lacks substance and is unrelated to their immediate survivalist needs. For the thousands of workers involved in the coal value chain, a just transition that is reduced to mean only the imminent closure of several coal-fired power stations is deeply threatening; "this Just Transition will kill us," one coal worker commented. In many communities in Mpumalanga, where most of the coal-fired power stations and coal mines are situated, there is a deep dependence on coal. Not only does it provide jobs, but coal workers provide a market for the many women who rely on informal sector activities. Government remains wedded to extractivism, which is at the centre of the "minerals-energy complex," a system of accumulation encompassing critical links and networks of power between the financial sector, mining and energy corporations and government" (Baker et al. 2015: 8). It defines the just transition in a social dialogue approach, "which poses no threat to the mainstream, pro-growth, business-dominated narrative, a narrative that was largely created by a global corporate elite" (Sweeney and Treat 2018: 27).

The current challenge is to emphasize the provocative potential of the concept of a just transition to mobilize for change and fill it with a shared vision of a postcapitalist social order. Fragments of such a vision are emerging from the labour movement, new civil society formations and ecofeminist organizations.

The current context in South Africa

South Africa demonstrates widespread and intense social insurgence. This is a response to environmental degradation and injustice, rising unemployment, inequality and deprivation, creating anger and defiance. In 2021 this exploded in chaotic mass protests, violence and looting with some three hundred deaths. Some protest actions are strongly gendered with young men predominating in localized actions such as burning tires to block access roads to extractivist sites, destroying buildings and other violent actions. Women are particularly active in formulating demands especially for participation in decision making. There also is a growing surge of organized collective action largely directed at the failure of local government to provide essential services such as water and sanitation. Increasingly this social energy involves communities organizing themselves, going beyond protest to issues such as allocation of sites for building shacks, "illegal" electricity connections and resolving disputes. Ngwane (2021: xx) has described how in shack settlements small committees termed amakomiti organize all community issues through "a grassroots form of democratic practice." Ngwane describes these as "democracy on the margins … a democracy of people pushed aside and neglected who are fighting to have their needs addressed" (Ngwane 2021: 157). While these uncoordinated struggles and initiatives are important in terms of mobilizing collective energy, they lack a vision of an alternative society.

At the same time, neoliberalism has eroded the power of organized labour. In addition to unemployment, it must cope with an increasingly casualized workforce, a budget of austerity, restrictive strike legislation, rising food, energy, and transport costs (Kenny 2020). The outcome is fragmentation. The largest trade union, the National Union of Metalworkers of South Africa (NUMSA), has long argued strongly for a just transition from coal to renewable energy that is socially owned and democratically controlled. However, a National Union of Mineworkers (NUM) media release on February 2, 2022 "vehemently supports the stance taken by Mineral Resources Minister ... that there will be a lot of coal generation in the country by 2030 or even after that." They maintain that "it will be very irresponsible and reckless for the country to stop the use of coal ... We have always suspected that there is an imperialist agenda in this whole thing." But there are also points of convergence such as support for renewable energy "for building environmentally friendly power stations and to investigate all technologies which can reduce the pollution of greenhouse gas emissions." However, according to the NUM president, "we have started a process of mobilizing communities to resist and oppose the move of getting rid of coal. Why do we have to appease the capitalists?" This perversely supports carbon capitalism. The labour movement seems caught in the crossfire between the challenging task of protecting workers' long-term interests by addressing the climate crisis and closing the coal plants to reduce carbon emissions, and protecting workers immediate interests by mobilizing to secure a just transition that includes income support, re-skilling and job replacement.

The provocative potential in the concept of a just transition

The concept of a just transition emphasizes the need for change and frequently operates as a provocative call to collective action, mobilizing a variety of protest actions on the streets — and on the beaches — as in the current protests about seismic mining for oil that threatens marine mammals as well as local fishing communities. While there is no mass-based movement for a just transition, no collective actor, nor master frame encoded in any blueprint (Swilling 2020), the concept is promoting new thinking and organizing about alternatives to neoliberalism.

The labour movement

Beginning in 2010, the labour movement in South Africa played a key role in introducing and promoting a radical understanding of a "Just Transition" as the driver of transformation, claiming that "A just transition provides the opportunity to deepen transformation that includes the distribution of power and resources" (COSATU 2012). The concept was both grounded in peoples' lived experience and aspirational; it was at the heart of a powerful narrative of hope for a more just and sustainable world, a compass for alternative forms of producing, consuming, and relating to nature.

The labour movement recognized that the expansionist logic of capitalism means it is not only unjust but, also, unsustainable. The Congress of South African Trade Unions (COSATU) 2012 climate policy framework was comprehensive, asserting that "climate change is part of a larger economic and ecological crisis which represents a serious challenge for the working class in general and the trade union movement in particular." It involved a set of twelve principles; the first stated that "Capitalist accumulation is the underlying cause of excessive greenhouse gas emissions" (COSATU 2012: 53). Endorsed by the Congress's Central Committee, this document linked sustainability and justice and was widely distributed. It currently forms the basis for trade union officials to argue for the revitalization of the labour movement.

This policy framework was the product of a reference group established by the research arm of COSATU in 2011, on which all twenty-two affiliate unions were represented, as well as activists from some environmental justice organizations. Drawing on "coalition power" this formed the embryo of a red-green coalition to drive a just transition strategy. However, there were differences between the National Union of Mineworkers (NUM) and the National Union of Metalworkers (NUMSA), which should have been addressed more directly. NUMSA organized for publicly owned and democratically controlled renewable energy. The NUM was increasingly defensive of the interests of coal miners in the face of the threats of job losses from mine closures, falling coal prices, mechanization, absolutist demands from environmental activists like "Keep the coal in the hole" and the divestment movement. Then (and now) the NUM continues to argue for "clean coal" from expensive and untested technological innovations such as carbon capture and storage.

However, in the subsequent years the labour movement, to some degree, retreated into a defensive position, focused on protecting existing jobs. This protective stance is wholly comprehensible in the light of South Africa's unemployment rate of 40 percent (one of the highest in the world), massive job losses in the mining industry (particularly gold and platinum) and high levels of poverty. Today this is changing and COSATU has produced a blueprint for a just transition that builds on the 2012 document and argues for labour to drive a radical transformation of the economy to ecosocialism. It identifies three principles of a "new African ecosocialism": 1) economic transformation towards democratic ownership; 2) sustainable work, livelihoods and wellbeing; and 3) a low-carbon and climate resilient economy" (COSATU 2022). The document has a strong ethical dimension, stressing that capitalism brings out the worst in people and glorifies self-interest and competition. Ecosocialism emphasizes mutual support, sharing, reciprocity and cooperation. There was an enthusiastic response to this document when it was launched in Johannesburg on March 10, 2022. This new approach involves moving from a social dialogue or social compact approach and is closer to the social power approach of the South African Federation of Trade Unions (SAFTU).

SAFTU, which broke away from COSATU and claims 800,000 members, is explicitly a socialist organization and supportive of "the politics of convergence." According to the president, "the lack of climate action from our government means we must take to the streets, build a broad and diverse movement and demand action for a just transition from fossil fuels. It is for labour and the climate justice movement to stand together for a just and sustainable world" (Vavi 2019: 5). It is particularly inclusive in that it is "in favour of a just transition … In a way that protects the livelihoods of mining and energy workers and the lives of communities most affected by environmental pollution" (SAFTU media statement June 2, 2018). This is significant as those mining-affected communities living next to coal mines and coal-fired power stations have suffered the most and been largely excluded from debates on a just transition. SAFTU has consistently advocated for the social power approach that involves militant class-based activism, in contrast with the social dialogue approach. In 2021 both COSATU and SAFTU were together striking against deteriorating conditions for the working class. Their demands are for a new economy "a socialist democracy where the economy is under common ownership, management and control of the working class" and "a healthier environment protecting the interest of workers in the energy mining, smelting and related industry" (SAFTU media statement August 3, 2021). SAFTU provides a compelling message though its charismatic founder Zwelinzima Vavi, especially regarding the African National Congress (ANC) state. He recently pointed out,

"When South Africa's President refers to the need for a 'just transition' in the same speech where he announced that the national public utility Eskom would be broken up or 'unbundled' to attract private investors we know the term has been captured, co-opted and corrupted" (Vavi 2019: 35). On October 7, 2020 both labour federations were together striking against deteriorating conditions for the working class, particularly job losses, corruption, and gender-based violence. This is the first time the two major labour federations have collaborated, putting rivalries and their bitter histories aside in over two decades. However, there is serious disconnect regarding the role of labour at the local level.

According to Matthews Hlabane, the founder of MACUA (Mining Communities United in Action), "COSATU are mainly active only at the national level" (Interview, Witbank June 21, 2018). Another environmental justice activist working with mining-affected communities recently met with the National Union of Metalworkers but "I felt they were trying to intimidate me. They said the job losses from the closure of coal mines was because we insist on environmental compliance ... they said the debates on a just transition are not connected to our experience and our struggle as workers" (Interview, Middleburg February 13, 2019). However, this disconnect is slowly closing as grassroots experience of how extractivism impacts negatively on both nature and on workers' livelihoods is growing.

There are environmental justice organizations promoting strategic agendas with labour towards a socioecological transformation. For example, in 2019, groundWork organized a "coal exchange," a meeting of environmental activists from mining-affected communities.[1] This event illustrates what has been called building "prefigurative activism: the participants are imagining alternative futures" (Marquardt and Delina 2019: 92). This event is also an illustration of how environmental activists in fenceline communities can act as "catalytic agents" working in partnerships that involve mobilizing resistance to coal (Nilsen 2010: 70). The report on the exchange states, "A just transition requires a transition to a democratic order supported by an economy based on economic, social and environmental justice rather than growth" (Hallowes and Munnik 2019: 112). Following the coal exchange some laid off mineworkers joined environmental activists, local trade union officials from NUM, NUMSA and the Transport and Allied Workers Union (SATAWU) and COSATU reference group Naledi to exchange views on a just transition. This event is a significant pointer to labour–environmental collaboration for substantive change which is building from below instead of imposing blueprints from above. However, there were "Sharp differences on the future of coal" (Hallowes and Munnik 2019: 183). A NUM official stated, "You green activists take a delight in ending coal, but coal means jobs and life for us." These differences have been intense recently in relation to renewable energy. The labour movement is not against renewables but increasingly defensive and adamant that the state's privatized renewable energy policy is a threat because it will involve job losses and increased energy prices. At the same time the environmental movement is increasingly adamant about the immediate closure of coal mines and coal-fired power stations and a shift to renewable energy (in whatever form) as essential to a just transition. It does not acknowledge that a deep just transition requires changes not only in the sources of energy, but also in who owns and controls various components of the energy system (Overy 2018: 8).

Emerging environmental and climate justice organizations

While the labour movement is radicalizing, new civil society organizations are emerging that centre on transformative versions of a just transition. Their statements are largely principled and aspirational rather than agendas that provide strategic direction. However, some do provide what could be building blocks for a transformative just transition driven from below: community-owned and controlled renewable energy plants, small-scale agroecology, communal kitchens and food, a basic income grant, alternative forms of construction and transport, and other social forms that are infused with a sense of solidarity.

The Climate Justice Coalition is one such organization that is potentially powerful in its wide range of members, which includes SAFTU. It has an inclusive agenda: "Together we are working on advancing a transformative climate justice agenda with workers to tackle the inequality, poverty and unemployment that pervades South Africa. We are advocating for a vision of climate justice which advances environment, energy, racial, immigrant, climate and economic justice together." However, it is not a community-based alliance and may not appeal to communities in mining-affected areas whose notion of justice prioritizes immediate concrete issues such as compensation for damage to their homesteads from blasting, mining blocking access to a water source and the employment of local people in the mines.

An older formation, the Alternative Information and Development Centre (AIDC) is focused on "Building alliances for a just transition to a wage-led, low carbon development path." There is some research cooperation between labour and other organizations — for example, between AIDC, NUMSA and NUM — in promoting a model of Eskom remaining a public entity with conditions that it transitions to renewable energy and no workers are retrenched. The organization drives the Climate Jobs Campaign and has identified over one million new, alternative "climate jobs," meaning specifically "those that help to reduce the emissions of greenhouse gases and build the resilience of communities to withstand the impact of climate change" (Ashley 2018: 27). Examples include developing renewable energy plants, public transport, and small-scale organic agriculture. However, one trade unionist insisted that the climate jobs campaign "to have any traction … should be driven by labour and housed within the SAFTU" (Key informant interview, Johannesburg March 14, 2018).

Another significant new civil society initiative is a detailed charter for "Climate Justice and a deep just transition," which is building a mass-based movement demanding that parliament adopt key principles for transformative change. The document stresses people's power and unity; stating "solidarity is central to the deep just transition and serves to unite all who are struggling for emancipation from oppression and for a post carbon world." The Charter consists of eight very broad principles: climate justice, social justice, ecocentric living, participatory democracy, socialized ownership, international solidarity, decoloniality and intergenerational justice. It presents a vision of an ecosocialist society, though socialism is not mentioned and the language (especially the notion of "Decoloniality") is inaccessible to grassroots communities.

The potential of ecofeminism

The aforementioned Charter, however, does not feature a strong gender perspective. This is provided by several women's organizations, particularly WoMin, an NGO committed to building a women's movement for climate justice and a just transition for Africa from an ecofeminist perspective.[2] WoMin is at present mobilizing for an African Feminist Just Transition Charter with grassroots women throughout Africa. In July 2018, a meeting of a group of ecofeminists resulted in a draft titled

The Mogale Declaration (WoMin 2019). This is a list of twenty-six principles, which could be claimed as socialist, namely: "ecological balance, social and economic justice for all, food sovereignty, socialized renewable energy which benefits women, clean air and water, valuing and reclaiming African traditional knowledge, living simply, living Ubuntu in our relations with each other and nature, land held in common, living well — not better, collective, democratic leadership … climate justice is critical because it demands that the unjust capitalist system be dismantled." These principles need to be aligned with the priorities of the labour movement.

Ecofeminism is defined not as an identity, but a set of practices. "It has become a theory and movement largely articulated by the activist themselves" (Gaard 1993: 6). While not always claiming the identity, Black working-class women in mining-affected areas are doing important ecofeminist work in their practices. An ethic of reciprocity, solidarity and sharing is evident in their daily lives. It means women sharing the onerous task of clearing land for planting, or harvesting, saving, and sharing seeds, collecting grass for thatching, collecting wild plants for food or medicine, fetching water or firewood, cultivating food gardens and generally performing the tasks of social reproduction. This ecofeminism involves a redefinition of "nature" in several senses: firstly, a rejection of "nature" as the source of gender identities that subordinate women by "naturalizing" qualities of submission, deference and exclusion; and secondly, a rejection of the dualistic view of "nature" as an externalized, discrete entity separate from society. The latter is not "new" in that it draws on integrated understandings of the nature-society relation as integral to many Indigenous cultures. These stress our connections with all life forms in a shared ecological community (Berkes 2008). Compared to the instrumentalist, expansionist logic of neoliberal capitalism, this work is promoting a new narrative about our relationship with nature, a revaluing of nature as something more than a store of natural resources for economic activity to be utilized for short-term gain without concern for long-term survival, or as a sink for waste products.

In South Africa and globally most environmental justice activists are women (Shiva 2014). The explanation of women's preponderance in these environmental struggles is not essentialist. It is not based on any natural affinity that women have with nature, but as Merchant wrote, "any analysis that makes women's essence and qualities special, ties them to a biological destiny that thwarts any possibility of [their] liberation" (Merchant 1990: 102). The explanation lies in the gendered division of labour — the unpaid care work that women are doing both in the home and in the community. As ecofeminist Vandana Shiva writes, "women are most directly involved with subsistence work and are the safeguards of the natural resources needed to sustain the family and community" (Shiva 2014: 65).

Many feminist theorists have insisted that feminism is anticapitalist because of capitalism's connection with patriarchy (Luxton 1980; hooks 2015). "A feminism that speaks of women's oppression and its injustice but fails to address capitalism will be of little help in ending women's oppression (Holstrom 2002: 8). As bell hooks wrote, "Feminism as liberation struggle must exist apart from, and as a part of the larger struggle to eradicate domination in all its forms" (hooks 2015: 22). Several feminist schools are explicitly anticapitalist (Fakier and Cock 2018). For example, one participant stated, "we looked at how capitalism and extractivism are bedfellows who rely on using women's labour while devaluing and oppressing them" (in Benya and Yeni 2022: 11).

Conclusion

The challenge is to create a shared, imaginative vision of a just transition to another world beyond neoliberalism. Building the connections between feminists, environmental justice activists and trade unionists has exciting potential for a postcapitalist world. Its foundations are the growing convergence between labour and environmental justice activists as well as the emergence of an ecofeminist framework that connects patriarchy, capitalism and environmental destruction. Despite its limitations, the concept of a just transition emphasizes the need for change, exposes competing interests and galvanizes collective action. New social forms involving relations of reciprocity, solidarity and cooperation are emerging and embody fragments of a vision of an alternative post-capitalist future.

Inspirational concrete examples of such a future are increasing. There is a powerful example of a democratic socialist commune established by Abahlali baseMjondolo, which was built on a land occupation and is run through democratic processes. Food is collectively produced and distributed. These practices are concrete examples of the spirit of solidarity that is at the core of a democratic socialism. Furthermore, at the time of writing, a press statement was issued by the Zabalaza Socialist Forum for Left Renewal, which states:

> The eastern cape is collapsing. Our people have had enough of failed promises and lies from the political elite … There is no other sustainable and workable alternative to the crises but a people-driven socialist vision and programme to transform society … the coming week-end more than eighty delegates representing trade unions, social movements, civics and youth organizations … will gather for a dialogue for rebuilding working class power and renewing the socialist agenda. (Zabalaza Press Statement, February 24, 2022)

This is an appropriate response to Ian Angus's (2009: 232) warning that "if capitalism (of whatever type) remains the dominant social order, the best we can expect is unbearable climate conditions, an intensification of social crises and the spread of the most barbaric forms of class rule."

Notes

1 See <groundwork.org.za/>.
2 See <womin.africa/>.

References

Angus, Ian. 2019. *Facing the Anthropocene: Fossil Capitalism and the Crisis of the Earth System*. New York: Monthly Review Press.
Ashley, Brian. 2018. "Climate Jobs and Two Minutes to Midnight." In Vishwas, S. (ed.), *The Climate Crisis*. Johannesburg: Wits University Press, 272–292.
Baker, Lucy. 2015. "The Political Economy of Decarbonisation." Energy Research Centre, University of Cape Town.
Benya, Asanda-Jonas, and Yeni, Sithandiwe. 2022. "Co-developing Local Feminist 'Conceptual Vocabularies' While Strengthening Activism through Critical Consciousness Raising with South Africa's Mine and Farm Women." *South African Review of Sociology* 52, 1: 72–89.
Berkes, Fikret. 2008. *Sacred Ecology*. New York: Routledge.
Brownhill, Leigh et al. 2022. "An introduction to eco-socialism." In *The Routledge Handbook on Ecosocialism*. London: Routledge, 1–11.
COSATU (Congress of South African Trade Unions). 2012. "A Just Transition to a Low-Carbon and Resilient Economy." Johannesburg.
_____. 2022. "A Just Transition for Workers." Johannesburg.
Cock, Jacklyn. 2014. "The 'Green Economy': A Just and Sustainable Development Path or a 'Wolf in Sheep's Clothing?'" *Global Labour Journal* 5, 1: 23–44.
Fakier, Khayaat, and Jacklyn Cock. 2018. "Eco-Feminist Organizing in South Africa: Reflections on the Feminist Table." *Capitalism, Nature. Socialism* 29, 1: 40–57.

Gaard, Greta. 1993. *Ecofeminism: Women, Animals, Nature*. Philadelphia: Temple University Press.
Hallowes, David, and Victor Munnik. 2019. *Down to Zero: The Politics of a Just Transition*. Pietermaritzburg: Groundwork
hooks, bell. 2015. *Talking Back: Thinking Feminist, Thinking Black*. New York: Routledge.
Holstrom, Nancy (ed.). 2022. *The Socialist Feminist Project*. New York: Monthly Review Press.
Kenny, Bridget. 2020. "The South African Labour Movement." *Tempo Sasi* 32, 1: 119–136.
Kovel, Joel. 2021. "The Ecofeminist Ground of Ecosocialism." In Brownhill et al. (eds.), *The Routledge Handbook on Ecosocialism*. London: Routledge, 32–38.
Löwy, Michael. 2021. "The Ecosocialist Alternative." In Legun, Katherine (ed.), *The Cambridge Handbook of Environmental Sociology*. Cambridge University Press, 143–151.
Luxton, Meg. 1980. *More than a Labour of Love: Three Generations of Women's Work in the Home*. Toronto: Canadian Scholars.
Marquardt, Jens, and Laurence L. Delina. 2019. "Reimagining Energy Futures: Contributions from Community Sustainable Energy Transitions in Thailand and the Philippines." *Energy Research & Social Science* 49: 91–102.
Merchant, Carolyn. 1990. *The Death of Nature: Women, Ecology, and the Scientific Revolution*. New York: HarperCollins.
Ngwane, Trevor. 2021. *Amakomiti: Grassroots Democracy in South African Shack Settlements*. London: Pluto Press.
Nilsen, Alf Gunvald. 2010. *Dispossession and Resistance in India: The River and the Rage*. London: Routledge.
Shiva, Vandana. 2014. *Making Peace with the Earth: Beyond Resource, Land & Food Wars*. Johannesburg: Jacana Press.
SAFTU (South African Federation of Trade Unions). 2018. Media statement, June 2. At <saftu.org.za/archives/4345>.
_____. 2021. Media statement, August 3. At <saftu.org.za/archives/6070>.
Sweeney, Sean, and John Treat. 2018. "Trade Unions and Just Transitions: The Search for a Transformative Politics." New York: Trade Unions for Energy Democracy.
Swilling, Mark. 2020. *The Age of Sustainability: Just Transitions in a Complex World*. London: Routledge.
Overy, Neil. 2018. "The Role of Ownership in a Just Energy Transition." Research Report. South Africa: Project 90 by 2030.
Uzzell, David, and Nora Räthzel. 2012. "Mending the Breach between Nature and Labour." *Interface* 4, 2: 81–100.
Vavi, Zwelinzima. 2019. "Their Just Transition and Ours." *Amandla* 66: 34–36.
Velicu, Irina, and Stefania Barca. 2020. "The Just Transition and its Work of Inequality." *Sustainability: Science, Practice and Policy* 16, 1.
WoMin. 2018. "Women Building Power." Johannesburg: WoMin.

WORKERS' STRUGGLES IN COLOMBIA

From the Defence of National Sovereignty to the Defence of Territory

Tatiana Roa Avendaño

For decades, the most visible demands of Colombian oil and mining workers were the nationalization of natural resources,[1] the defence of national patrimony and the promotion of their own industry to meet the needs of the country (Roa Avendaño 2013). However, in recent years, several trade union organizations in the mining and energy sector have joined the local and national struggles against extractivism and for territorial defence.

In the early years of this century, the public services union (Sintraemsdes) joined the call and promotion of the Referendum for Water, which encouraged a multisectorial alliance demanding the recognition of water as a fundamental right and its cultural dimension, the universal guarantee of a free vital minimum and the prohibition of water privatization. This initiative was frustrated by the lack of political will of the Congress of the Republic. A decade ago, in the Guajira region of northern Colombia, Sintracarbón, the coal workers' union linked to the El Cerrejón company (owned by BHP Billiton, Glencore and Anglo American), which operates the mine of the same name, joined the social movement that has been fighting for several years against the company's expansion that wants to divert the Ranchería River and the Bruno Stream to exploit the minerals underneath them. At the end of 2019, an assembly of oil workers, the main body of the Unión Sindical Obrera (USO, Workers' Trade Union), the most important oil union in Colombia, decided, by majority, to condemn fracking[2] in shale rocks, and to join the hundreds of organizations that have questioned this technique and are fighting for its prohibition in Colombia.

In Colombia, as in other Latin American countries, the so-called commodity boom[3] exacerbated the extraction of natural resources and increased environmental conflicts. These conflicts have been nurtured by the changes in the general social dynamics: actors have joined the actions in defence of the territory with new demands and narratives. Together with the resistances that demand the recognition of rights for Nature, new proposals arise to suspend or put a moratorium on extractive activities, and narratives such as the demand for the non-exploitation of oil as the blood of the Earth are recognized. In addition, they promote "new ecosocial pacts" seeking a profound transformation that transcends dependence "on oil, coal and gas, mining, deforestation and large monocultures."[4] Maristella Svampa (2012) speaks of an ecoterritorial turn, in collective action, understood as the convergence of a common language between Indigenous community and environmental and territorial defence struggles.

In this context of national mobilization and multisectorial articulations against extractivism, the Mesa Social Minero Energética y Ambiental por la Paz (Mining, Energy, Environmental and Social Roundtable for Peace), hereinafter referred to as the "Social Roundtable," emerged in Colombia. This space, which was promoted by USO workers, has facilitated debate among social organizations in Colombia that have questioned a development model based on plunder, violence and dispossession, giving rise to struggles against extractivism and in defence of territory, water and life.

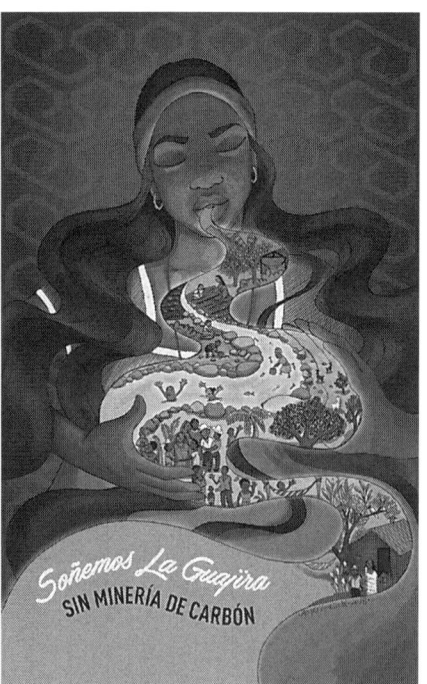

"Let us dream La Guajira without coal mining." By Angie Vanessita.

This article reflects on the efforts of Colombian workers in the energy mining sector to articulate with environmentalists, Indigenous and peasant communities, local communities and other organizations to confront extractivism, based on the experience of the Social Roundtable. It seeks to understand the motives that lead the workers to realize these multisectorial articulations against extractivism, even when this may affect their source of work, the inclusion in their narratives of issues such as the defence of the environment, and the respect for harmonious relations between society and Nature.

The First and Second Peace Assemblies

Colombia is the most dangerous country in the world for trade union activity. In the last three decades, hundreds of union leaders have been assassinated for their activity in defence of labour and territorial rights (ENS 2020).[5] Even in this adversity, the conquests of a sovereign oil policy in favour of the country are the work of the oil industry workers. At the beginning of the twentieth century, by clandestinity, the USO, the main union of oil industry workers, fought to create a national company that would guarantee that the oil wealth would remain in the country for the benefit of the Colombian people, instead of transnational companies. The strike of 1948 made it possible for the national Colombian oil company Ecopetrol to be created on August 25, 1951, taking advantage of the assets seized from the private Tropical Oil Company. The struggle of the workers and democratic and nationalist sectors also guaranteed state participation of 50 percent in all oil contracts and improved the oil income. Ecopetrol became the most important oil company in the country. This struggle, amid an armed conflict, had a hard cost for the oil union: many of its leaders were assassinated. For this reason, the search for peace and a negotiated political solution to the armed conflict has been present in the demands and struggles of Colombian workers, particularly those associated with the USO, but has also contributed to the strengthening of the union's articulation with other social sectors.

In this perspective, the USO convened and held the First National Assembly for Peace in 1996. It was called *Para que Colombia viva: Petróleo, Paz y Progreso* (For Colombia to Live: Oil, Peace, and Progress) and was attended by a large number of social organizations, workers and political leaders. The central objective of the Assembly was to place at the centre of the debate the role of energy and mining wealth for the construction of regional development and peace. This First Assembly was held under difficult conditions for the social leadership, which was suffering the ravages of the armed conflict. The USO called on the armed actors to remove oil, its workers, and communities from the armed conflict, and on the national government to advance in the resolution of the conflict. As a result of this event, the Permanent Assembly of Civil Society for Peace and the Development and Peace Program for Magdalena Medio emerged.[6] However, repression and criminalization against the Colombian labour and social movement continued, and almost two decades passed before a new assembly convened.

In mid-2015, the USO held the Second National Assembly for Peace with the purpose of "contributing to a political solution to the social and armed conflict in Colombia; generating scenarios for dialogue at regional and national level between the different sectors of society, the government and the insurgency, to address conflicts through broad and democratic dialogue; explore ways for a post-agreement to turn into development for the communities, towards a truly stable and lasting peace; promote a mining-energy policy that respects human beings and the environment, and that guarantees that the profits from these activities are invested for the good of the communities; and disseminate the proposed Hydrocarbon Framework Law that was drafted by the USO" (USO 2015). The proposed law sought to improve the conditions of oil contracts and oil rent, as well as social investment and environmental requirements for oil companies.

This call came during a favourable political climate. A few years earlier, the Colombian government and the FARC and ELN guerrillas had begun talks to negotiate a way out of the armed conflict, and peace debates were intense.[7] Because of the negotiations, the new winds of peace opened important debates on the role of land, natural resources, and peace building. This added to the intense resistance against the extractivist model that began to deepen in the first decades of the twenty-first century.

The Second National Assembly for Peace was held between November 19 and 20, 2015 in the city of Bogotá. Prior to the national meeting, around fifty sub-regional assemblies and thirteen regional assemblies were held in different parts of the country, mainly in regions where mining and energy projects were being promoted. In this multitudinous series of events, around 10,000 people and around 1,800 local, regional and national organizations participated. This allowed for a broad debate on the Colombian extractivist model, and the elaboration of proposals

March against fracking organized in 2016. Photo credit: Rafael "Felo" Alvarez (Cuba)

for territorial development and the construction of an integral peace. The interesting thing is that, for the first time, an event organized by workers in the mining-energy sector did not revolve around the problems of mining-energy income, the nationalization of mining wealth, or the ownership of companies, but around environmental issues: the problem of water and other environmental impacts of mining, territorial dispossession, and the right to participation.

By mandate of the Second Assembly, the Social Roundtable was created, a broad space for the convergence and articulation of social, environmental and workers' movements related to the debates and struggles against the extractive model and the government's mining and energy policy.

The Mining, Energy, Environmental and Social Roundtable for Peace

The Social Roundtable was created with the purpose of promoting a broad deliberation on the need for a sovereign and democratic public policy of the mining and energy State that would contribute to the construction of peace, to respect the rights of nature, of workers and of those affected by dams, and to guarantee the good living of communities in the territories.

> **Objectives of the Mesa Social Minero Energética y Ambiental por la Paz (Social, Mining, Energy and Environmental Roundtable for Peace)**
>
> - To build an agenda with civil society, to present to the country a new proposal for a new alternative energy mining model that guarantees the rights of workers, the good living of communities, respects nature and makes energy sovereignty viable.
> - To build peace from the territories to defend the rights of communities and respect for nature as part of the construction of a true integral peace, with social and environmental justice.
> - To contribute to the construction of a shared vision of a nation that leaves behind the anachronistic structure of social and economic inequality that has been at the root of the armed conflict.
> - To overcome these inequalities through the search for a common ground, guaranteeing fundamental and political rights.

At the beginning of the twenty-first century, as mentioned above, the intense struggle against extractivism deepened. The divergence in the proposals of the social sectors generated strong tensions, mainly between workers and unions in the mining-energy sector, and social and environmental organizations. In response, in 2011 an attempt was made to create a broad and diverse coalition called Red Colombiana Frente a la Gran Minería Transnacional (RECLAME). The Network brought together environmental, civic and community movements, labour unions, small and medium-sized national miners, students, academics and artists fighting against large-scale transnational mining, and set out to promote efforts to stop open-pit mining projects promoted by the government through its mining-energy locomotive policy. However, RECLAME dissolved after two years because of the divergent views these groups had on mining.

With the lessons learned from RECLAME, around one hundred organizations formed the Social Roundtable, which brought together various social sectors of the country, including environmentalists, Indigenous peoples, Afro-Colombians, small and medium-sized miners, peasants, women, workers, artists, and young people. The initial leadership of the Social Roundtable was held mainly by workers in the mining and energy sector, among them the USO, the Coal Workers Union, Sintracarbón, the Electrical Workers Union (Sintraelecol) and the Central Unitaria de Trabajadores. A broad coordination of unions and representation of social movements was created through the Movimiento en Defensa de los Territorios y Afectados por Represas — Movimiento Ríos Vivos (Movement in Defence of Territories and People Affected by Dams — Living Rivers Movement).

The functioning of the Social Roundtable was not easy. As in the case of RECLAME, there were several tensions and ambivalences among the sectors that made it up. On the one hand, the communities demanded a moratorium on mining activities, the rejection of fracking, and a halt to large hydroelectric projects, while the workers saw their jobs threatened and argued that mining and energy activities could be carried out if there was strict compliance with environmental legislation and contracts were renegotiated. Reconciling these divergent positions was complex. However, the incursion of extractive projects with the "commodity boom" raged against the territories and the bodies of women and workers, which forced them to join forces to halt the advance of the mining-energy transnationals. The violence with which these projects were imposed resulted in the assassination or criminalization of several social and union leaders, displacement of populations, and mining regions becoming true sacrifice zones. Extractivism stripped peasant and agricultural vocation regions of their ways of life, destroyed rivers and polluted extensive areas (Roa Avendaño 2012; Roa Avendaño and Navas 2014; Roa Avendaño and Duarte Abadía 2012; Toro Pérez et al. 2012). The leadership of the Social Roundtable sought to put common interests first to keep alive the social articulation that was gradually becoming a reference in the national debate against extractivism.

The fight against fracking and dams

In 2016, resistance to fracking and large dams took on important steps. In San Martín, Cesar, three massive mobilizations took place that same year. In addition, a national articulation began forming that called for a National Day against fracking, managing to mobilize dozens of activists to the Magdalena Medio region, the epicentre of fracking projects. The Colombian Ministry of Mines and Energy had given the green light to this technique, despite the warning function of the Comptroller General of the Republic, which, using the precautionary principle, had pointed out the risks of this activity. The anti-fracking movement managed to put this debate on the national agenda, questioning this technique with an intense mobilization and rigorous arguments.

On the other hand, the construction during the first decades of this century of three large dams (El Quimbo, Ituango and Hidrosogamoso) mobilized thousands of people who saw how their territories were transformed as the gigantic walls rose, damming the Magdalena, Cauca and Sogamoso rivers, respectively. For the first time, the questioning of hydroelectric projects made its way to the national level, transforming the imaginary of broad social and political sectors for whom the dams represented the progress and energy that the country required for national development.

"No to fracking, not here, not there, not today, not ever." By Angie Vanessita.

These debates reached inside the Social Roundtable and challenged workers in the sector. In the heart of the USO's rank, file and leadership, the anti-fracking debate became difficult. Some sectors considered that fracking was an opportunity to reactivate the oil activities that were in decline after the end of the commodities boom, that it was only necessary to improve legislation and make a change in contracting, while other sectors advocated for a moratorium. Similarly, Sintraelectol's leadership faced difficulties with sectors that questioned the country's hydroelectric development. These two issues, although there were many more, made evident the complexity of the functioning of the Social Roundtable, which had to settle the differences between those who understand mining and energy projects as a threat to the territories and conversely, the workers or sectors of small-scale miners, who understood them as an opportunity for employment and development.

On the road to a just energy transition

To break out of the polarization in which the Social Roundtable found itself, the Ríos Vivos Movement, which brings together the anti-dam struggles, and Censat Agua Viva wrote the document *Energy Transition: Reflections, Debates and Proposals*.[8] As a result, the debate in the Social Roundtable was reoriented towards a just energy transition, which manages to break the energy dependence on fossil fuels and solve questions such as: Energy for what and for whom? Colombia is a country with energy surpluses (it is the largest exporter of coal in the continent, has great hydroelectric, wind and solar power and oil/gas reserves); however, large sectors of society cannot access energy or are disconnected from the system due to difficulties in paying the bill.

The organizations taking part in the Social Roundtable understood that transforming the energy model requires a process with broad involvement of citizens and their social movements. Thus, the Social Roundtable became a tool to open and promote this debate. The just energy transition was understood as an opportunity to transform the power relations of the current energy model, a democratization, decentralization, de-patriarchization, and de-privatization, linked to cultural transformations that include the relocation of activities, including those related to the agrifood system, the reconfiguration of cities, the creation of massive, public and dignified mobility systems and in general, to reduce energy and material consumption of certain sectors of the country. In this sense, the transition proposal also demanded rethinking the roles of the national oil company, Ecopetrol, the Colombian Petroleum Institute and the faculties of mining and petroleum, orienting them to become institutions that contribute to research, management and training for the energy transition. In addition, the sector's workers' unions, committed to the energy transition, understood as a process under construction, decided to create the Centre for Research and Innovation for the Just Transition of the Mining and Energy Sector, CIPAME.[9]

The Social Roundtable proposed in 2018 that these and other alternatives be discussed in a national mining-energy dialogue in which the different social and political actors would converge (MESMEAP 2018). Although the dialogue was not welcomed and supported by the last governments, the truth is that some of these proposals became part of the national political agenda and have even enriched the last two electoral debates.

"Energies for the transition". By Angie Vanessita. See https://angievanessita.wordpress.com.

However, in recent years, particularly due to the pandemic, the Social Roundtable has reduced its activities, but may find its way in the new political moment of the country, with the Petro-Marquez government, which has proposed to suspend the new oil and gas exploration contracts and to advance in an energy transition; it has also opened spaces to discuss these and other proposals such as the Great National Dialogue and binding territorial dialogues that will be fundamental in the construction of the National Development Plan. This new context may be an opportunity to raise again its political and thematic agenda.

Conclusion

Throughout its history, the Colombian state has placed national wealth at the service of corporate capital, even using violence and legal and illegal military structures to destroy any social expression that opposes this economic logic. The mining-energy policy has been formulated to favour the extractivist model while communities are dispossessed of their territories and livelihoods. This condition of plundering has radicalized the class consciousness of the workers in the sector, which is why they have fought to ensure that mining wealth is used for the welfare of the poor majorities of the country and have demanded policies and contracts that are more favourable to the nation. In more recent times they have taken even more radical decisions, such as opposing fracking, the advance of coal projects in La Guajira, or mining in the *páramos*. Their socio-environmental concerns have been brought into dialogue with the rest of the social movement, through spaces that they have promoted and defended, such as the Social Roundtable. In addition, the advances in the debate on the just energy transition that have taken place in Colombia are closely related to this and other spaces promoted by workers in coordination with broad sectors. Even President Gustavo Petro's proposal to suspend new oil exploration has to do with the social consensus that this proposal has gained from within the Colombian social movement. Undoubtedly, the struggle of Colombian workers is paradigmatic and could provide elements to broaden the debates on extractivism and enable an active role of workers and their trade union organizations in other regions of the continent.

Notes

1. Although I do not share this concept to refer to natural assets, I call it this way because it has been the way workers have named them.
2. Hydraulic fracturing or fracking is a technique used in the extraction of hydrocarbons in the source rock. These geological formations (usually shales) have a low permeability. For this reason, horizontal wells are drilled in different directions until the shale containing gas or oil is reached. Once there, the rock is fractured by injecting a mixture of water, sand and chemicals at high pressure, which forces the hydrocarbons to flow out of the pores. Since the pressure drops very quickly, new wells must be drilled to maintain reservoir production. For this reason, hydraulic fracturing involves the occupation of vast extensions of territory, demands an intense amount of water and generates a high level of socio-environmental conflict.
3. The commodity boom or commodity super cycle is the period between 2000 and 2014, characterized by a sharp rise in the price of a large number of raw materials (food, energy, metals and chemicals). The growing demand for materials and energy from emerging economies, mainly China, had a strong impact on Latin America and Africa, exacerbating the extraction of natural resources and provoking strong socio-environmental conflicts.
4. See Ecosocial and Intercultural Pact of the South, <pactoecosocialdelsur.com>.
5. The National Labor Union School has recorded, from January 11, 1973, to November 30, 2020, "some 15,317 violations of the rights to life, liberty and integrity committed against trade unionists, of which 3,277 are homicides, 7,541 threats and 1,952 forced displacements" (ENS 2020).

6   The Magdalena Medio is a region in the extensive inter-Andean valley in the central part of Colombia formed by the Magdalena River between the surrounding rapids with Honda (Tolima) and the entrance of the river to the sheets of the Caribbean region in Colombia. It is distributed among several departments in the centre of the country. Barrancabermeja, considered the oil capital of the country, is located there.
7   On November 24, 2016, the government of Juan Manuel Santos and the FARC signed an Agreement for the Definitive Termination of the Conflict in the city of Bogotá. Following this Agreement, members of this guerrilla group created the political party Los Comunes and currently participate in politics. The ELN and the government of Juan Manuel Santos broke off negotiations at the beginning of 2019 and dissolved the Negotiation Table. This guerrilla group is still active as an armed group.
8   See <co.boell.org/es/2018/03/01/transicion-energetica-en-colombia-aproximaciones-debates-y-propuestas>.
9   CIPAME was created with legal status in Bogotá in January 2022 by the Sintraelecol and Sintracarbon unions. The USO joined last July with the authorization of its national assembly of delegates.

References

ENS (Escuela Nacional Sindical). 2020. "Violencia contra el sindicalismo en Colombia preocupa a la OIT." At <ail.ens.org.co/opinion/violencia-contra-el-sindicalismo-en-colombia-preocupa-a-la-oit/>.

MESMEAP (Mesa Social Minero Energética por la Paz). 2018. "21 propuestas desde el sector minero energetico para la paz y la transicion hacia un proyecto compartido de país." At <transiciones.info/wp-content/uploads/2020/02/21-PROPUESTAS-DESDE-EL-SECTOR-MINERO-ENERGETICO-PARA-LA-PAZ-Y-LA-TRANSICION-HACIA-UN-PROYECTO-COMPARTIDO-DE-PA%C3%8DS.pdf>.

Roa Avendaño, Tatiana (ed.). 2012. *Conflictividad en el sector minero-energético en Colombia*. Censat Agua Viva, Cinep, Cetec, Synergia. At <issuu.com/cinepppp/docs/documento_conflictos_minero_definitivo>.

_____. 2013. "De la fábrica al territorio. Dimensiones sociales y ambientales en las resistencias de los trabajadores colombianos." In M. Lang, C. López and A. Santillana (Grupo Permanente de Trabajo sobre Alternativas al Desarrollo) (eds.), *Alternativas al Capitalismo / Colonialismo del Siglo XXI*. Quito: Fundación Rosa Luxemburg.

Roa Avendaño, Tatiana, and Luisa María Navas (eds.). 2014. *Extractivismo. Conflictos y resistencias*. Bogotá: Censat Agua Viva.

Roa Avendaño, Tatiana, and Bibiana Duarte Abadía. 2012. *Aguas represadas: El caso del proyecto Hidrosogamoso en Colombia*. Bogotá: Censat Agua Viva.

Svampa, Maristella. 2012. "Consenso de los commodities, giro ecoterritorial y pensamiento crítico en América Latina." *Observatorio Social de América Latina (OSAL)* 32.

Toro Peréz, Catalina, Julio Fierro-Morales, Sergio Coronado, and Tatiana Roa (eds.). 2012. *Minería, territorio y conflicto en Colombia*. Bogotá: Universidad Nacional de Colombia.

Unión Sindical Obrera. 2015. Hydrocarbons Framework Law (unpublished)

BELONGING BY CONFRONTATION

Living, Working and Struggling next to a Mine in Halkidiki, Greece

Giorgos Velegrakis and Danai Liodaki

The mines now wrought are about half an hour from Nizvoro, between two hills, in a deep ravine, where a stream of water serves for the operations of washing, as well as to turn a wheel for working the bellows for the furnace. The whole is conducted in the rudest and most slovenly manner. The richest ore is pounded with stones upon a board by hand, then washed and burnt with charcoal; the inferior ore is broken into larger pieces and burnt twice without washing. The lead, when extracted from the furnace, is carried to Kastro, where the silver is separated, in the proportion of two or three drams to an oke of 400 drams. When the present shafts are exhausted, the mines will probably be abandoned. (William M. Leake 2010 [1835]: 164)

Already since the nineteenth century, large-scale ore extraction had been carried out in various mines in the region of Halkidiki, Northern Greece — as English historian, geographer and traveller William M. Leake recorded in detail in his four-volume book *Travels in Northern Greece* (1835). The extractive activities were massive in terms of production but unregulated, with significant negative effects on the health of the inhabitants and the environment. Working conditions for the miners were particularly painful, as Leake describes. There were also frequent riots by the workers and the local communities, because of the unfavourable working conditions, the unpaid work, and the regular deaths of workers or local inhabitants due to accidents.

The so-called "newer history" of the mines begins in 1893 when mining rights were granted by the Ottoman Empire to the famous

Franco-Ottoman Company. As was the case in several areas in Greece at that time (e.g., the mines of Lavrio near Athens, the Cycladian islands of Serifos, Milos, etc.), the lack of Greek capital and the lack of extractive expertise paved the way for international companies, mainly European, rushing to exploit the rich mining reserves of the Greek land. This situation has continued until current times. Since its birth, mining in Greece is internationalized, in which the place of extraction is merely a hub to international speculative interests. The mining explorations have always been invariably accompanied by a vocal and widely propagated discourse, wherein notions of underground metals as "subterranean treasure," "instrument of fiscal salvation" and "method of geopolitical empowerment" are firmly intertwined with opaque technical terms borrowed from geology (Karampatsos et al. 2022).

In the long mining history of Halkidiki, several discontinuities can be observed. Let us remember, for example, that on March 14, 1977, the company's metal workers went on strike for twenty-eight months, highlighting their harsh working conditions and low pay. From 1995 to 2003, the residents resisted the installation of a gold plant in the area by the then-Canadian company TVX Gold. The mobilizations were hit hard by the state repression, both in the 1970s and the 1990s.

Following a history of transfers from company to company, Eldorado Gold, a Canadian gold and base metals producer with mining, development and exploration operations worldwide, became the owner of Halkidiki mines in 2003. In 2011, the Greek government approved the company's business and exploration plan. It granted Eldorado Gold rights over land, permits for mining, fiscal incentives, and a fast-track approval procedure for the expansion and intensification of gold extraction. Despite the delays of the project between 2015 and 2020, the company got a renewed permit in early 2021.

The project has faced great opposition locally since 2011. Concerns about environment, health and quality of life aside, in a region where the economy mainly depends on tourism, farming, beekeeping and fisheries, increasing gold extraction puts into serious jeopardy the sustainability of existing local economic activities.

These short excerpts show that mining has always been an economic, social and political capital for Halkidiki in different periods. But there is no seamless mining history. On the contrary, mining has been and still is a history of conflicts, contestations, and intersections of labour and

The Skouries mining project in Halkidiki as of September 2022. Source: <hellas-gold.com>.

the environment, whereas local communities and/or the workers have been organized in social movements to defend their rights. It is, in other words, a class history where the subaltern classes have brought up their demands and, occasionally, have come up with alternative visions for local development, the environment and everyday life.

These visions are not always shared by everyone and create a terrain of conflict even among the locals. Local environmental activists mobilize against the project as it excludes them from access to collective goods and resources (e.g., the environmental commons), while it unequally distributes environmental and social costs precipitated by intensive resource extraction and appropriation of land.[1] In sharp contrast to them, pro-mining actors, mainly miners working in the company, demonstrate their indispensable bonds with their work and place by supporting the project. "Mining is the only future of the area," argues Nikos, a 43-year-old miner (personal communication, March 2015).[2]

The understanding and analysis of these visions, and their meanings, is at the core of this chapter. We shed light on how a socioenvironmental conflict acts as a terrain for generating diverse and conflicting future visions of local development for the area. We also inquire into if and how social conflict and confrontation to mega-projects creates a feeling of "belonging by confrontation" for the locals, which cuts through their visions and conceptualizations of well-being, everyday life, and above all, of the future. We argue that a feeling of environmental, social and political suffocation is generated, influencing imaginaries and transforming everyday life. We, then, analyze (how and by whom) the environment is socially constructed, deconstructed, and reconstructed in Halkidiki because of the conflict. We bring up the concept of "the conflictive negotiation of the environment" as a key focal point for understanding place-specific environmental conflicts and the position of the main actors within them. Finally, we revisit workers' alienation as a key concept for their (positive, in many cases) attitude towards the growth imperative, which is entrenched not only in existing institutions but also in overall societal norms, values and discourses to the point to how it operates as a mental infrastructure or a subtle mode of subjectivation (e.g., Brand et al. 2021; Adloff and Neckel 2019). In this chapter, we attempt to enlarge the discussion on labour environmentalism by understanding it also as a terrain of conflict. We rely on qualitative research, interviews and informal conversations with local actors, pro and against the mining project, and on participatory observation.

Living by confrontation and suffocation

As Robbins (2004: 173) notes in his well-known "thesis on environmental conflict," there are two main aspects that are recognized and studied in the field of political ecology. The first concerns the politicization of environmental problems when state agencies or private capital control and have exclusive access to collective goods (natural resources) at the expense of some or all local communities. The second concerns the "ecologization" of pre-existing conflicts because of changes in policies for development or access to resources.

Mobilizations against the gold mining projects in Halkidiki, Greece in 2014. Source: <efsyn.gr/>.

Both aspects are obvious in Halkidiki. For over a decade now, the local social movement challenges the legality of the environmental permit issued to the project by the Council of State (Greece's highest administrative court) by organizing protests, scientific and cultural events, and solidarity actions with other national and international movements. In this process, through their direct engagement with everyday political action, they make sense of the world and develop new socioenvironmental relations, in ways that transform their everyday life and subjectivity (Velegrakis et al. 2022). Conversely, the employees of the company also build active and conscious socioenvironmental relations. For them, environmental protection cannot take precedence over work, labour power and income.

These conflictive performativities of the local activists and the miners takes place in the forest of Halkidiki where the mines are located, in their villages, in the streets of big cities where they demonstrate, in the courtrooms, in their public discourse and in their everyday life. Therefore, the conflict is formed by many small and daily conflicts. Through this process, the locals create and support not only different claims about the here and now, but also different narratives and reproductions about the identity of the place, its history, and visions of its future development.

Maria, a 65-year-old pensioner (personal communication, November 2014) argues: "I have three children, two boys and a girl. My sons are both migrants in Germany. Once they thought about coming back. I don't want them to return if they are going to work for the mining company and betray our community." On the contrary, Alexis, a young miner of twenty-five, illustrated the general feeling of the miners: "Our grandfathers were miners, our fathers were miners, and we will be miners as well. It is our only option to survive in our villages; our only alternative to migration" (personal communication, March 2015). Each side brings to the public discourse their personal stories, their own considerations, representations based on their social status and on their gender.

Within the conflict, the demand for immediate action is the dominant one. The protesting locals are prepared, at any moment, to clash with the police, to stop with their bodies a truck or a company machine, and to enter the company's "private" and restricted areas such as the mine in the Skouries forest. The belief that "we are right" is predominant among the local activists: "I feel that the state is unfair to me. I feel the police are unfair to me. I feel the court is unfair to me. But I say we're right, it can't be otherwise. Justice is all we have left. And that is what we will continue to fight for" (Lina, 25-year-old university student, personal communication, November 2014).

However, workers for their part also consider that they have been subjected to violence and injustice by members of the anti-project movement. This sense that there is a community that puts them "against" is important in interpreting their attitude. As one miner puts it: "A few months ago, my mother went down to the village for shopping. Some people stopped her on the street and spoke badly to her. Just because her son works at the mine. Is this fair?" (Elias, thirty-two years old, personal communication, March 2015). The various personal, social and political identities of both the activists and the miners were troubled and transformed, even ephemerally, in the emerging space of conflict, violence and a constant feeling of injustice from both sides (see also Tsavdaroglou et al. 2017).

Moreover, they bring up their different interpretations of the environment:

> For us, the local forest is not just an image. It relates to our everyday life, it's where we go on weekends to collect herbs, it's where we keep our beehives, it's where we enjoy the landscape. Therefore, our fight is both symbolic and material. If we lose, we will not just lose a forest, we will lose our life and place. (Kostas, 50-year-old teacher, personal communication, November 2014)

In contrast, Stefanos, a 48-year-old miner, argues: "Do you think we don't want the best for our place? We too breathe the same air, drink the same water. But technology has advanced. There is not much environmental harm by mining. We can't lose our jobs for ten, twenty, one hundred 'environmentalists'" (personal communication, March 2015). Local activists understand the environment as "what defines our place and life" and that which "we are called upon to protect" against a project that "encroaches on it, destroys it and denies us access to it." On the contrary, again, the supporters of the project believe that mining wealth, "the deposits of hope," should be continuously exploited, since it is a comparative advantage for local prosperity and development. This so-called "hidden treasure" describes the area.

A discourse of "mining as the only possible future" influenced the movement's approach. Those who oppose mining range from the long-unemployed, low-income unskilled workers to seasonal employees in the local tourist industry, to young people with no job opportunities locally. It is a diverse group of people united in struggle for their livelihoods and future lives in this region. Therefore, local activists have problematized issues of development and elaborated alternative proposals for the development of Halkidiki, critically approaching austerity-driven pathways of development. The alternative they elaborated is based on the creation of jobs within a sustainable economy and environment through the promotion of small-scale agriculture, ecotourism, local fisheries and forestry activities, and a network of local cooperatives. In creating a space for experimenting with alternative visions of local development, the local integrates in its struggle a philosophy of praxis for forging an alternative conception of the world beyond furthering of neoliberal natures:

> Anyone who thinks that the company only steals the environment is wrong. It steals our land, our lives, and our future. And the state supports it. And the police are beating us … All of them, apart from poisoning our environment, they also made sure to poison the society of our villages so that they could impose themselves. (Eleni, 45-year-old entrepreneur, personal communication, November 2014)

For their part, miners who are forced into a very specific specialization far from other possibilities of utilizing their labour power, identify their reproduction, their well-being, and their working and social future with the viability of the extractive activities. There are several stories worldwide on how difficult it is for many workers to even consider the possibility of losing their job, no matter how dirty and dangerous, in the absence of viable alternatives (see for instance Barca 2019). As Aris, a 55-year-old miner argues,

> The question is not whether I am for or against the mine or the company. The question is how I can and want to live in my place. And rightly or wrongly I must work in the mines. That's what I learned to do and that's what I can do. That's the history of the region." (personal communication, November 2014)

All the above stories show that in Halkidiki a lingering feeling of suffocation is historically being cultivated.[3] The local communities, for or against the extractive activities, learn to live in and next to the mines and at the same time learn or are forced to live with a feeling of suffocation that is translated into a constant confrontation. Suffocation is primarily environmental. Very often the members of the socio-environmental movement use the word "crime" to describe what is happening in their area. A crime that begins with the destruction of the environment. A specific economic activity poisons the land, the forest, the waters, and the wider natural landscape of the region while undermining their right to nature and access to the environmental goods and natural resources.

Suffocation is also social. A discourse of "mining as the only possible future" influenced both the movement's and the miners' approach. The actions of the company, the state and the police create a generalized feeling of injustice, which has a direct relation to the space of everyday life of the local population. Violence, conflict, tear gas, special police forces, criminalization and repression has invaded into that space.

Finally, suffocation is political. Local repertoire of action includes a performative political act, a collective "indiscipline" against the consensus processes surrounding the project. The inhabitants of Halkidiki have implicitly sought to create "subaltern geographies of connection" and to expand their struggle. The social movement itself and the alliance-building with other movements give content to the "dynamic geographies of subaltern political activity and the generative character of political struggle" (Featherstone 2013: 66). Solidarity-making is embedded in a philosophy of praxis that empowers participants to critically approach and actively struggle against an undemocratic and violent development pattern that overlooks social needs and local practices. In the process, they go beyond particularistic and limited local interests and bring forward alternative ideas and practices of land use, local development, and society-environment relations (Calvário et al. 2017: 84). The great social mobilization, the long duration, the transcendence of locality and the development of legal and "illegal" practices (from all actors) are signs of a political suffocation.

The conflictive negotiation of the environment

The environment in Halkidiki is socially constructed, deconstructed, and reconstructed. Locals involved in the socio-environmental movement create an imaginary of the environment as the land for their reproduction and well-being, a place for enacting socioecological transformation, practising resistance and articulating counterhegemonic demands. The miners, on the other hand, socially construct it merely as a source that needs to be constantly modified and remade for providing raw materials, the objects that labour power utilizes to make its products. The company constructs the environment as a mere host of its extraction. The state constructs it initially with the institutional framework of land use and protection, only to revise it later to the benefit of the private company. It also constructs it as the terrain for the movement's oppression and violence.

In this way, the environment is not only constructed but in fact negotiated between the different actors through conflict and confrontation. The activists, through their own limitations, contradictions, excesses and omissions, adopt, as Gramsci (1971: 346) puts it, a "new, systematic — contextual and logical — conception of the world." This new conception is produced through and because of the conflict. The other subaltern group, the miners, within the conflict and through their labour, also develop "active and conscious relationships [and] an understanding of social relations and of themselves in nature and in the world" (Gramsci 1971: 352).

Nevertheless, the struggle goes beyond a simple standoff between the forces of "development" and environmental-local protection concerns. It is an active and ongoing challenge to development patterns and an articulation of diverse visions for local development and sustainability. As Barca (2019) notes, when we study cases around investments and projects that rally both the residents who oppose them and the workers of the company in question, we must never forget the alienation that the mode of production "imposes" on the latter. In most cases, as in the case of Halkidiki, the local activists form and shape a narrative "for their place," their well-being and what can be understood as "development of their region."

For their part, workers — especially those in the extractive industries who are forced into a very specific specialization far from other possibilities of utilizing their labour power — identify their reproduction, their well-being, and their working and social future with the viability of these industries. In many cases they know and experience the environmental consequences in their locality and the impact on their health and well-being, but they consider it a necessary price to pay for the benefit of employment. They also produce different and highly contested imaginaries of the future. These imaginaries then structure their distinctive practices of sustainability in the fields of politics, local economy and development and everyday life.

Alienation, as a constitutive and corrosive element of capitalist mode of production (Harvey 2014), can be held responsible for such logics, narratives, and imaginations. The miners are alienated (estranged) from the products of their labour as well as from nature and all other aspects of social life during their contract and usually beyond. A state of deprivation and dispossession is internalized as a sense of loss and frustration of creative alternatives foregone. This process takes different forms in the different geographies of the global political economy and production.

But this is not enough, and we should look beyond. We cannot understand the corresponding conflict around resources, common goods, or the environment without also considering the voices of workers who depend for their reproduction exclusively on activities and companies that — sometimes in the name of development — lead to extensive accumulation and waste of resources and the creation of high environmental and social costs. The catalytic political problem that derives from all this and remains is to identify, confront and overcome the many forms of alienation while supporting the subaltern to gain control over not only the labour process and product, but also the political process where decisions are made over the best route to prosperity and local development. This is a process of (re)politicizing both the environmental issues and the local development questions.

This is, in our view, one of the least discussed, yet core elements of labour environmentalism. Labour environmentalism should not be limited to a convergence of environmental and labour struggles. It should be broadened up. It should be understood, conceptualized, and practiced as a constant attempt to criticize the hegemony of traditional growth imperative while being connected to community and the making of communal relations. This approach builds upon an understanding of the environment as a contested concept that crosses through labour and environmental fields, being conceptualized and acted upon in different ways within each (Barca 2019). Therefore, labour and environmentalism are two composite fields of political action that are highly differentiated within themselves, and whose areas of intervention are overlapping in several ways.

This is important for: a) the in-depth understanding of place-based socioecological struggles that rally locals in different ways according to their conflicting interests (environmental protection or securing of employment); and b) the rethinking of ecological politics in class terms today. As the Halkidiki case illustrates, labour environmentalism and alternative imaginaries of the future are always created, practiced and supported around a symbolic and political stake: the conflictive negotiation of both the environment and labour. The outcome of this conflictive negotiation remains open.

Notes

1   On the unequal distribution of social and environmental costs, see also Beltrán et al. 2016; Robbins 2015; Martínez-Alier 2002.
2   To secure anonymity of the interviewees, we use fictional names.
3   We use the term "suffocation" in dialogue with Ahmann and Kenner's concept of "Breathing late industrialism" (Ahmann and Kenner 2020).

References

Adloff, Frank, and Sighard Neckel. 2019. "Futures of Sustainability as Modernization, Transformation, and Control: A Conceptual Framework." *Sustainability Science* 14.

Ahmann, Chloe, and Alison Kenner. 2020. "Breathing Late Industrialism." *Engaging Science, Technology, and Society* 6.

Barca, Stefania. 2019. "The Labor(s) of Degrowth." *Capitalism Nature Socialism* 30, 2.

Beltrán, María Jesús, Panagiota Kotsila, Gustavo García-López, Giorgos Velegrakis, and Irina Velicu (eds.). 2016. *Political Ecology for Civil Society*. Rome: CDCA.

Brand, Ulrich, Barbara Muraca, Éric Pineault et al. 2021. "From Planetary to Societal Boundaries: An Argument for Collectively Defined Self-Limitation." *Sustainability: Science, Practice and Policy* 17, 1.

Calvário, Rita, Giorgos Velegrakis, and Maria Kaika. 2017. "The Political Ecology of Austerity: An Analysis of Socio-environmental Conflict under Crisis in Greece." *Capitalism Nature Socialism* 28, 3.

Featherstone, David. 2013. "Gramsci in Action: Space, Politics and the Making of Solidarities." In M. Ekers, G. Hart, S. Kipfer, and A. Loftus (eds.), *Gramsci: Space, Nature, Politics*. Malden, MA: Wiley-Blackwell.

Gramsci, Antonio. 1971. *Selections from the Prison Notebooks of Antonio Gramsci*. G. Nowell-Smith and Q. Hoare (eds.). London: Lawrence & Wishart.

Harvey, David. 2014. *Seventeen Contradictions and the End of Capitalism*. London: Profile Books.

Karampatsos, Christos, Spyros Tzokas, Giorgos Velegrakis, and Gelina Harlaftis. 2022. "Is There Oil in Greece? Oil Exploration and Scientific Conflict during the First Years of the Greek Geological Survey (1917–1925)." *Historical Review/La Revue Historique* 19, 1.

Leake, William Martin. 2010 [1835]. *Travels in Northern Greece, Volume III.* Cambridge: Cambridge University Press.

Martínez-Alier, Joan. 2002. *The Environmentalism of the Poor: A Study of Ecological Conflicts and Valuation.* Cheltenham, UK: Edward Elgar Publishing.

Robbins, Paul. 2004. *Political Ecology: A Critical Introduction.* Malden, MA: Wiley-Blackwell.

_____. 2015. "The Trickster Science." In T. Perreault, G. Bridge, and J. McCarthy (eds.), *The Routledge Handbook of Political Ecology.* London and New York: Routledge.

Tsavdaroglou, Charalampos, Konstantinos Petrakos, and Vasiliki Makrygianni. 2017. "The golden 'salto mortale' in the era of crisis: Primitive accumulation and local and urban struggle in the case of Skouries gold mining in Greece." *City* 21: 3–4.

Velegrakis, Giorgos, Rita Calvário, and Maria Kaika. 2022. "The Politicised Ecologies of Austerity: Anti-Austerity Environmentalism during and after the Greek Crisis." In R. Calvário, M. Kaika, and G. Velegrakis (eds.), *The Political Ecology of Austerity: Environment, Social movements, and Economic Crisis.* London: Routledge.

CONCLUSIONS

Undisciplined Environments Collective

We have planned this book as an experiment in doing political ecology differently — "from below and to the Left," as the Zapatista would put it — in two main ways. First, a political ecology that moves beyond simply analyzing, describing or denouncing environmental injustices and conflicts, daring also to address questions of counterhegemonic strategy faced by movements. The issues of whether political ecology should be "relevant" — and of where "the political" is in "political ecology" — have long been posed (Walker 2007). Yet, they often reduced politics to influencing *policy*, thereby disavowing the possibility of a truly revolutionary horizon of change, beyond the capitalist state (Graeber 2004; Swyngedouw 2011). In this sense, we suggest rethinking *the political* in political ecology as a focus on transformative strategy — a political ecology embedded in the collective praxis of a radical ecosocialism, positioning the ecological question at the centre of class, antiracist, anticolonial, and feminist struggle.

Second, we have strived for a political ecology that does all this not based on abstract theorizing, but from below, grounded in dialogue and collaboration with activists and subaltern or grassroots environmental movements. Writing political ecology "from above" is no longer tenable. We do not claim that our book is above the political detachment and coloniality of mainstream academic knowledge: it is written in English, inevitably targeted at "international" audiences with relatively high levels of formal education, and the majority of its editors are white(ish) people based in Europe who earn a living as university researchers, however precarious. At the same time, we have tried to overcome at least some of the most glaring contradictions of much academic work on environmental movements, by centring our book on stories told from the places of struggle, and by or with those who have participated in such struggles.

This points to the importance of learning from and theorizing socioecological transformation out of embodied experiences of struggle, in a two-way reinforcing process between theory and practice. The oppressed, subaltern, and dispossessed must always be at the centre, as active participants of such theorizing. Some of the movements whose ideas and voices are represented in this book — from La Vía Campesina to the Kurdish Freedom Movement — are impressive examples of such ability to collectively define their horizon of struggle, elaborate their strategies, learn from victories as well as mistakes, and adapt to changing conjunctures by reflecting on their practices.

What are the main lessons we can derive from the stories told in this collection, and how are they useful for our understanding of radical ecosocialist strategy today? We can let readers draw their own insights — certainly some of the experiences and reflections offered in the book will resonate more with activists, others will speak more vividly to students or fellow researchers — but we want to close the collection by briefly sharing a few reflections that emerged from conversations among us editors.

First, the possibilities of enacting radical socioecological transformation remain shaped and constrained by place-specific and conjunctural factors. In situations with high degrees of injustice, oppression and violence against racialized and sexualized body-territories — such as typically settler colonial contexts, authoritarian states or extractive peripheries — counterhegemony remains a horizon rather than an immediate possibility. Where the power balance is overwhelmingly in favour of the oppressor, the main struggle is for survival — to exist is to resist. Yet, even in the direst situations, we see this struggle for social reproduction being articulated time and time again into broader fronts of resistance, counterpower and re-existence. Furthermore, the stories in this book illustrate how place-specific socioecological struggles create the needed space for (re)thinking counterhegemonic or revolutionary change.

Second, solidarity is key, and specifically solidarity from below, as practiced by movements from the scale of the community, to "national popular" and internationalist solidarity, as many cases of struggles detailed in the book show. Solidarity plays out not across places and across diverse concerns — as we saw, for instance, in cases of labour and feminist movements converging with antiextractivist struggles; in North-South alliances for climate justice (stopping fossil fuels, claim reparations, climate debts, climate litigation); or in broad-based coalitions for food sovereignty. To the extent that creating divisions and cleavages is a colonial strategy, solidarity is a tool of resistance and disruption of this strategy: "your struggle is my struggle" is the cornerstone of solidarity.[1] At the centre of such practices of solidarity is a recognition that, even though the immediate demands may differ, the struggle is fundamentally the same — as cis-hetero-patriarchy, racism and colonialism are deeply embedded into capitalism, and sustain its extractivist and ecocidal compulsion to accumulate wealth, control bodies and enclose and contaminate territories.

Third, sovereignty over land, territory and other key means of production and social reproduction is often a key claim of transformative struggles. Several chapters in this collection highlight how people in conditions of settler colonialism, as well as land-based "working peoples" — to refer to those who make a living from their work on land, rivers, oceans, among others — organize, mobilize, and come together in struggles against the violence of enclosures and extractivism. These socially differentiated "peoples" include peasants, fisherfolks, forest dwellers, pastoralists, and farmworkers, in other words, individuals, collectives and communities who are directly affected by capital-driven land and ocean transformations, but also urban people whose lives are disturbed by metabolic rifts in the relationship between land, the environment, and territory. Sovereignty is a framework that captures much of these struggles and efforts for building a post-capitalist society. However, the emancipatory potential of these movements arises from their ability to engage in a cross-fertilization between critique of capitalism, political action, and everyday lived experiences, to which a "politics as translation" is key.

Fourth, feminist theories, activism and praxis are central to resist and confront patriarchy, extractive capitalism, growth and modernization at all costs and to imagine and co-enact alternatives (more inclusive, safe, diverse and just socionatures) — to fight against gender-based injustices, the de-valuing of the work of socioecological reproduction and related health issues affecting particularly specific bodies: of rural, Indigenous, Black and impoverished women and gender nonconforming people.

Fifth, class matters. The diversity of struggles considered throughout this collection cannot be considered separate from their common structuring around class. Disconnecting antiracist and feminist politics from class struggle risks reducing them back to a liberal identity politics and apolitical interpretations of "intersectionality." Similarly, as argued above, and throughout this book, ecological struggle is class struggle through and through — as Nancy Fraser has argued, bourgeois environmentalism is a historical exception rather than the norm: from sixteenth-century peasant revolts in Europe to the panoply of subaltern environmental struggles that take place globally today, defending, reclaiming, and remaking socionatures is deeply entangled with reaffirming life and community against the predations of a colonial-patriarchal capitalist class project. Issues of class are relevant in relation to wage labour in urban and rural contexts, but also to the shifting and complex relationship between commodified and non-commodified labour as it relates to women's unpaid work, migrants' forced labour, peasants' caring activities towards nature, and urban people's activism for protecting the commons.

Sixth, climate does "change everything." The stories in this book confirm, and add empirical substance to, the thesis famously put forward by Naomi Klein (2014) and others, which also became a core claim behind radical Green New Deal-type proposals (e.g., Planet to Win): that tackling the ongoing climate catastrophe is both predicated upon, and likely to foster, previously unlikely alliances across diverse movements, typically labour movements with communities on the "frontline" of extractivism and ecological destruction. This is not to deny that the destruction brought by climate change is nothing new for communities and social groups that have experienced "the end of their worlds" many times over, having lived with the disastrous effects of colonialism and extractivist capitalism for a long time. This is a reminder that the "climate catastrophe" is highly uneven (and combined): a threatening future for privileged places and classes, but a reality for the most part of humanity, where climate disruptions add to the predations of (ecological) colonialism and imperialism. However, unmitigated climate change will first and foremost impact the most marginalized, turning harsh conditions into hellish ones. The most vocal on the need to step up mitigation, adaptation and finance are states, communities and movements from the Global South, including Indigenous people. All struggles are and will be touched by the climate spiralling out of control, alongside capitalist machinations to profit from climate change responses (electrification, offsetting, new extractions, adaptation, nature financialization and the like). The fact that climate change calls into question the privilege of the North built on colonial genocide, the need to redress such injustices, and the need for globally coordinated solutions, makes it necessary to pursue a platform of convergence for anti-imperialist and anticapitalist movements across the Global North and South.

Finally, we hope the stories of struggle shared in this book show that the work of (re)imagining other worlds where all people may live "a life that is worth living" is not a utopia, but is at the centre of any strategic politics aiming at pushing the boundaries of the impossible.

Notes

1 See the webinar "Post-Extractive Futures: Networks — How Can We Build Relationships of Solidarity across Borders and Silos?" at <youtube.com/watch?v=Z20DpyOhUyA>.

References

Graeber, David. 2004. *Fragments of an Anarchist Anthropology*. Chicago: Prickly Paradigm Press.
Swyngedouw, Erik. 2011. "Interrogating Post-Democratization: Reclaiming Egalitarian Political Spaces." *Political Geography*, 30, 7.
Walker, Peter A. 2007. "Political Ecology: Where Is the Politics?." *Progress in Human Geography* 31, 3.

Building upon an inheritance of cultural resilience and collective organizing passed down for generations, Appalachian community groups are speaking out and standing up for the mountains and the miners! Educating their folks about mountaintop removal's health impacts, hosting vigils, and organizing rallies and marches, these activist "pollinators" are fighting for their homes, their mountains, their livelihoods, and their lives at great personal risk.

—**BEEHIVE DESIGN COLLECTIVE** (2008)

Cutoffs from "True cost of coal" poster, by Beehive Design Collective (2008).

INDEX

*Note: image locators are shown in **bold***

Abahlali baseMjondolo (South Africa), 244–5
Abdul Hadi, Sundus, 67–8, 78n5
ableism, 8; *see also* disability justice
Abu Aram, Harun, 25, 28, **30**, 32
Abya Yala, 214–16, 218, 223–4
accumulation, 27, 147, 153, 268
    capital, 3–4, 140, 170–1, 212, 231
    by dispossession, 130–1, 166
    extractivist, 59, 234–5, 238, 273
    parasitic, 28–8, 30, 35
    reproduction of capitalism, 8, 13, 20, 27
Agarwal, Bina, 216
agrarian reform, 54, 58, 84, 103
agri-food systems, 86, 100–1, 108
agroecology,
    artisanal fishers and, 114, 118, **119**, 122
    food sovereignty and, 84–5, 103, 70, **71**, 126n1
    movements, 57, 70, 109, 144, 241
agro-industrial model, 112
    extractivism, 52, 57–9
    mobilizing against, 103, 107–9
Alazzeh, Ala, 33–4
allyship, 140, 213, 226n4
    comradeship versus, 6–9
Al-Sanah, Riya, 28–9
Alternative Information and Development Centre (AIDC — South Africa), 242
anarchism, 8, 16, 102, 137, 144
Andalusia (Southern Spain),
    agricultural reliance on migrant workers, 103, 109–10
    food sovereignty movements in, 101–4, 108
    see also Sindicato Andaluz de Trabajadores/as (SAT — Andalusian Workers' Union; Spain)
Angus, Ian, 245
Anker, Elisabeth, 157
Anthropocene, 85, 215
anticapitalist critiques, 5, 150, 153, 244
    movements, 51, 234, 275
    specific struggles, 48, 63, 137, 206, 214
anticolonial critiques, 5–6
    diverse ecological struggles with, 13, 20–3, 67, 214, 226, 271
    social reproduction and, 26–7, 32, 35
    sovereignty movements with, 51–2, 63, 68, 137
anti-imperialist critiques, 5, 144, 275
    sovereignty movements with, 51–3, 63
anti-neoliberal critiques, 6
    community-territorial sovereignty, 23, 52–7, 60–3
    food sovereignty, 107, 114
anti-patriarchal critiques, 62–3, 215, 226
antiracist critiques, 4, 6
    ecological struggles with, 68, 102, 141, 152, 271–4
Armiero, Marco, 164
autogestion, 23, 69–71
autonomist struggle, 21–3
    direct action and, 138, 140–2, 147
    feminist, 62, 198–202, 204, 223
    food production, 105–7, 111
    just transition, 133, 156, 161
    politics of, 8, 28, 41, 52

Barca, Stefania, 230, 267
body-territories (-land), 184–5, 221–2, 225, 272
    cartography/healing of, 76–8
    notion of, 14, 217–18
Bolivia, 217
    feminist movements in, 53, 62–4
    Gas War in, 55–6
    movements' decolonial articulations, 23, 52–3, **59**, 63, 64n1
    neoliberalism in, 53, 55, 58–9, 63–4
    plurinational constitution in, 53, 56–8
    political crisis in, 53, 63–4
    Tariquía, struggle against extractivism and violence, 62–3
    Unity Pact, 56, 58
    Water War in, 55

Bookchin, Murray, 22, 39–40
Brazil, 87, 226n3
    fisher-peasant mobilizing in, 116–17, 120–5

capital,
    accumulation, 3–4, 13, 20, 140, 147, 170–1
    commons of, 84, 157, 160–2, 273
    destructive forces of, 9, 31, 67, 121, 176, 223
    false "fixes" to crises, 3, 130, 175, 262
    lobbying/investment interests of, 44, 47, 57–8, 64, 256
    transnational, 52, 59–60, 212–13, 231
capitalism,
    alternatives to, 10, 20, 40–1, 244–5, 271–5
    coloniality and, 22, 26, 32, 273–4
    crony, 166–7
    destructiveness of, 5, 8, 38–9, 234, 238–9, 268
    disaster, 73–4, 144
    entrenchment of, 4, 13, 20, 44, 152
    extractive, 7, 14, 58, 84, 154, 157
    food sovereignty versus, 118, 120–1, 124, 209
    fossil, 14, 130–2, 140–1, 147
    green, 89, 175–6, 235; *see also* greenwashing
    movement organizing under, 49, 85–6, 88, 234, 238–9
    pluriversal resistance to, 8, 60–1
    racial-patriarchal, 6, 7, 183–4, 205–9, 215, 231
    siege of, 212–13, 216–17, 221
    state, 22, 50, 166
    transformation beyond, 3–4, 63–4, 231, 236
    see also anticapitalist critiques
capitalist class, hegemony of, 4, 8, 274
carbon, 173, 237
    atmospheric concentrations of, 134, 139, 155, 168, 177n2
    envisioning a world post-, 140, 235, 242
    sequestration, 3, 238
    transition from, 14, 130, 139–41, 152–3, 163
    see also CO_2 emissions; hydrocarbons
Caribbean,
    climate crisis impacts, 67
    colonialism/imperialism in, 21, 66–7, **69**, 72, 75
    community solidarity across, 23, 71, 138, 202
    exploitation of, 67, 69

Chile, 63, 68
Chipko movement (India), 160
civil society organizations, 187
    advocacy of, 48, 104
    climate justice work by, 145–6
    energy sovereignty, 250, 252
    isolation of Palestinian, 33–4
    Israeli state criminalization of, 34
    just transition focus, 232, 234, 236, 241–2
    mobilization of, 26, 45, 57, 117
class,
    ecological politics and, 15, 105, 140, 230–1, 269
    entrenched capitalist power, 4, 8
    exploitation, 13, 75, 84
    food sovereignty and, 199, 203, 209
    intersectional analysis and, 183, 186, 189, 216, 222
    just transitions and, 144, 150, 230, 235, 239–40, 243
    movement convergence through, 6–7, 35, 54, 257, 261, 273–4
    ruling, 6, 20, 58
climate change,
    discourse, 89, 237, 274–5
    impacts, 67, 142, 152, 242
    system change, not, 14, 130, 134
climate crisis,
    intersecting with social crises, 3, 9, 151–5, 238, 274
    as learning opportunity, 7, 74, 157, 231
climate justice,
    lawsuits and, 145–6
    movements, 14, 130, 150, 182, 234
CO_2 emissions, 173, 177n2
    forest monocultures and, 89
    litigation and international agreements, 145–6, 168, 173
    narrow focus on, 3, 151, 154, 237
coal power plants, 15, 40, 255, 257, **276**, **279**
    campaigns against, 46, 71, 137–8, 141, 176, 234, 247–8
    just transitions from, 154, 168, 235–41, 252
    persistence of, 140, 152, 237–41
Colombia, 63, 138, 226n3, 232
    Assemblies for Peace, 249–51
    CIPAME (Centre for Research and Innovation for the Just Transition of the Mining and Energy Sector), 255, 258n9
    energy/mining worker mobilizing, 247–8, **256**
    Magdalena Medio region damming, 253–4, 258n6

Ríos Vivos Movement, 253, 255
Roundtables for Peace, 248–9, 251–7
Sintracarbón (coal workers' union), 247, 252, 258n9
Sintraelecol (electrical workers' union), 252, 254, 258n9
colonialism,
    capital accumulation and, 4, 20, 84, 88–9, 151–4
    climate, 23, 68
    as ecological project, 20, 69, 134
    epistemologies, 12, 271, 273
    hurricane of, 66–7, **69**, 72
    legacies of, 38, 41, 52, 130, 164
    neo-, *see* neocolonialism
    resistance to, 12, 64, 72–5, 185, 214
    settler, *see* settler colonialism
    struggles for land sovereignty versus, 13, 20–2, 34, 160
    violence of, 3, 38, 70, 212–13, 222–5, 274–5
commodification,
    labour, 8, 86, 88, 102, 274
    land/food, 13, 85, 102, 113, 119
commodities boom, 59, 176, 248, 253–4, 257n3
commons, the,
    (capitalist) enclosure of, 156–7, 160–2
    defence of, 7, 74, 133, 182, 261, 274
    plunder of, 86, 90–1
    re-establishing, 13, 93, 96, 163
communism, 68
comradeship, 6–9, 11, 13
Confederation of Indigenous Nationalities of Ecuador (CONAIE), 54, 60
Congress of South African Trade Unions (COSATU), 238–40
cooperatives,
    building of, 41, 140, 174, 265
    economy based on, 108, 133, 156, 160, 162
COP21 meetings, 114, **115, 119**
corporations,
    destructiveness of, 31, 40, 130, 199
    mobilizing against, 136–7, 139, 145, 164, 184–5
    responses to climate crisis, 3, 154, 158, 235–6
    state support for, 60, 130, 158, 199, 236, 256
    transnational, 13, 22, 60, 88
Correa, Rafael, 55, 57, 59–61
Corretjer, Juan Antonio, 77
counter-cartographies, 76–7, 219, **220, 221**

counterhegemony,
    environmental/social movements', 6, 54, 167–9
    notion of, 6, 16n1
    strategies, 117, 124–5, 131–2, 175–6
COVID-19 pandemic,
    activist organizing amid, 143, 158, 195, 256
    migrant farmworkers amid, 86, 102, 109–11
    state-capital projects amid, 31, 60

Dakota Access Pipeline (DAPL), 137, 148n1
decarbonization, 153, 166
decentralization,
    energy production, 14, 29
    food production, 106, 108
    industry, 39–40, 133
    as organizing approach, 141, 155, 255
decolonial ecologies, 23, 67, 69, 72, 77, 183
decolonial movements,
    capitalism versus, 20
    climate justice/just transition and, 132, 137, 141, 242
    historical, 21, 58, 183
    notion of sovereignty in, 13, 74–5
decolonial theory, 2
    and the body, 217–18
    influence of, 8–9, 12, 150, 153
    Northern academia versus, 4
degrowth, 5
democracy, 3, 236, 239
    deep, 152, 161–2, 176
    energy, 133, 157, 160
    radical, 13, 22, 40–1, 45, 63, 242
Democratic Confederalism, 39–40, 44, 49–50
Democratic Society Congress (KCD), 44–8
direct action, 6, 174
    climate justice and, 14, 131, 135–7, 143–7
    concept and critiques of, 136, 139–41
    convergence through, 33, 131, 136, 138, 147–8
    tactics for, 93–4, 131, **135**, 138–47, 194
disability justice, 133, 163
dispossession,
    accumulation by, 131, 166, 177n3
    body-territorial, 212, 217–19, 225
    colonial, 22–3, 134
    movements against, 13, 118, 182, 234–5, 272
    resistance to, 7–9, 11, 33–4, 231, 248–51
    social reproduction versus, 21, 27–8, 30, 199
    violence of, 62, 184, 256–7, 268

Earth First!, 139, **140**
ecocide, 8, 41, 67, 146, 273
ecofeminism, 79n17, 215
  feminist environmentalism versus, 182–3, 216
  just transition and, 234–6, 242–4
ecological crisis,
  conceptualizations of, 130, 142, 155
  need for tangible action amid, 49, 130, 142
  other crises and, 9, 238
ecology, 85, 192
  decolonial, *see* decolonial ecologies
  environmentalism versus, 40
  industry of, 40
  insurgent, 102
  integration into governance structures, 45–8
  movement focus of, 45, **46–7**, 132, 150–1, 173–6
  as permanent economy, 160
  political, *see* political ecology
  social, 22, 39
Ecology and Society Workshop (ECOSOC), Portugal, 77
Ecology Union (Turkey), 48, 176
ecosocialism, 5, 8, 271–2
  just transition in, 231–2
  new African (transformation to), 239, 242
  notion of, 234–5, 239
Ecuador,
  agrarian reform/anti-neoliberal mobilizing, 54–5, 60, **61**, 62, 214
  economy of care in, 61–2
  feminist movements in, 53, 61–2, 64, 226n3
  movements' counterhegemonic articulations, 23, 52–5, 63, 64n1
  neoliberalism in, 53–4, 58–61, 64
  plurinational constitution, 53, 55–7
  political crisis and responses, 60–1, 63–4
electricity generation,
  economies based on, 166–70, 172–3
  settler colonial attacks on, 25–31, 35
  see also hydropower projects
emissions, *see* CO_2 emissions
environmentalism, 141, 252
  ecology versus, 40
  feminist, 182–3, 216
  labour, 15, 230–2, 248, 262–4, 268–9
  mobilizations involving, 53, 89, 137, 166–70, 175, 274
  queer, 184
Environmental Justice Atlas project, 5

environmental justice struggles, 243
  decolonial sovereignty in, 23, 51, 63
  freedoms, vision of, 157–8
  frontline/fenceline, 132, 150–2, 157–9, 240
  convergence with, 69, 73, 151, 161–3
  labour movements and, 15, 132, 230–4, 238–40, 252
  need for focus on strategy, 4–5, 151
  queer, 183, 186–8, 195
Erdoğan, Recep Tayyip, 131, 166–9, 171, 175
escalation (direct action tactic), 131, 138–40, 147
ethnic cleansing, 22, 26, 32, 34
ethnography, 11, 187
Europe, 43, 90, 260, 274
  accession to, 189, 196n2
  climate justice in, 136, 139
  energy production in, 166–7, 172
  food production in, 103–4, 107–8, 126nn1, 2
  settler colonialism, 21, 88
  Southern, *see* Andalusia (Southern Spain)
exploitation, resistance to, 248
  capitalist hegemony versus, 7–8, 22, 134, 146, 162
  Indigenous communities', 26, 54–6
  labour/worker, 102–4, 106–8, 234
  pluriversal, 9, 11
Extinction Rebellion, 49, 137
extraction, resource,
  building/maintaining infrastructure for, 31, 84, 212, 257nn2,3, 267
  climate justice action versus, 134–8, 141, 152–3, 158–60, 232, 261
  colonial logics of, 68–9, 72, 259–60
  "green," 14, 131, 274
  narrow focus on, 3, 248, 267
  worldview of, 151, 154, 156, 164
Extractive Economy, 154, **155**, 156, 162
  Living Economies versus, 151–2

Fanon, Frantz, 6, 75
farmers,
  advocacy organizing, 101–6, 108–9, 117, 210n1
  food sovereignty and, 100, 102–3, 108, 112–13
  land politics and, 71, 84–5
  movements of, 13, 120, 124, 126n1
  small-scale/family, 100–1, 105–6, 124, 184, 199
  threats to, 25, 28–33, 71, 205, 260
  see also agroecology; migrant farmworkers

far-right groups/governments, 44, 53, 60, 196n2
Faz₃a campaign (West Bank), 33
femicide, 62–3, 219–20
feminisms,
    Abya Yala, 214–16, 218, 223–4
    eco-, *see* ecofeminism
    food sovereignty and, 123–4
    hegemonic, 216–17
    importance of, 73, 78n11, 183, 273
    integration in local governance structures, 45, 49
    just transition and, 152, 242
    La Vía Campesina on, 198–200, 201, 202–10, 226n3
    struggle convergence with, 6, 57, 68, 272–3
    territorial community, 184–5, 215–19, 222–6
feminist economics, 215–16
feminist movements, 49, 53, 61–4, 182, 196n4, 272
feminist political ecology, 4, 6, 215–16, 271
feminists,
    autonomous struggles, 62, 198–202, 204, 223, 244
    Black, 183, 215–16, 242–3, 273
    consensus on capitalism's harm, 5, 164, 213, 216, 244
    Indigenous, 64, 184, 215–16, 225, 273
    mobilization of, 14–15, 64, 213–14
    on settler colonial violence, 27–9, 214, 223–4
    trans-, 73
Ferdinand, Malcom, 66–7, 75
fishers, artisanal, 265
    agroecology and, 114, 118, **119**, 122
    food sovereignty mobilizing, 85, 87, 114–18, 120–5
    movements of, 69, 114–18, 123–5, 126n2
    threats to, 13, 118–19, 121–3, 237, 273
    women, 123–4
    see also Movimento dos Pescadores e das Pescadoras Artesanais (MPP — Artisanal Fisherfolks Movement)
food sovereignty, 243
    climate crisis responses and, 133, 150, 157, 160, 204
    farmers' needs in, 100, 102–3, 108, 112–13
    fishers and, 13, 85, 87, 114–18, 120–5
    introduction and importance of concept, 57–8, 73, 117–18
    movements, 86–7, 101, 133, 150, 162, 273

    peasants, 13, 114–18, 120–5, 198, 202
    pillars of, 117, 126n6
    women's/feminist involvement in, 70–1, 123–4, 184, 198–**201**, 202–10
fossil capitalism, 140
    confronting, 14, 130, 147
fossil fuels, 130, 272
    direct action targeting, 136–7, 140, 145–6
    divestment campaigns, 156, 161, 231
    government subsidies/support for, 67, 167–8
    just transition from, 231, 235, 239, 255
    narrow focus on, 3, 140, 151–4
fracking, 49, 257n2
    campaigns against, 46, 247, 251–3, **254**, 257
Franco, Francisco, 90–1, 96
Fraser, Nancy, 274
Freire, Paulo, 12
Fridays for Future, 49, 138, **143**
frontier land,
    anti-indigenous infrastructural violence, 25–6, 28–32
    social reproduction on, 32–5
frontline communities,
    climate justice and, 131–2, 134, 150–2, 157–8, **159**
    fossil capital versus, 61, 131, 147, 175
    land defence, 7, 34, 94, 161
    tactics for convergence, 138–43, 147, 166
    worker struggles and, 274
FuoriMercato (Italy),
    Campobello di Mazara organizing, **111**, 112
    Contadinazioni, 106, 108
    amid COVID-19 pandemic, 109–11
    genesis and work of, 105–8
    migrant farmworkers' rights activism, 101–2, 108–9, **111**, 112
    participatory guarantee system, 109
    SOS Rosarno, 105–6, 108

Galicia (Spain),
    Common Land in, 86, 90–1, 96–7
    De-eucalyptising Brigades, 86, 90, 92–4, **95**, 96–7
    eucalyptus tree monoculture expansion, 86, 89–90, **91**, 92, 95
    land use shifts, 90, 96
Gandy, Matthew, 189–90
García-Lamarca, Melissa, 10
gender,
    critiques of, 41–2, 150, 186–90, 207, 217, 242–3

impacts of climate crisis, 183
inequities, 8, 14, 75, 89, 164, 222, 244
justice, 199, 235, 273
movements' discourse on, 48, 123–4, 183, 195–6, 198–210
power relations, 84, 164, 198, 205–9, 214–15
representation based on, 42, 44, 94, 203, 236, 263
resource access based on, 30, 182–3, 216
gendered violence, *see* violence
gender-non-conforming people, 14, 184
gentrification, 43, 47–8, 77
Georgia (Republic of),
Green Party in, 195–6
LGBTQIA+ discrimination in, 187–9, 195, 196n2
Tbilisi redevelopment, *see* Tbilisi, Georgia, redevelopment
geothermal energy, 131, 166–73, **174**–7
globalization, neoliberal, 51, 88, 114, 156
Global North,
movement discourse/critiques in, 15, 22, 49, 276
panoply of struggles, 3, 84, 89, 137–8
tree monocultures/plantations in, *see* Galicia (Spain)
unequal relations with South, 14, 132, 147, 232
Global South,
discourse critiques by, 133, 150, 163
movement struggles in, 4, 22, 84, 131, 166, 274
representation from, 74, 89, 133, 234
unequal relations with North, 14, 132, 147, 232
Gramscian critique, 73
political ecology and, 6, 267
politics as translation, 116–17, 122, 124–5
universal horizon of struggle, 6, 8, 21, 272
Greece, mining in, *see* Halkidiki, Greece
Green New Deal, 132, 157, **159**, 274
greenwashing, 3, 67, 130, 142, 186
mineral extraction, 14, 131
redevelopment, 184, 186, 193–4
Guzmán, Adriana, 217

Haider, Asad, 10
Haiti, 21, **71**
Hakların Demokratik Partisi/People's Democratic Party (HDP — Bakûr), 42, 45–8
Halkidiki, Greece, 269

anti-mining mobilization, 259–61, **262**, 263–8
mine worker experiences in, 263–8
mining history, 259–61
Skouries mining project, 232, **261**, 263
Hammami, Rema, 32–3
Hansen, Bue Rübner, 140
Haraway, Donna, 187
heteropatriarchy, 14
Hlabane, Matthews, 240
hooks, bell, 244
How to Blow up a Pipeline, 6
human rights, 119
constitutional recognition of, 57, 145
documenting violations of, 34, 55, 146, 199, 204
movements/organizations, 26, 199
hydrocarbons, 55–6, 62, 250, 257n2
hydropower projects,
campaigns against, 43, 45, **46–7**, 168–71, 175–7, 251–5
community displacement from, 39–40, 92, 121, 131
run-of-river, 166–7, 170

Indigenous people, 117, 79n22, 89, 243
Afro-, 75–6
colonialism, impacts of, 20–2, 34, 212
direct action, 137, 140–1
dispossession, land, *see* dispossession
extractivism versus, 134–8, 141, 152–3, 232, 261
movements, 21–2, 96, 184, 199, 252–3, 274
political ecology involvement, 2, 4–5
social reproduction, 27–8, 32–5
sovereignty, struggles for, 13, 51–63, 133, 160–2, 248
uprisings, 54–5, **61**, 214
women, 184, 214–18, 222, 225, 273
see also decolonial movements; Land Back movement
infrastructure, 262
destruction of community/indigenous, 22, 25–9, 31, 34
direct action targeting of, 136–7
fossil fuel, 14, 62, 131, 168
insurgent, 32–5, 141, 145, 147
rebuilding/maintenance of, 32–5
social reproduction and, 27–8, 32–5, 187, 194
state-driven projects, 39, 43, 47–8, 169
insurgency,
counter-, 137–8

ecological, 85, 102
   notions of, 9–11, 16n2, 70, 102
   practices of, 10, 73, 164, 225
   social reproduction and, 26, 32–5, 141, 145, 147
   subaltern movements', 10, 15, 20–2, 66, 133, 250
International Day Against Homophobia, Transphobia and Biphobia (IDAHOT), 188, 195
internationalist solidarity, 6, 133, 138, 147, 272
International Labour Organization, 89, 235
Israeli state, 22
   anti-Palestinian infrastructural violence, 25–9, 31, 34
   support for Jewish settler colonialism, 25, 27–8, 30–1
Italy, 141, 164
   farmworkers in, 101–2, 108–10, **111**, 112
   food sovereignty movement, 86, 102–3, 105–6, 108, 112–13
   solidarity economy, 101, 105–9

Jordan Valley (Palestine), 25, 28–**30**, 32–3
Juris, Jeffrey S., 9–11
Justice and Development Party (AKP; Turkey), 44, 171
just transition, 74
   charter, 242–3
   direct action on, 131, 142–3, 255
   narratives of, 130, **159**, 234, 240
   notions of, 147, 151, 161, 231–2, 235–7, 244–5
   framework, 132–3, 150–6, 160–4
   movements, 13–14, 130–2, 158, 237–9
   Resilience-based Organizing, 161

Khasnabish, Alex, 9–11
Khirbet a-Rakeez (Palestine), 25–6, **30**
Klein, Naomi, 157, 274
Kubaneishvili, Kote, 194
Kurdish Freedom Movement (KFM), 272
   electoral success and policy implementation, 42–5
   social ecology framework, 22–3, 38–41, 44–5
   Turkish state policies versus, 43–4, 46–50
Kurdistan, Northern (Bakûr),
   introduction of capitalism to, 38, 44
   self-determination struggles, 21, 42–4
   support for KFM in, 42–5
Kurdistan Workers' Party (PKK), 38–40, 45, 50
Kusiani, Tornike, 184, 187

labour, 75
   agricultural waged, 86, 100, 274
   divisions of, 139, 147
   environmentalism, 15, 230–2, 241, 260–2, 268–9
   exploitation, 38, 102, 110, 151–4, 234
   forced, 88–9
   migrant, *see* migrant workers
   organized, 140, 236, 263
   precarious, 30, 60, 101–3, 106, 112, 271
   rights, 13, 101–3, 107–12, 151–4, 200, 249–52
   women's/queers'/sex workers', 94–5, 189, 195, 244, 274
labour movements, 112, 249–50, 272
   ecosocialism and, 234, 242–3
   environmental justice, 15, 132, 151–2, 239, 274
   South African, 237–43
   struggles for land, 13, 35, 86
   see also just transition
land,
   centrality of infrastructures on, 27–8
   decolonial struggles and, 21–2, 67, 69, 72, 77, 84, 183
   frontier, *see* frontier land
   grabbing, 52, 118, 130
   notions of, 13, 21, 85, 102, 113, 119
   plurality of struggles for, 13, 20–2, 34, 51–63, 94, 160–2
   politics, 13, 84–6
   privatization, 13, 85–6, 172, 186, 255
   relationality with, 13, 23, 184–5, 221–2, 225, 272
   socioecological movements for, 21–3, 51–4, 84–7, 267–9
   sovereignty, 13, 20–2, 34, 133, 160–2, 248
   theft, 21, 26, 31, 158
Land Back movement, 21, 84, 163
Lasso, Guillermo, 53, 60
Latin America,
   neoliberalism in, 53, 63, 68, 148, 157n3
   sovereignty struggles in, 21, 51–2, 63, 71, 160
Leake, William M., 259
leftists,
   anti-imperialist, 51–2
   mutual aid organizing, 144, 213, 219, 271
   political parties, 56–7, 63, 195
   tensions with other groups, 23, 52–3, 189, 196
LGBTQIA+ people, 207
   discrimination in Georgia, 187–9, 195, 196n2

see also queer movements/mobilizations; transgender people
Liberation Ecologies, 4
liberation movements, 67–8, 75, 139, 151
  Black, 150, 184
  national, 49, 51
  Palestinian, 33–4
  queer, 133, 150, 163
  women's, *see* women
litigation (direct action), 33, 131, 138, 145–7, 273
Malm, Andreas, 6
Marxist critique, 102
  political ecology and, 4–5, 40
Masafer Yatta (Palestine), 25, 28–**30**, 32–3
Mascarenhas-Swan, Michelle, 152
Mesopotamia Ecology Movement (MEM), 45–6, 48–9
migrant farmworkers, 85, 199, 273
  advocacy/mobilizing for, 100–6, 109–10, **111**, 112–13, 184
  in COVID-19 pandemic, 86, 109–12
  poor working/living conditions, 86, 103–4, 106, 109–12
  strikes by, 107–8, 110
  trade unionism, 103–4
migrant workers,
  farming, *see* migrant farmworkers
  mobilizing for, **111**, 112–13
  strikes by, 107–8, 110
  trade unionism, 103–4
militarism, 10, 16n2, 67, 151, 154–6
mining sector, 45, 122, **135**
  Assemblies for Peace, 249–51
  extractivism of, 39, 151–2, 247–51
  history, 259–62
  just transition and, 236–40, 247
  movements against, 52–5, **59**, 70, 137, 247–53, **262**, 263–6
  nearby communities, 93, 232, 240–3, 262–6
  open-pit, 135, 252
  policy discussions, 248–52, 257, 262
  rights, 259–60
  Roundtables for Peace, 248–9, 251–7
modernization, 14, 183, 273
Mohanty, Chandra Talpade, 214
monocultures, 41, 58, 75
  tree, *see* tree monocultures/plantations
Morales, Evo, 56, 59
Moreno, Lenín, 59–60
more-than-humans, 8, 15, 76, 182; *see also* non-humans
Morocco, workers from, 103

Movement Generation: Justice and Ecology Project,
  genesis and theory of change, 133, 150–3, 155–6
  Just Transition (JT) framework, 132–3, 150–4, **155**–6, 160–4
Movimento dos Pescadores e das Pescadoras Artesanais (MPP — Artisanal Fisherfolks Movement),
  agroecology and, 118, **119**, 122
  convergences with peasants, 114–16, 118–25
  food sovereignty mobilizing, 114–18, 120–5
Movimento dos Trabalhadores Sem Terra (MST — Landless Workers Movement), 123–4, 160
Mujeres Transformando Mundos (Women Transforming Worlds — MUTRAM), 213, 218, 226n4
mutual aid, 33, 110, **111**
  autogestion, 69–70
  disaster relief, 72–3, **74**, 143–4

Naqab (Palestine), 25, 28–9, 31–3
nationalism, 48
  patriarchy and, 41–2, 188
  workers' struggles and, 102, 249
nationalization, resource, 52, 56, 59, 247, 251, 260
National Union of Metalworkers of South Africa (NUMSA), 237–8, 240, 242
National Union of Mineworkers (NUM — South Africa), 237–8, 240–2
nature, 150, 177n4
  colonialism versus, 20, 27
  conservation, 43, 45, 96, 122
  dualistic views of (/culture), 157, 183, 186, 215, 243
  ecological notions of, 27, 41, 122
  exploitation of, 38–41, 122, 183, 265–6, 274
  labour/workers and, 230–2, 238–40, 243, 268
  queering notions of, 183–4, 190–1
  recognizing rights of, 57–8, 146, 248–52
  socio-, 9, 171, 176, 182–4, 267, 273–4
  urban, 186–8, 190–1, 194
  women as representative of, 41, 215–16
neocolonialism, 13–14, 20, 51–8, 184
neo-fascism, 3
neoliberalism,
  energy production, 166–7, 170–1
  feminist resistance to, 14, 205–6, 209, 243

food production and, 100, 103, 107, 114
labour conditions under, 236–7, 243–4
social/sovereignty movements versus, 51, 53–63, 117–21, 198–9
state implementation of, 26, 39, 43–4, 53–7, 59–63, 265
urbanism and, 184, 186, 192–4
see also anti-neoliberal critiques
Ngwane, Trevor, 236
non-humans,
    oppression of, 4, 67, 164
    relations with, 8, 52, 136, 157, 175, 215–16
    see also more-than-humans
nonviolence, 137, 139-40, 150

Öcalan, Abdullah, 39–41
Occupy movement, 144, 160, 170
oppression,
    class, 6, 152, 195–6
    colonial/capitalist, 130, 134, 138, 212, 217, 244
    intersecting forms of, 7–9, 74, 130, 183, 203
    political, 43, 157, 195, 267
    racial, 152, 272
    resistance to, 11, 77, 164, 184–5, 231, 242
    women's/gendered, 41–2, 189, 195–9, 208–10, 213–15
Oyěwùmí, Oyèrónkẹ́, 218

Pacheco, Federico, 103
Palestine,
    Israeli state infrastructural violence, 21–2, 25–9, 31, 34
    Jewish settler colonialism, 25, 27–8, 30–1
    liberation movements, 33–4
    Naqab, 25, 28–9, 31–3
Paris Agreement, 168, 235
patriarchy,
    anti-, *see* anti-patriarchal critiques
    feminists/women versus, 63, 205–19, 223–6, 244, 273
    gendered oppression under, 182–3, 209, 218–19
    hetero-, *see* heteropatriarchy
    intersectional oppression and, 4, 41–2, 208–9, 255, 274
    mobilizing against, 13–14, 75, 86, 123, 199
    racial capitalism and, 4–7, 183–4, 205–10, 215–18, 231
    structures of, 64, 144, 205–6, 212, 255
    violence of, 62–3, 205–6

peasants,
    food sovereignty, 13, 114–18, 120–5, 198, 202
    mobilizing with fishers, 14–15, 114–17, 119–25
Peet, Richard, 4
Pinto, Josana, 114, 116, **120**, 121
plurinationality, 52–4, 56–8, 60, 64
pluriverse, concept of, 8–9
political ecology,
    core axes of struggle, 8, 231, 262
    focus of, 4–7, 183
    feminist, *see* feminist political ecology
    Northern academic dominance, 4, 12, 271
    organic struggle involvement, 4, 7, 12, 176, 271
    practitioners, 5, 77, 176, 230
    urban, 184, 186
    see also ecosocialism; Gramscian critique
populism, right-wing, 3, 177
possibilities for revolutionary change, 4–6, 10, 142, 177, 217, 272
"Post-Extractive Futures" encounter, 74–5
precarity, 3
    workers', 30, 101–3, 106, 271
prefiguration (direct action), 131, 140–2, 147, 240
preparation (direct action), 131, 138, 143–5
privatization, 255
    energy production, 235, 241
    land, 13, 85–6, 172, 186, 205
    neoliberal, 54–5, 60
    water, 55, 247
Puerto Rico (Borikén), 138, 144
    Casa Pueblo (People's House), 70–3
    Colmena Cimarrona (Maroon Hive), 70, **71**, 72
    colonialism in, 68–9, 72
    community mutual aid/organizing, 68–73, **74**
    decolonial ecologies in, 23, 69–70, 77
    governor resignation, 73
    hurricane US disaster response, 72–3, 74, 75
    Jobos Bay Eco-Development Initiative (IDEBAJO) struggles, 70–2
    Vieques/Operation Bootstrap, 68–70

queer movements/mobilizations, 73, 196
    environmental justice and, 14, 186, 188, 193, 195–6
    liberatory, 42, 131–3, 150, 163
    sex workers', 186–95
    state violence/lack of safety, 188–91

urbanism and, 186-7, 192
queer theory/perspectives,
  cruising spaces, 186-7, 189-92, **193**, 194-5
  political ecology and, 4, 6, 14, 183-4, 186-7
  questioning of social constructs, 186-7, 189-90
  unruliness of, 184, 186, 190, 195
  see also transgender people

racism,
  capitalism and, 4-7, 183-4, 205-10, 215-18, 231
  class exploitation and, 8, 58, 75, 110, 154-5, 215
  intersectional oppression and, 75, 144, 183, 209, 215-16
  mobilizing against, 86, 123, 150, 215
  state-based/structural, 3-4, 58, 73
  struggles against, 13, 56, 84, 154-5
  violence of, 67, 104, 187, 222, 225, 273
  see also antiracist critiques
radical transformation,
  implications for movement success, 12, 15, 147
  mobilizing for, 103, 230-1, 239
Red Colombiana Frente a la Gran Minería Transnacional (RECLAME), 252-3
regenerative economies, 14, 130, 132, 154, 160-2
renewable energy,
  extraction rush, 14, 131, 176
  false branding of, 170
  geothermal, 131, 166-73, **174**-7
  legislation, 169, 241
  struggles for democratic ownership, 166, 168, 175, 237-8, 241-3
renewable products, 3, 132, 157, 166, 171, 241
  energy, *see* renewable energy
reparations, 135, 150, 272-3
  climate, 67, 76, 79n18, 130, 138, 146
research, 143, 271
  activist, 4-8, 45, 79n17, 187, 262
  collaborative, 94, 232, 242, 255
  feminist, 213, 226n3
  militant, 11-12, 16n2, 226n3
revolutionary change,
  discussion of strategies for, 5-7, 272
  possibilities for, *see* possibilities for revolutionary change
rights, 48, 251
  assertions of, 112-14, 158, 163, 248, 261

  collective, 54, 57, 85, 91-2, 119-22, 188
  human, *see* human rights
  Indigenous, 52, 55
  to land/food, 13, 58-9, 100, 269-70, 198, 266
  mining, 259-60
  of nature, 57-8, 146, 177n4, 251
  violations, 108-10, 121-4, 146, 199, 157n5, 257n5
  women's 123-4, 195, 208
  workers', 13, 101-3, 107-12, 151-4, 200, 249-52
Robbins, Paul, 262
Rose, Deborah Bird, 32
rural areas/communities,
  construction/extraction projects in, 44, 84, 85-6, 89-97, 169-71
  exodus from, 30, 38, 90-1, 175
  food struggles in, 84-7, 117, 123-5, 184-5
  mobilization of, 13-15, 47, 61, 93-7, 141, 225
  political divisions in, 31, 34, 177
  urban activist connections, 13, 34, 56, 105, 109, 214-19
  women in, 94-5, 198-202, 205-9, 225
  workers in, 100-9, 274

self-defence, struggles for, 6-8
self-determination, 28, 39, 75
  demands for, 51, 54, 58, **111**
  movements, 13, 15, 21-2, 68, 137
self-organization,
  activist, 94-6, 143-5, 208
  importance and functions of, 6-7, 100, 141-2
  worker, 86, 104, 111-12
settler colonial capitalism, 26, 32
settler colonialism,
  depletion of indigenous worlds, 26-7, 30-1
  movements versus, 7, 13, 21, 35, 273
  violence of, 20, 272-3
  see also colonialism
sexism, 42, 196n2
  violence of, 8, 187, 201, 206-7
Sindicato Andaluz de Trabajadores/as (SAT — Andalusian Workers' Union; Spain), 101
  in COVID-19 pandemic, 109-12
  food sovereignty activism, 102-3, 108, 112-13
  Godoy Hortalizas strike, 107-8
  migrant worker trade unionism, 103-5
  organizing strategies, 107-8, 110-12

Sindicato de Obreros del Campo (SOC), *see*
  Sindicato Andaluz de Trabajadores/
  as (SAT — Andalusian Workers' Union;
  Spain)
social reproduction,
  anticolonial resistance through, 32–5
  climate crisis and, 9, 132–3
  Israeli state depletion of Palestinian, 22,
    25–9, 31, 34
  movement integration of, 14, 22, 140–1,
    243, 272–3
  settler colonial capitalism versus indigenous, 26–7, 30, 51
socioecological relations,
  anticapitalist struggles, 4, 166–71, 173,
    230–2, 240
  counterhegemonic articulations, 10–12,
    15, 20–1, 97, 188
  (de)valuing reproduction, 14, 72, 134,
    164, 182, 272–3
  sovereignty in, 51, 53, 84–5, 267–9
socioeconomic upheaval, 54, 63, 138, 231
solidarity, 92
  campaigns, 32–3, 69–**71**, 72–7, 104, 263
  economy, *see* solidarity economies
  feminist, 204–10, 241–4
  focus on building, 23, 130–1, 187, 241,
    273
  from below, 7, 272
  international, 86, 107–8, 138, 144, 147, 242
  municipalities, 43, 105
  not charity, 72, 144
  practices of, 8, 11, 15, 119, 143, 231, 266
solidarity economies, 57, 70, 141, 199
  Southern European, 100–1, 105–9
South Africa, 232, 234, 236
  Climate Justice Coalition, 241–2
  climate justice/just transition charters,
    242–3
  just transition/labour movement, 235,
    237–41
  women's activism in, 242–4
South African Federation of Trade Unions
  (SAFTU), 239, 241–2
sovereignty,
  community-territorial, 51–3, 58, 62–3
  food, *see* food sovereignty
  from below, 7, 21, 23, 126n1
  indigenous-peasant movements for, 13,
    20–2, 34, 51–63, 74–5 160–2, 248
  movements' decolonial ambitions, 13, 23,
    51–2, 63, 68, 137
  national-popular, 51–3, 58
  notions of, 13, 20–1, 51, 87, 121, 273

  plurality of struggles for, 21–2, 51–2, 63,
    71, 86, 160
  popular, 20–1, 55
  theory of, 20
Spain, 54, 68, 104, 203
  extractive industry, 89–90, **91**, 93, 96
  food production in, 86, 107, 109–10
strikes, 236
  cases of, 34, 239–40, 249, 260
  migrant farmworker, 104, 107–8, 110, 112
  school, 138
structural adjustment plans, 53–4, 60
subaltern classes,
  alliances among, 14, 56–7, 64, 266–8
  ecological movements of, 3, 9–10, 22, 51,
    230–1
  notion of, 6, 8, 85–6
  theory from below, 12, 261, 271–2, 274
Svampa, Maristella, 248
systemic change, 235
  climate justice and, 4, 14, 130, 134
  consensus on, 5, 14
  strategic organizing for, 5, 11

Tbilisi, Georgia, redevelopment, 184, 186
  City Hall/Council actions, 187, 191–5
  Heroes Square, 186–7, 189–92, 193,
    194–5
  queer and trans sex workers in, 186–95
  state violence/lack of safety, 188–91
  see also queer movements/mobilizations
trade unionism, 15, 86
  activism beyond, 230–2
  danger of, 249, 253
  lack of, 55, 89
  migrant worker, 101–6, 108, 111
trade unions, 44, 237
  agricultural/peasant, 33, 56, 101
  Colombian, 247–9, 252, 255–7
  extractive industry, 55, 247–9, 252
  just transition organizing and, 142, 151–2,
    230–2, 235–44, 255
  resistance to neoliberal privatization,
    55–62, 235, 240–1, 252
  social movement alliances, 15, 33–4, 57,
    61, 151, 245, 252–7
  South African, 237–45
transgender people,
  women, 189–96
  sex workers, 190–4
  spaces for, **193**, 194–5
tree monocultures/plantations, 13, 86, 248
  as extractivism, 86, 89–90, **91**, 92, 95
  forced/poor labour conditions, 89

green capitalism rationale, 89
resistance to, 86, 90, 92–4, **95**, 96–7
Turkey,
    counter-hegemonic flows, 131–2, 166–8, 175–6
    energy industry in, 131, 166–172, 175
    environmental/ecologist movements in, 48–9, 131–2, 166–73
    Gezi Park protests, 132, 170, 176
    occupation of Northern Kurdistan, 22, 38–42, 43–7, 49

Undisciplined Environments (collective), 12
Union of Agricultural Work Committees (UAWC South Africa), 33–4
Unión Sindical Obrera (USO, Workers' Trade Union — Colombia), 247–50, 252, 258n9
Unity Intifada, 34
universality,
    insurgent, 9–11
    political visions of, 7–8, 41
urban areas/communities, 53, 140
    contestation of, 184, 186–92, 194
    feminist organizing in, 53, 206, 214, 218, 222, 225
    land sovereignty struggles and, 84–6, 170, 195, 273–4
    mobilization of, 14–15, 47–8, 56, 152
    nature, 186–8, 190–1, 194
    rural area alliances, 13, 34, 94–6, 102–5, 109–10
    rural exodus to, 29, 31, 44–5, 90
    warfare in, 26, 28

Vavi, Zwelinzima, 239–40
Vía Campesina, La, 108, 184, 272
    Bangalore Conference, 202–3
    emergence of, 103, 126n1, 199–200
    feminist politics of, 198–200, **201**, 202–10
    fisherfolk and, 114, **115**, 116–18, **119–20**, 122–5, 126n2
    on food sovereignty/workers, 101, 198–200, 204–10
    on gender-based violence, 204–6, **207**
    Maputo Declaration, 205–6
    women's commission/assemblies, 201–2, **203**, 204–5
violence,
    anti-LGBTQIA+, 187–9, 195
    capitalist/extractive, 8, 84, 103–5, 156–8, 225, 256–7
    environmental, 4, 152, 236, 248, 264–6
    forest monocultures and, 85, 88–9
    gender-based, 3, 27, 182, 187, 195, **206–7**, 240
    infrastructural, 22, 25–9, 31, 34
    movements countering, 9, 137, 139, 214, 219–24
    patriarchal, 62–3, 200–5, 208–9, 272
    privatization of the commons, 9, 67, 184–5, 273
    settler colonial, 3, 25, 32–3, 35
    see also nonviolence

water, 64n1
    campaigns for, 45, **46–7**, 168–71, 175–7, 251–5
    commons, 154, 157, 160, 243
    community mobilizing for, 42–3, 55, 111, 236, 251
    destruction/lack of infrastructure for, 25–9, 88, 103, 121–2, 241, 266
    forums on, 49, 114, 118–19, 247
    privatization of, 55, 247
    sovereignty struggles for, 22, 31–3, 35, 69, 75, 141
    see also hydropower projects
Watts, Michael, 4
Wilson, Japhy, 9
women,
    Black, 14, 73, 184, 215–16, 242–3, 273
    food sovereignty, 70–1, 123–4, 184, 198–201, 202–10
    Indigenous, 184, 214–18, 222, 225, 273
    labour of, 94–5, 189, 195, 244, 274
    liberatory movements, 22, 40–2, 45, 244
    oppression of, 41–2, 189, 195–9, 208–10, 213–15
    organized, 214, 216, 222–4
    as representative of nature, 41, 215–16
    rights, 123–4, 195, 208
    rural, 94–5, 198–202, 205–9, 225
    trans, 189–96
    violence facing, 3, 27, 182, 187, 195, **206–7**, 240
workers,
    exploitation of, 102–4, 106–8, 234
    migrant farm, *see* migrant farmworkers
    participation in anticolonial alliances, 35, 132, 137, 141, 242
    precarity, 30, 101–3, 106, 271
    rights of, 13, 101–3, 107–12, 151–4, 200, 249–52
    rural, 100–9, 274
    self-organization, 86, 104, 111–12
    sex, 186–95
    strikes by, *see* strikes

waged, 86, 100–1, 274
women/queer, 94–5, 189, 195, 244, 274
World Bank, 55, 712
World Forum of Fisher People, 120, 123, 125
    COP21 meetings, 114, **115**, **119**
    food sovereignty organizing, 116–18, **119**, 126n2

youth movements, 44, 47, 199, 245
    climate, 14, 132, 138
    Palestine, 34

Zabalaza Socialist Forum for Left Renewal (South Africa), 245
Zapatistas, 160, 219
    organizational ontologies, 8, 75, 213, 226n2, 271